Sybase Architecture and Administration

ELLIS HORWOOD SERIES IN COMPUTERS AND THEIR APPLICATIONS

Series Editor: IAN CHIVERS, Senior Analyst, The Computer Centre, King's College, London, and formerly Senior Programmer and Analyst, Imperial College of Science and Technology, University of London

Series continued at back of book

SYBASE ARCHITECTURE AND ADMINISTRATION

JOHN KIRKWOOD

ELLIS HORWOOD

NEW YORK   LONDON   TORONTO   SYDNEY   TOKYO   SINGAPORE

First published 1993 by
Ellis Horwood Limited
Campus 400, Maylands Avenue
Hemel Hempstead
Hertfordshire HP2 7EZ
and
Market Cross House, Cooper Street
Chichester
West Sussex, PO19 1EB
A division of
Simon & Schuster International Group

Printed and bound in Great Britain at
the University Press, Cambridge

Library of Congress Cataloging-in-Publication Data

Available from the publisher

British Library Cataloguing in Publication Data

A catalogue record for this book is available from
the British Library

ISBN 0-13-100330-5

4   5   97   96   95   94

Contents

Appendices

Foreword by Mark Hoffman, President, Sybase Inc.

Sybase introduced the first client/server online relational database product to the market in 1987. Since then the rapid acceptance of Sybase's technology and the company's meteoric worldwide growth have been testimony to the changing face of the computer industry.

Upon Sybase's arrival in the UK, John Kirkwood was one of the very first IT professionals to recognise the potential of the client/server approach. His subsequent evaluation of SYBASE for a client resulted in his recommendation of SYBASE as the "optimum platform for future development."

At Sybase, we welcome the arrival of an independent expert guide to the SYBASE architecture and the SYBASE SQL Server relational database management system. John has produced a most readable book which will be invaluable to readers who are contemplating, or currently involved in the application of client/server technology.

Preface

I have long held the view that we are not very ably served by the literature of the mainframe and mid-range environment. The books directed at the PC market seem much more interesting to read and appear to try to tell you things that are not straight from the vendor's documentation. Of course this is a generalisation and there are exceptions in both areas. However, especially in the database environment, I believe that this is substantially true and so I have tried to make this book a treatment of Sybase which goes beyond the manuals.

I have been working with Sybase since 1987, providing several of the Sybase training courses and I have tried to include the tips and problems to watch out for that I have encountered or have been related to me over this time. Not every "feature" that you have experienced will be in this book and I would like you to contact me if you have such information, as I am also trying to collect these together for distribution to the user community.

I have intended the book to be as useful to beginners as it is to experienced users. I also hope that the style and presentation of the material does not send you to sleep. Those who know me will understand that I try not to produce such "cures for insomnia", but the subject of System Administration is a difficult one to liven up: the bottom line is that System Administration is boring. I have attempted to brighten each chapter with extracts from "IT's a Funny Thing". The "O'Reilly's Laws" and the "And finally ..." are extracted from this book with the permission of the editor, Roger Frampton. This book is still available and all proceeds go the Great Ormond Street Hospital: so buy it.

You can dip into the material at any point but, if you want a structured approach, I would recommend reading chapters 2-4 in sequence: installation, disk space management, user management. The other chapters may be taken in any sequence: chapter 1 - architecture, chapter 5 - recovery and backup, chapter 6 - concurrency and locking, chapter 7 - optimiser, chapter 8 - problem solving. Chapter 7 borrows heavily on my previous book - High Performance Relational Database Design - and the rest of the material is based on practical experience and the Sybase literature, both training

the material is based on practical experience and the Sybase literature, both training manuals and official documentation. The appendices are straight from the manuals and add nothing, but I have included them for completeness in an attempt to create a single reference source.

The material describes the Sybase server as at system 4.x. This does not include the new system 10 servers: backup, replication, navigation and OmniSQL gateway. I have not had a great deal of hands-on experience with system 10 and therefore the comments beyond the manuals are based on version 4.0.1 and above. Read the upgrade notes on system 10 to see what has changed but, from my experience, you should assume that the pre-system 10 "features" will still be there.

John Kirkwood

Chapter 1

Architecture

This chapter takes a general look at the Sybase client/server architecture and then discusses the detail of Sybase storage structures and indexes.

The basic client/SQL server connection is covered and expanded to the more general open client/open server environment.

The two forms of Sybase B-tree index - clustered and non-clustered - are then investigated in detail, covering the data storage structures, the index structure and the processing involved in insert/ update/ delete against each combination of index. The other types of page structure - allocation, distribution and text/image - are also discussed.

O'Reilly's First Law

It works better if you plug it in.

1

1.1 **Introduction**

Sybase is one of the youngest entrants into the Unix relational database world and made its initial impact by claiming to be the first relational database to be constructed with high performance in mind. Whether there are sufficient success stories to support this claim is neither the subject nor the aim of this book, but my personal opinion is that there are many design traits - such as stored procedures, sparse B-tree indexes - which give Sybase a distinct performance advantage over its peers to enable it to achieve a consistent high level of throughput and fast response time.

However there are a few design blind spots - page level locking, no hashed access and a heavy overhead on updates - which indicate that Sybase does not have everything tuned for maximum performance. Only makes them human and makes you work for your money as performance designers.

In my opinion the debate between the vendors over whose product goes fastest is interesting and ensures that the vendors do not neglect the performance of their products, but in general each product is as good as the other in specific circumstances which benefit the product. However performance is no longer the only requirement of the software and having achieved and sustained an acceptable level of performance, other architecture aspects become more significant. It is in the area of client/server that Sybase is beginning to make major advances and create a gap between the other mainstream Unix databases. Not a big gap and the others are doing their usual catch up, as in V7.0 of Oracle but, until the other vendor's latest offerings are proven in serious operational environments, Sybase appears to have an edge.

Sybase exhibits a truly independent client/server architecture in its ability for each node of the network to support an independently functioning client and/or server which communicates with the other nodes in the network via SQL calls. So what? I'll explain as I cover the architecture in this chapter but the independence of the clients and servers between SQL calls and responses is fundamental to true, high performance operation in a client/server environment. Sybase has - probably - the best fundamental design to operate in this environment. Records retrieved by a client from a server are retained at the client without the server having any knowledge of which records are at the client or in fact which client the records are at. Once the records have been sent by the server it forgets about them. Therefore there are no locks retained on the records while they are at the client. You would be surprised how many systems read with a shared lock which remains on until it is escalated to an exclusive lock - or use select for update which exclusively locks - over the server/client interface. I know that you can write your software to keep the lock off, but Sybase does this automatically and you have to write your software to keep the lock on. Unfortunately this is complicated by the buffering mechanism between the server and the client. If Sybase fills this buffer before reading all of the records, then the last page read at the buffer full condition has the shared lock retained until the buffer is emptied and the client requests more records. Therefore try never to leave results pending in Sybase as shared locks will be retained at the server.

High performance of a database owes as much to the talents of the database designer as it does to the features of the database software. Optimum operation in a network environment by minimising network traffic, maximising processing locality and never having transaction dependence across the network is possible only if the database software recognises the problems and has an underlying design which supports this optimum network operation. Sybase certainly recognises the problems although most of the effort has to be expended by the application developer to provide solutions.

1.2   Client/server architecture

Let me first of all define client/server from a database viewpoint. Client/server is a term which has lost a singular meaning as it has been applied to any and every situation where one resource requests work from another resource. Therefore it is worth making a specific definition for each situation. Basically they are all the same: the client requests a service from the server. This means that a node in a network should be capable of functioning as both client and server at different times, depending on whether it is making or servicing a request.

My database definition is: the server does all of the processing associated with database access and the client does all of the processing not associated with database access. So the server actions all SQL against the database ensuring the data integrity, concurrency control and the ability to recover from any failure. In addition the server stores and maintains the data dictionary which defines the server database environment and all objects in the databases. The client actions all screen interaction at the user's terminal and carries out all processing which is not involved in accessing data on the database. Screen based processing at the user's terminal such as input character echoing, cursor movement and function key mapping are obvious client functions. However some of the non-data access processing such as field validation is more of a problem as the server definition includes the maintenance of the dictionary where such field validation definitions may be held.

So even this simple definition has potential problems based on the maintenance location and the execution location of the processing. It is all very well supporting a dictionary which provides a central repository of information to minimise redundancy and optimise modular programming if the actual processing is done at remote clients which have no direct access to the dictionary. But that's a wider problem than I have time for here and it's not a Sybase specific problem - so back to the main theme.

Sybase very adequately supports client software running on a network node communicating with the server which controls the database as shown in figure 1.1.

Of course the client and the server may be on the same hardware node but this is trivial and my discussions of client/server are based on connection across the network. Similarly the client software may have several terminals attached - which is usually the case when the client and server software are on the same hardware. This is not important to the discussion as all comments are between the client and the server and are independent of how many terminals the client is supporting. I shall discuss and diagram as if the client was a workstation situation with software supporting one terminal. This does not restrict the discussion as the other client/server scenarios are the same as far as the software goes: it simply makes the diagramming easier.

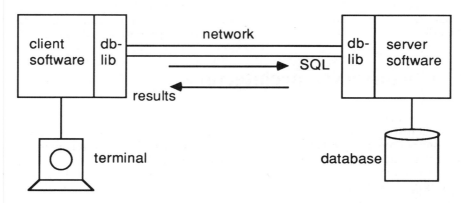

figure 1.1: client/server connection

Figure 1.2 illustrates several client/server connections: the same hardware; workstations and local processors with attached terminals.

Remember that client/server is a software architecture so the hardware configuration which supports it simply needs to be able to run the software.

The server software is, of course, Sybase. The client software may be anything which is capable of interfacing to Sybase - and there are a large number of third party products - but I shall confine my discussions to the Sybase client products.

isql Interactive SQL. A programmer's line edit tool which allows SQL to be submitted interactively. This has no screen handling support and is strictly for data processing use.

dwb Data workbench. A window based - Sybase specific windowing - menu driven environment, mainly for ad hoc data processing use but containing user oriented support for SQL submission and report generation. The SQL/reports may be submitted as raw SQL or built up using a "point and pick" method. This should be released to the users with care and only after in-depth training.

apt Sybase's 4GL development environment. A windows based - again Sybase specific as for dwb - development environment to create forms based, event driven menus and screens. Includes a code generating prototyping tool but is more a high level language based environment.

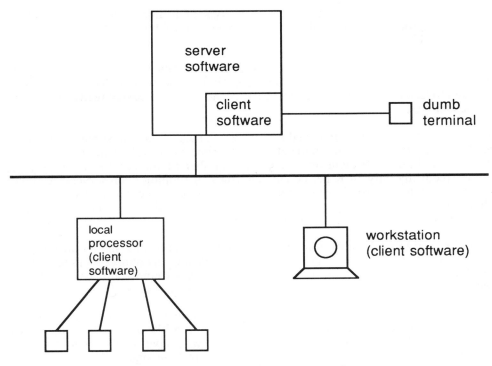

figure 1.2:   client/server connections

All of these, as well as 3GL programs, interface to the server via a Sybase specific component - db-library - as illustrated in figure 1.1. This is a set of functions which controls the transfer between client and server across the network, assembling and disassembling the messages and presenting the information at each end in the appropriate format.

The client talks to the server in Transact-SQL (T-SQL) a Sybase specific extension of ANSI standard SQL and the server talks to the client in Tabular Data Stream (TDS) a Sybase specific protocol for presenting the results of the T-SQL.

The interface between the non-3GL client software - isql, dwb, apt - and db-library is hidden from the user. Submission of a T-SQL command in any of these environments results in the display of the results with column headings, data fields and control information presented and formatted by the appropriate client software.

A 3GL program, however, has to make the input and output interfaces to db-library explicitly by function/subroutine calls. Establishing a connection to the server, submitting the command, processing the results row by row and handling the heading and control information has to be done by the programmer with calls to db-library functions/subroutines. APT has a measure of this type of db-library interface depending on how much processing you wish to be under your control but it is not all mandatory as it is in a 3GL.

Sybase does not fully support embedded SQL: the 3GL function calls are part of the source code with one compile phase. There is client code support for precompiled, embedded SQL but this does not support cursors and therefore cannot really be classed as embedded SQL.

The Sybase server is a multi-threaded server, which means that one server program is capable of supporting several clients at the same time by threading them through its code. This is highly efficient as regards the number of threads per megabyte of memory, requiring only 34 K per connection (64 K if running open server). A client transaction may have several connections so it is not a one to one ratio and a useful rule of thumb is 2-3 connections per client transaction. (It depends what you are doing but you might as well overestimate when sizing memory.)

Sybase is effectively taking the role of TP monitor by establishing and monitoring the connections to the client and controlling the activities of each connection in the server code. Each connection is allocated CPU resource on a round robin basis until its timeout period or it makes an external request such as a disk access.

Sybase - as mentioned above - does not support the cursor mechanism favoured by other relational database software but uses a connection like a cursor. To have two dependent searches of two tables a Sybase client will have to open two separate connections, one for each search, instead of declaring two cursors.

The client/server architecture as discussed is really no more than the traditional message pair environment with the client sending a message to the server and receiving a reply. As regards the relationship between the client and the server this is all that they are capable of: the client sending messages and the server processing and replying to them. The client is not capable of receiving independent output from the server which it is not expecting because it did not initiate the dialogue.

To make full use of the client/server architecture we need to permit this type of dialogue where the server sends messages to the client for action to be taken. We really need the client to look like a server and the server to look like a client when we want them to.

Sybase implements this with two pieces of software: open client which resides on the client and allows it to function as a server and open server which resides on the server and allows it to function as a client.

We are now able to initiate events at other clients based on the results of a transaction as shown in figure 1.3.

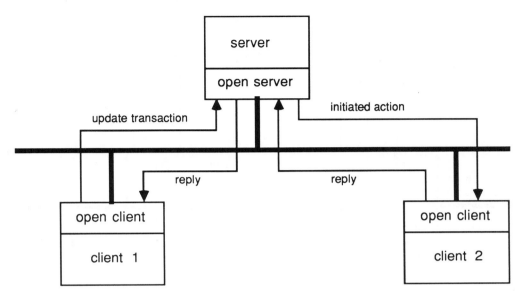

figure 1.3:   open client / open server configuration

Now the update from client 1 is replied to by the server which then initiates action on client 2 by open server talking to open client. Of course you do not need the open client and open server software to achieve this - you can do it yourself as both the client and the server are programmable devices. But why reinvent the wheel when it is already round and fits the car? (Note that Sybase still refer to open client as db_library for historical reasons but in practice, any references to db_library should be replaced by open client.)

The benefits of the open client/open server environment - which I shall call client/server from now on - is that each node of the network is capable of independent function as a client or a server depending simply on the processing requirements at the specific time. This simple, symmetric architecture allows inter-server communication as well as client to server communication as shown in figure 1.4 by a server making open client calls to another server. The processing between servers is done with remote procedure calls (RPCs).

1.2.1 Open server

Open server is a library of 'C' functions - called the server-library - which unifies the way that an application talks to multiple systems. By incorporating both open client and open server, a program can act as both a client and a server. The open client component makes the application a client application which initiates requests and the open server component makes the application a server application which responds to requests.

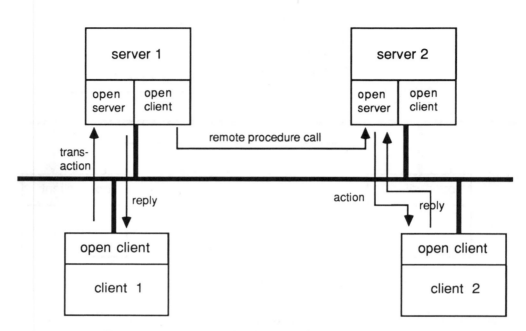

figure 1.4:   server to server client communication

Open servers look like normal servers as far as the client application is concerned, receiving T-SQL via open client function calls and returning TDS. The important addition is that the open server now allows server to server communication by remote procedure call (RPC). So a request from a client to a server can make an RPC to another server to execute the application from more than one server. In the configuration of figure 1.5 proc_2 on a remote server may be accessed from the client in one of three ways.

In the first two cases the client is connected to the local server_1 (via the environment variable DSQUERY which I explain in chapter 2) and the client makes a normal execution of a procedure on server_1 which has an embedded RPC to execute proc_2 on the remote server_2. In the second case, although the client is connected to server_1, the RPC qualifies the procedure_name with the server_name and so the RPC executes proc_2 on server_2. The call is:

exec server_name.db_name.owner_name.proc_name

In the third case the client is connected to the remote server_2 and can make a direct

RPC of proc_2. In this third case a local procedure call would have accomplished the execution of proc_2, but there is no overhead in making RPCs to local procedures. The results returned to the client look the same independent of how the procedure is executed.

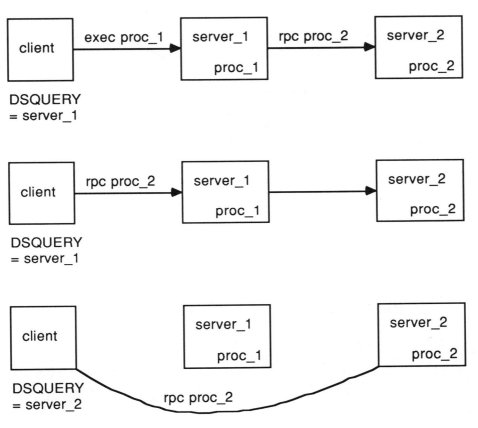

figure 1.5:   remote procedure calls

This is an excellent environment to facilitate gateways to other database software. By using an open server, the Sybase T-SQL can be converted into the appropriate database SQL calls and the results converted into TDS to return to the client. This is being implemented by Sybase in their Omni gateway server.

It is also an important component of a distributed database in that the client applications can be independent of the database distribution by routeing the client calls to the appropriate server as in figure 1.6.

A request to retrieve data from tab_1 and tab_2 in the same SQL command is directed to the open server which knows the locations of tab_1 and tab_2 and can make RPCs to them to retrieve the appropriate records. The open server then merges the separate returns from each server into the single reply to the client.

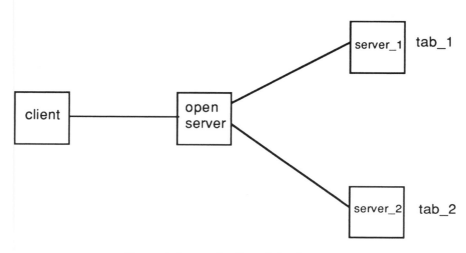

figure 1.6:   distributed database

1.3 Storage structures and indexing

It is impossible to separate the index method of a Sybase table and the underlying storage structure. Sybase uses B-tree to index the tables and has two types: clustered and non-clustered. The clustered B-tree is a sparse index where the records are held in sequence of the index values and only the first record in each data page has an index entry. The non-clustered B-tree is a dense index where each record in the table has an index entry.

Therefore a Sybase table with a clustered index has the data records maintained in sequence of the index field values. So records are placed in specific pages depending on the value of the index field. A Sybase table which has only non-clustered indexes has the data records added to the last page of the table with no notice taken of the index field value. So only the index entries of the non-clustered index are maintained in sequence: any sequencing of the data in a non-clustered table is coincidental.

Therefore a Sybase table may have 1 clustered index but may have up to 250 non-clustered indexes. Clustering one index on a table is not mandatory as all indexes may be non-clustered but the storage and processing of the data records is significantly different if a table has a clustered index defined on it.

1.3.1 **Clustered index**

I believe the easiest way to understand any index method it to go through how it is
built, but if you are happy with the layout of sparse B-trees then you may skip the
initial discussion.

The likelihood is that the data table already has records in it when we create the index so
we shall start with a set of records as in figure 1.7.

1		22		19		18		26
16		8		6		11		12
3		2		28		4		27
17		20		7		24		14

figure 1.7:   initial record population

The first thing that the clustered index requires is the records in sequence of the key as
in figure 1.8.

1		6		12		18		24
2		7		14		19		26
3		8		16		20		27
4		11		17		22		28

figure 1.8:   data sequenced for clustering

To index these records we now have a traditional sequenced storage - ISAM is the most
typical - where not every record needs to be indexed. We need only index the first
record in each data page as we know that the sequence is being maintained and
therefore all records from 1 up to, but not including, 6 must always be in the first page,
all records from 6 up to 12 must always be in the next page and so on. So we can build
a first level of index entries which simply point to the first record in each data page as in
figure 1.9.

(I have put 4 index entries per index page to illustrate the index build. In reality there
will be many more index entries in an index page depending on the size of the index
field. We shall look at sizing shortly.)

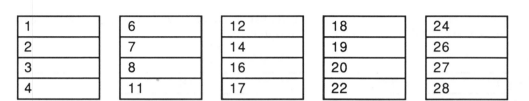

figure 1.9:   first level clustered index

To locate a record (say 19) we can now browse along the index level until we find the index entry for the page that the record is in (18 - 24) and read that page to locate the record. Note that we do not know if the record exists until we have read the data page. Not uncommon in sparse indexes. This is clearly more efficient than reading all of the data pages but still not as efficient as we can make it because we are usually talking of a reduction of one order of magnitude only between the number of data pages and the number of first level index pages.

The B-tree solves this by continuing to index each level until it reaches a level with a single index page. In our small example this is reached at the second index level as shown in figure 1.10.

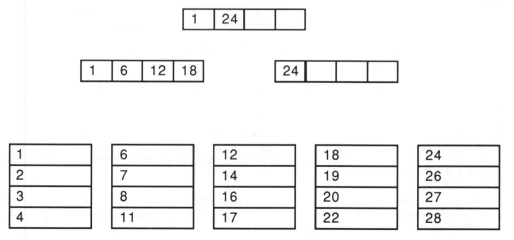

figure 1.10:   clustered B-tree index

Now to locate record 19 we read in at the top level and find that 19 is in the left hand branch of the tree (between 1 and 24). We read the index page at the next level and find that 19 is in the page beginning with 18 and we read that data page to locate the record.

The Sybase clustered index is one of the best examples of a sparse index that I have seen.

The index is called **sparse** because not every data record has an index entry.

The single index page entry point is called the **root node**. The page number of this is held in the field "root" in sysindexes.

The level at which the entries (data or index) are first in sequence is called the **leaf level** or **sequence set**.

Any other levels between the leaf level and the root node are called **intermediate levels**.

Each index page is called an **index node**.

Each level in the index is linked horizontally by page pointers. So if a range of records is required (10 - 20) once the first record is located vertically via the index levels, the leaf level may be browsed horizontally to locate the subsequent records without retraversing the index.

This is a very significant benefit of the clustered index. Because the data records themselves are in sequence of the key, once the first record is located only the data pages need to be read for a range enquiry. (I'll come back to this later when comparing the two indexing methods.)

Let's take a closer look at the pointers of the clustered index. Every index entry of the clustered index is a page pointer. A page pointer in Sybase is 4 bytes plus a 1 byte overhead: so every index entry in the clustered index is the key value plus a 5 byte pointer. Introducing page pointers to our index looks like figure 1.11.

The root node is page 65, the intermediate level pages 60 and 55 and the data pages 20, 100, 45, 223 and 80.

Now to locate record 27 we read the root node page 65 - from sysindexes - which tells us that record 27 is in the right hand branch which starts at page 55. This page tells us that record 27 is in page 80 which we need to scan to locate record 27.

Similarly to read all records greater than 6 takes us via page 65 and page 60 to page 100 and then to pages 45, 223 and 80 via the page pointer chain which links each level in the index - in this case the data records.

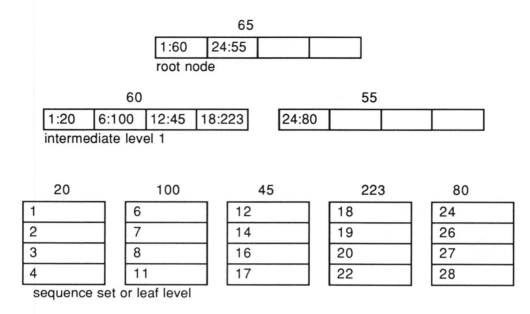

figure 1.11:   clustered index pointer structure

1.3.2 Non-clustered index

The start point is the data table of figure 1.7. For the non-clustered index we do not move the data but create a leaf index level containing an index entry for every record in the table as in figure 1.12.

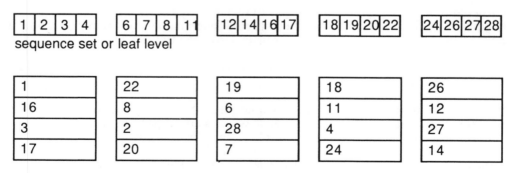

figure 1.12:   non-clustered index leaf level

This is the level of the non-clustered index which is maintained in index value sequence. This is a **dense** index as every record in the table has an index entry. The data records do not need to be maintained in key value sequence so new records are simply inserted at the end of the table.

Now the B-tree is completed by creating further index levels on top of the leaf level until a single root node is reached as shown in figure 1.13.

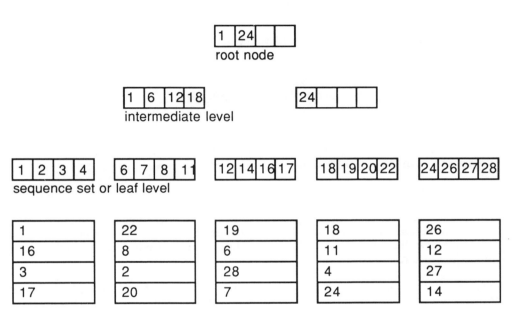

figure 1.13:   non-clustered index

Because the leaf level entries are always in sequence we can use the first record in each index page as we did before in the clustered index to create the intermediate and root levels.

To locate record 14 we read the root node which tells us record 14 is in the left hand branch. The intermediate level index page tells us that record 14 is in the leaf level starting with 12. This leaf level index page tells us the data page that record 14 is in. Note that we need only read as far as the leaf level of the non-clustered index to determine if the record exists. Every record has an index entry in the leaf level so if there is no entry in the leaf level, the record does not exist.

Again each level is linked horizontally via a pointer chain so browsing for a range of values is readily supported. However there is a considerable difference in the amount of logical accesses between the two types of index when a range of values is required.

To read records 10-20 from the non-clustered index we need to:

>   read root node
>   read intermediate index page
>   read 3 leaf level index pages
>   read 8 data pages

Using the clustered index of figure 1.10 we need to:

>   read root node
>   read intermediate level index page
>   read 3 data pages

This is already an advantage of 8 logical accesses in such a small table and we shall emphasise this in the optimiser chapter 7.

An SQL command which retrieves many records from a table need never do more than read every page in the table ie scan the complete table. However the non-clustered index generates a data page read for every record retrieved and clearly has the potential to try to make more page accesses than there are pages in the table. The Sybase optimiser does not allow this mistake but it does affect how indexes are used and which indexes should be clustered.

Let's look in detail at the non-clustered index pointers. The leaf level pointers are record pointers which are 6 bytes + 1 byte overhead. This is composed of a page pointer + a row number within the page (see index record discussion in section 1.4.2) ie 4+2 bytes.

The root node pointers are page pointers as before ie 4 bytes + 1 byte overhead.

The intermediate level pointers need only be page pointers as before for the clustered index but Sybase adds the record pointer of the first record in the leaf level page pointed to by the intermediate page. So the intermediate level pointer is 4(page) + 6(record) + 1(overhead) ie 11 bytes.

Our index now looks like figure 1.14.

To locate records 10-20 we read page 150 - the root node from sysindexes - which tells us that 10 is in the branch page 200 which tells us that the leaf entry is page 70 which tells us the first record is record 11 at page 30 record 2. We then browse the leaf level reading record 12 at page 100 record 2, record 14 at page 100 record 4 and so on until we get a key value greater than 20 when we stop.

The Sybase optimiser will not allow us to do this as the total number of data page reads is 7 but there are only 5 pages in the table and so the optimiser would force a table scan.

But that's how it locates records via the non-clustered index.

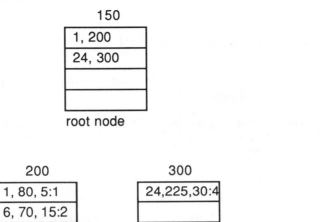

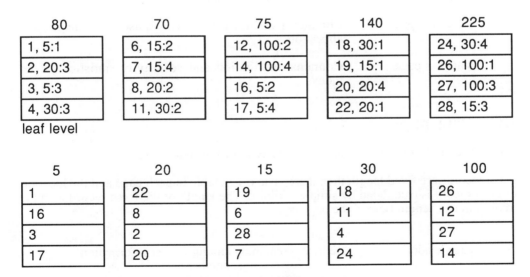

figure 1.14:   non-clustered index pointer structure

Sybase allows up to 16 fields in an index to a maximum of 256 bytes. These fields may be non-consecutive, non-contiguous in the record: they may come from anywhere in the record, in any sequence. The only thing you cannot do is to put a portion of a field or a calculation into the index: the index must contain complete, unaltered fields.

1.4   **Page and record layout**

Before we continue with the indexes it is worth looking at the data and index record layouts and the associated page structures.

The page size varies depending on the hardware/software but the most common size is 2 K bytes and so I shall use this all of the time. Sybase holds the page value for the installation in spt_values.

There are 5 types of page:

data page	Contains data rows or log rows. Log rows are laid out differently from data rows but the construction of the page is the same.
index page	Contains index rows.
text/image page	Contains text/image data.
allocation page	Contains a set of extent structures used to manage page allocation.
statistics page	Contains distribution and sensitivity statistics for an index.

1.4.1   **Data page**

A data page is composed of three elements as shown in figure 1.15.

If the records are fixed length then there is no offset table in each page and the location of each record is calculated by simple addition. The length of the fixed record is in the minimum row length field of the page header.

page header	32 bytes containing amongst other information logical page number next logical page number previous logical page number object_id that page belongs to next available row number in page

offset of free space
minimum row length

data rows   An integral number of rows as a data row is not allowed to cross a page boundary.

offset table   A set of offsets from the start of the page giving the location of each row. This set grows backwards from the end of the page and is present only when the records are variable length.

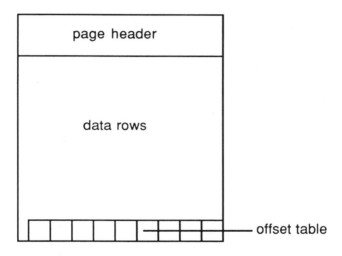

figure 1.15:   data page layout

The data record is laid out as shown in figure 1.16.

Each record in the page is allocated a row number. This is a 1 byte field and so has a maximum value of 255 which restricts the number of records in a page to 256. The record_id used in the non-clustered index is a combination of the page number and the row number in the page.

$$record\_id = page\_number : row\_number$$

The 2 byte row length allows the record to occupy the full page. So there is no minimum row length but the maximum number of rows in a page is 256. The maximum length of a row is 2048 - 32 : 2016 bytes.

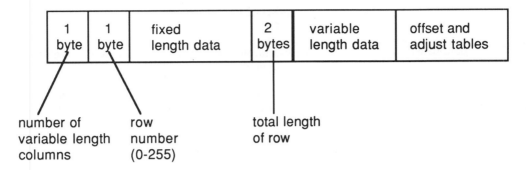

figure 1.16:   data record layout

If the records are fixed length then the first byte is set to zero and the record stops after the data. The table:

```
create table tab_1
       ( a   int,
         b   char(20))
```

has a record layout as shown in figure 1.17.

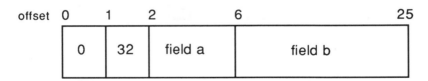

figure 1.17:   fixed length record layout

No variable length fields, a row number of 32 and no record length as it is in the header (minimum record length - they are all the same). The fields are arranged in the record in the same order as they are defined.

If the record is variable length the fixed and variable fields are separated irrespective of how you have defined them in the table.. The table:

```
create table tab_2
       ( a int,
         b varchar(20),
         c char(30),
         d varchar(10))
```

has a record layout as shown in figure 1.18.

0	1	2	6	36	38	48	54	55	56

2	40	field a	field c	57	field b	field d	1	38 (b)	48 (d)

figure 1.18:   variable length record layout

2 variable fields
a row number of 40
fixed length fields in sequence of definition
record length of 57 bytes
variable length fields in sequence of definition
offset table adjust byte
offset table of variable field locations from start of record

Each offset in the offset table at the end of the record is the displacement of the start of the field from the start of the record. As the offset is a 1 byte field the maximum offset value is 255 so a 1 byte adjust field points to additional sets of offsets for each 256 bytes.

Searching for a record based on the record_id is done by a binary search of the records. If the records are fixed length the search is done on the records in the page as positions may be calculated. If the records are variable length, the search is done on the offset table at the end of the page which contains the displacement of the record from the start of the page.

Locating record 9 in a page of fixed length records as in figure 1.19 is done as:

determine number of records from next row in page header

determine record length from minimum record length in header

start in middle of page and repetitively half in direction of record_id to locate record

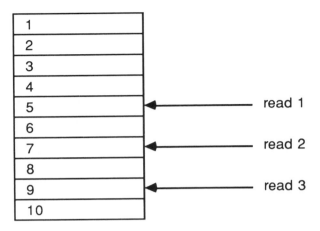

figure 1.19:   fixed length record search

So locate record 5, then record 7, then record 9. Remember that it is the row number in the page that we are searching on, not the record key.

When the records are variable length the search is made on the offset table as in figure 1.20. The record number is then the entry in the offset table which contains the location of the record.

The zero offset for row 1 means that the record has been deleted. The next insertion to this page will reuse row number 1 although the record itself is added to the end of the data in the page.

When records are deleted the records in the page are shuffled up to keep the free space at the end of the page. New records are added to the end of the records in the page ensuring no space fragmentation within a page.

If the records are fixed length the row numbers are not reused as there is no offset table to keep track of the row numbers.

If the records are variable length the row numbers are reused as the entries are not deleted from the offset table but simply given an offset of zero. This is illustrated in figure 1.21.

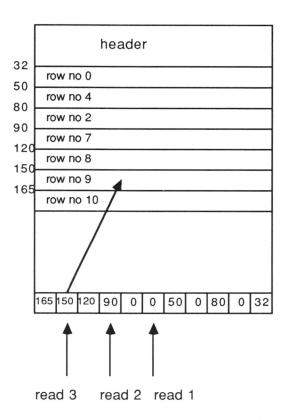

figure 1.20:   offset table binary search

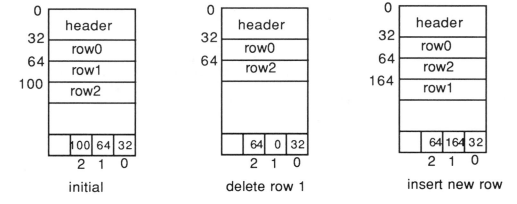

figure 1.21:   variable row deletion and insertion

Deletion of row number 1 moves row number 2 up to take up the free space, changing the offset value of row 2 and setting row 1 offset to zero. Addition of a new record to the page uses row number 1 and so in an active table it is more than likely that the rows will not be in sequence of the row number in the page. This is the internal row number of the record in the page, not the real key to the record. If our example were keyed on name the actual records could be as in figure 1.22.

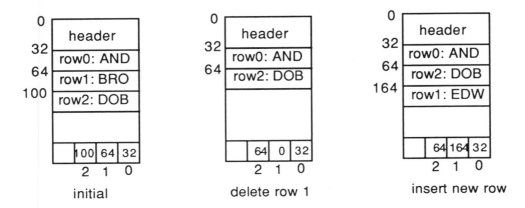

figure 1.22:   key values v row number

Note that all Sybase updates are done as deletion followed by insertion which means that an update can quite easily result in a change to the row number of the record. We were lucky in this example but take figure 1.20 and update row number 2. After deletion the first available row number for the insertion will be row number 1. Nobody else can use row number 1 as the update has the page locked. This is extremely important as the row number is part of the record_id and therefore any update to a Sybase record has to delete and reinsert all non-clustered index entries for the record.

The offset table applies only to variable length records but Sybase tends to store all records like this as it treats null as a variable length field (length 0). So any field which allows null is considered to be variable length and therefore the record is considered to be variable length. Therefore only tables which have all fixed length, non-null fields are held by Sybase as fixed length records. There are not many of these around and usually they tend to be static look-up tables which are not subject to any significant update anyway.

1.4.2 **Index page**

Index pages have 2 components as shown in figure 1.23.

```
┌─────────────────────────┐
│                         │
│         header          │
│                         │
├─────────────────────────┤
│                         │
│                         │
│       index rows        │
│                         │
│                         │
│                         │
└─────────────────────────┘
```

figure 1.23:   index page

header   32 bytes containing amongst other information
                                logical page number
                                next logical page number
                                previous logical page number
                                object_id that the page belongs to
                                index_id that the page belongs to
                                offset of free space
                                minimum row length on page
                                offset of last row in page
                                index level

index rows   key value and pointer combinations

Index rows have no row number in the page and so there is no offset table at the end of the page. Because there is no row number the index rows are located by different search algorithms than the data rows.

The index row layout is basically the same as the data row layout except that it does not have a row number and contains a page pointer to the next level of index and/or a record pointer to the record in the page. The actual structure depends on the type of index page.

Clustered index row

This contains a page pointer of 4 bytes as in figure 1.24.

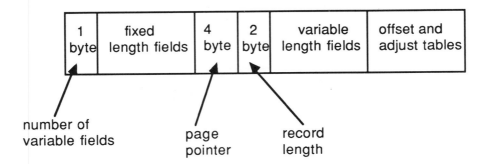

figure 1.24:   clustered index row structure

Again if the index field(s) are fixed length the index row is smaller - and easier to process - than variable length index rows.

The table and indexes:

```
create table tab_1
       (  a int,
          b int,
          c varchar(20),
          d char(10),
          e varchar(20))

create clustered index ind_1
       on tab_1(a, d)

create clustered index ind_2
       on tab_1(e, b)
```

have index rows as in figures 1.25 and 1.26. (Remember that you cannot have 2 clustered indexes on a table - this is only for illustration of the row layout.)

The overhead of the clustered index when the fields are fixed length is 5 bytes.

The overhead of the clustered index row when a field is variable length is 8 bytes + 1 byte per variable field. There is only the one adjust field as you cannot create index entries greater than 256 bytes.

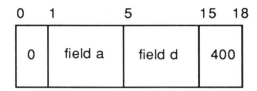

figure 1.25:   fixed length clustered index row

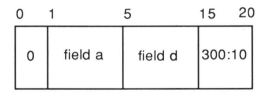

figure 1.26:   variable length clustered index row

Non-clustered index row

The non-clustered leaf row contains a record_id instead of the logical page number as it points to the individual record.

Using the previous table and defining the same fields as non-clustered indexes we now have the two row layouts as shown in figures 1.27 and 1.28.

```
0    1         5         15    20
┌────┬─────────┬─────────┬──────────┐
│    │         │         │          │
│ 0  │ field a │ field d │ 300:10   │
│    │         │         │          │
└────┴─────────┴─────────┴──────────┘
```

figure 1.27:   fixed length non-clustered leaf row

The overhead of the non-clustered leaf row when the fields are fixed length is 7 bytes.

The overhead of the non-clustered leaf row when a field is variable length is 10 bytes + 1 byte per variable field.

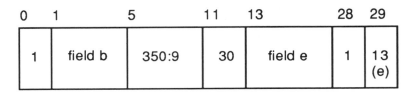

figure 1.28:   variable length non-clustered leaf row

Non-clustered intermediate rows

The non-clustered intermediate rows contain both a logical page number and a record_id. The record_id is for the first record of the node that the intermediate index is pointing to. So the non-clustered intermediate rows look like figures 1.29 and 1.30.

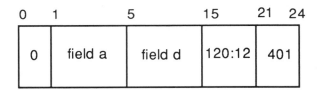

figure 1.29: fixed length non-clustered intermediate row

The overhead of the non-clustered intermediate row when the fields are fixed length is 11 bytes.

0	1	5	11	15	17	32	33
1	field b	1234:15	658	34	field e	1	17 (e)

figure 1.30:   variable length non-clustered intermediate row

The overhead of the non-clustered leaf row when a field is variable length is 14 bytes + 1 byte per variable field.

In summary, the index entry overheads on the key length are:

	fixed	variable
clustered	5	8 + n
non-clustered leaf	7	10 + n
non-clustered intermediate	11	14 + n

where n is the number of variable length fields in the index.

(I normally ignore most of this detail and use 10 bytes overhead for any index entry. The percentage error on variable length fields or number of records usually swamps any error on index size by using 10 bytes overhead all of the time.)

1.4.3 **Allocation page**

Allocation pages contain 4 components as shown in figure 1.31.

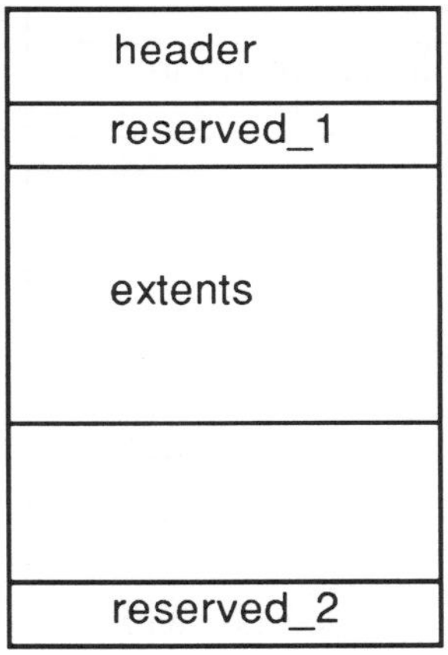

figure 1.31: allocation page

header   32 byte page header for compatibility but little of it used
                            logical page number
                            database_id of allocation

reserved_1   a 16 byte Sybase reserved area

extents   32 extent structures each of 16 bytes which control page
                            allocation. Each extent controls 8 pages so an allocation
                            page controls 256 pages.

reserved_2   a 32 byte Sybase reserved area

The allocation page is at the start of a 256 block of pages called an **allocation unit**. The allocation page controls the following 255 pages in the allocation unit as shown in figure 1.32.

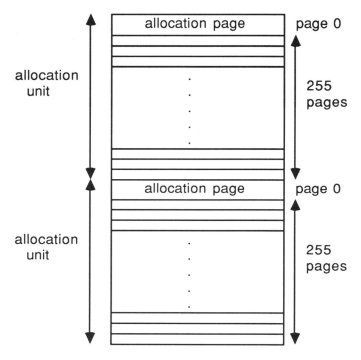

figure 1.32: allocation unit

The page numbers are logical numbers starting at zero, so allocation units are multiples of 256 pages. The physical pages are not necessarily contiguous. They may be contiguous at the start with an empty disk but once you start using the disk and adding extra space to the database you should never assume that free space is allocated contiguously (unless you ask for it in VMS).

The logical database pages start at 0 and are in units of 256 pages, the first being the controlling page. Allocation pages control physical Sybase pages which are mapped to user databases in a possibly non-contiguous manner. Therefore the logical page numbers in a user database will probably not map to physically contiguous pages.

The pages in the database are controlled by the extent structures in the allocation page. Each extent structure is a 16 byte structure containing:

> **extent**
>> next extent_id in chain
>> previous extent_id in chain
>> object_id
>> allocation bit map
>> deallocation bit map
>> index_id
>> status

The allocation bit map is one byte with each bit setting representing the allocation status of one of 8 pages as shown in figure 1.33.

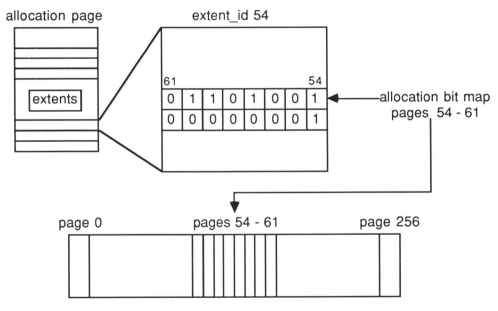

figure 1.33:   extent structure

If the bit is on in the allocation bit map the page is allocated to an object. If the bit is off the page is reserved for the object but not currently is use.

The deallocation bit map indicates those pages which have been identified during a transaction for deallocation ie they have become empty and are no longer currently needed. As with any update, the deallocation is not carried out until the commit at the end of the transaction. The deallocation bit map registers which pages have to be deallocated at the end of the transaction to prevent them being allocated by another transaction before the transaction is complete ie an allocation lock.

So database space is allocated as an allocation unit of 256 pages ie 512 K and the database object space is allocated in extents of 8 pages ie 16 K.

Allocating space to records goes through the algorithm:

> use current page if sufficient space
>
> use free page in current extent
>
> get new extent from current allocation page
>
> search allocation pages for object by following extent chain
>
> allocate new extent from next allocation page

V4.8 assists in the searching of allocation pages by holding a Global Allocation Map (GAM) which has a bit setting for each allocation page of 0: free space, 1: no free space.

V4.8 also has an Object Allocation Map (OAM) containing the page_id of each allocation page used by an object. When a new allocation page is required for an extent allocation, the OAM is checked for free space in the last entry. The OAM entries are held in sysindexes - which accounts for the new sysindexes layout in 4.8.

1.4.4 Index statistics page

The statistics of an index which are used by the optimiser are stored in a single page called the statistics page which has a 32 byte header for compatibility and the rest available to store index field values. Each entry in the page is an index key value so the number of entries is:

$$\text{number of distribution entries (n)} = \text{page size} / \text{key size}$$

The table is sampled n times and the value of the index key at each nth position is then recorded in the statistics page. This sampling and the use of the statistics by the optimiser is covered in detail in chapter 7 on the optimiser.

The index statistics page also contains a sensitivity figure - called the **density** - which is the percentage of duplicate values in the index. This is used in joins to estimate the number of records per join value, as explained in chapter 7.

1.4.5 Text/image page

Sybase has two datatypes - text and image - which permit the data record to hold a field larger than the page size record limit. Normal character based datatypes are limited to 255 characters but 'text' allows any size of variable length character string up to 2 G bytes. (Image is simply a binary equivalent of text.)

This is achieved by Sybase in a standard fashion of holding the text/image data in a separate chain of pages linked to the standard data record. So the data record contains a pointer to a set of 2 K pages containing the text or image as in figure 1.34.

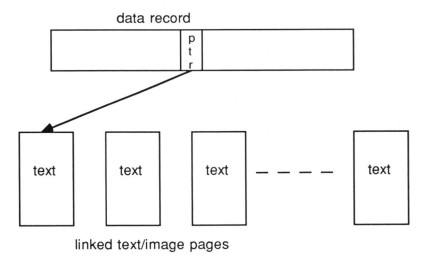

figure 1.34:   text/image pages

The text/image page is a standard data page with a 32 byte header and no offset table at the end. So the minimum size of a text/image field is one page - 2K or 2016 bytes to be more precise.

Select from such a field is quite efficient as the pages are linked together so once the data record is located there are embedded pointers to follow to retrieve the text ie no further index accesses. However update is horrendous as it is a standard Sybase update of delete followed by insert. So to update 4 bytes of a 12 K text field the 6 pages must be deleted and the new 6 pages inserted.

Try not to update text/image fields.

1.5   Buffer cache management

When a disk page is cached it shares cache with all pages from all databases in the server. Each disk page in cache is identified via a hash key based on the database_id and the logical page number. As the logical page number is unique within a database this uniquely identifies each page in cache. As with any hashing access method collisions will occur mainly because the available cache will be smaller than the total number of database pages which need to be cached. So there will be an overflow situation where each hash result has several disk pages linked to it. When a disk page is requested the hash table is checked to see if it is in cache.

Prior to V4.8 the number of hash buckets was fixed at 1024. A cache larger than this has 1024 lists of cache pages, which must be searched once the server has calculated the hash bucket number. From V4.8 the number of hash buckets is calculated based on the size of cache so that a hash bucket has no more than 2 cache pages linked to it.

Each page in cache has a corresponding buffer controlling its stay in cache.The buffers are part of a doubly linked chain: a least recently used (lru) chain and a most recently used (mru) chain. When a new page needs to use cache a free buffer is obtained from the lru chain to manage it. The buffer is linked into the mru chain so that pages which are referenced frequently tend to remain in cache.

Prior to V4.8 there is no difference between an index page and a data page as regards cache usage: only the extra use of the index page tends to keep it in cache longer than a data page. This applies most obviously to the root nodes and intermediate index levels: leaf levels of the clustered index are data pages anyway and the leaf level of the non-clustered index is used more often than the data page only in the ratio of index entries per page to data records per page. So it depends mostly on the ratio of the size of the index field to the data record. However the mru chain is most likely to contain data pages because these are always the last pages read, so from V4.8 Sybase ages index pages slower than data pages which is clearly extremely useful.

Finally when a page is modified the buffer is linked to a "dirty" buffer chain. There is one dirty buffer chain for each object and they are used by the checkpoint routine to assist it in finding all the used pages quickly.

So, under control of the buffer, each page is in:

> a least used chain and a most used chain: the page is always in these chains
>
> a hash table if the cache page is being used by a disk page
>
> a dirty page chain for the object if the page has been updated

1.6   **Index processing**

Now we know how everything is stored in the pages, let's have a detailed look at what happens when we maintain records in tables - insert/ update/ delete - and the processing required by the various index combinations. We shall look at no index, non-clustered only, clustered only and a clustered, non-clustered combination.

1.6.1   **No index**

This is standard heap storage where there are no indexes to impose a layout on the data and the data records are simply heaped onto the end of the table. The last logical page number of the table is held in sysindexes and all new records are placed in this page until there is no room left when a new page is obtained from the existing allocation or a new extent is requested from free space. Figure 1.35 illustrates this.

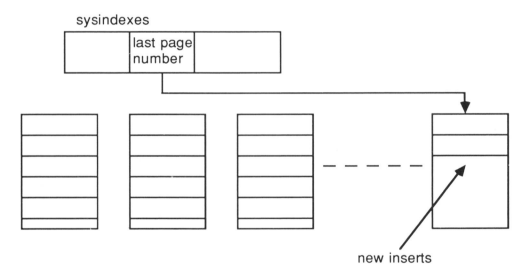

figure 1.35:   heap storage

This is the fastest method of adding new records to a Sybase table as there is no index overhead. However in a multi-user environment there will be considerable contention for the last page, so if you have an audit style table and decide not to index it be careful of the locking (page level) contention on the last page. If all you are doing is bulk loading records into a table then this is the optimum method of storage for the load and you should use fast bulk copy (bcp) to load the records. Do not have the indexes on when building a table. Do not have the triggers on when building a table. If you don't believe me, try it. It will take several seconds per record ie in the order of 1 hour per thousand records. Yes it is a long time. Create the table as heap, load the table with bcp and then build the indexes and check integrity. (There is a case for presorting the data into the clustered index sequence and loading it with the clustered index already created. You will have to balance the cost of the record sort against the clustered index build on this one. However it is only valid when the table has no other indexes.)

So the no index heap structure for fast insertion - checking the overhead of last page contention - but what about update and delete. Not a thing to do without an index unless the table is small - 3 or less pages. With 3 or less pages the disk activity with an index and the disk activity to read the whole table are about the same, so an index is not essential for such small tables. (This is a disk access argument only. If - as in Sybase - the easiest method of enforcing uniqueness is via the index, then define an index for every table which requires a unique primary key index.)

However for large tables without an index a full table scan is required to read one record. Because there is no sequence to the data and/or no index with entries in sequence, the server does not know when to stop. Even if you are looking for record 1 and it is the first record in the table, there is nothing to tell you that it is the only record 1 in the table or that, even if the next record is record 2, that there is not another record 1 in the table. In the absence of data or index sequence the server has to read the complete table to locate the required record. This is unacceptable for almost every application and therefore an index is created on a suitable key field or fields.

1.6.2 **Non-clustered only**

The first logical step from the no index heap structure is to leave the data untouched in the heap structure and create an index onto the data records. This applies only when there is no clustered index on the table ie when all indexes are non-clustered.

This gives the dense B-tree structure of figure 1.13 with the data still as heap storage and a dense B-tree index built on this with every data record having an index record_id pointer in the leaf level.

To insert a record (say 5) as in figure 1.36 it is placed on the end of the table - in this case a new page - and a record_id pointer is added to the leaf level node.

In this case there has not been enough room in the leaf node so it has split into two to accommodate the new index entry and still maintain the sequence. As there is now a new leaf node it requires a new entry at the intermediate level where again there is no room and so the node splitting continues until the new index entries can be accommodated in an existing index page - in this case at the root node.

This node splitting is clearly a significant overhead if it occurs frequently and therefore it should be minimised by not filling the initial index pages to capacity but leaving some free space for index growth. This is done in Sybase by applying a fillfactor to the index pages. This is the percentage full that the pages will be created to. The fillfactor is set as a system wide value by sp_configure or for an individual index in the create index command.

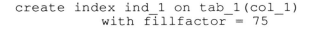

```
create index ind_1 on tab_1(col_1)
           with fillfactor = 75
```

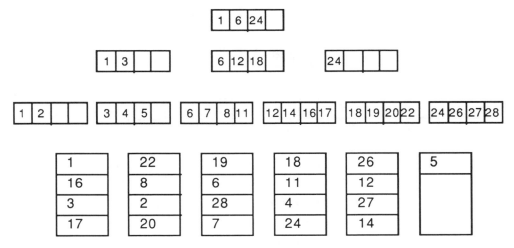

figure 1.36:   insert record 5 to non-clustered index

When the index is created this fillfactor is adhered to as in figure 1.37. The data pages are not disturbed and they remain 100% packed as in any heap structure.

This now gives us space in the index pages for table growth and an insert of record 5 no longer causes node splitting. If we had a 10 byte key the leaf level overhead is 7 bytes which gives 110 index records per page. So a 75% fillfactor will give room for 28 records per page which simply allows us 25% growth - reasonably distributed throughout the key range - before we hit any significant node splitting. Of course it is dependent on the allocation of key values but not an unreasonable assumption.

If your non-clustered Sybase table has a large insert rate always use a reasonable fillfactor to minimise node splitting.

Deletion from a non-clustered table is simple. The record is located via the index, deleted from the page and the index entry deleted. This is a reasonable overhead as the deletes are logged but it is leaf index and data page activity only. You do not go above the leaf level for the deletion as it is a sparse index of first record in the page. Even if you delete the first record in the leaf page it is unusual in B-trees to delete the sparse pointer. (You do not delete it, you update it and it is not worth the bother as it is only a pointer of the lowest value which should be in the page - so normally not deleted/updated. I do not know the actual Sybase processing - one for you to research.)

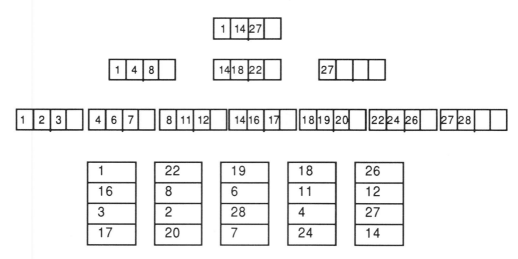

figure 1.37:   non-clustered with fillfactor

However the update in Sybase non-clustering is a totally different matter.

All Sybase updates are done as a deletion followed by an insertion. In general very few are done in place and normally the Sybase update will cause the record to move. Only fixed length field updates have any chance of being done *in situ* and even then the other rules against it are usually overwhelming.

For a table with no clustered index, Sybase update will remove the record from its current page and add it to a new page at the end of the table under the following conditions.

- if a field being updated is variable length

- if a field being updated allows null

- if a field being updated is part of an index

- if the table has an update trigger

- if more than one record is being updated

(Single record update is known to the optimiser if there is a unique index and the update command has a where clause with equality on the index.)

In general one or more of these is difficult to avoid and so you should always assume that the record will not be updated in place (unless you have gone to great lengths to ensure that it is). In the non-clustered table when update in place does not happen the record is deleted from its current page and inserted at the end of the table. This means that the record_id of the record changes - it is made up of the logical page number and the row number in the page - which means that all non-clustered index entries for that record must be updated.

This is a significant overhead which is exacerbated by the Sybase update to the index pages also actioning as a delete followed by an insert.

To update a record:

- the index is searched to locate the leaf entry

- the record is located via the leaf entry pointer

- the record is deleted and the contents of the page shuffled up to ensure free space is at the end of the page

- the leaf entry pointer is deleted and the index entries shuffled up to ensure that free space is at the end of the page

- the updated record is inserted in the last page in the table

- the leaf entry is inserted in the leaf index page

- all the data and index changes are logged

Note that Sybase is unflinching in its adherence to an update being executed as a deletion followed by an insertion. Even if update is done in place the record delete is done and then the record insert is done.

- locate leaf entry

- locate record entry

- delete record and shuffle data

- delete index entry and shuffle index entries

- insert record in same page

- insert leaf index entry

- log all changes

So take great care of update overhead when a table has several indexes. It is very high.

1.6.3 **Clustered**

If the table has only the one index then the index overhead is less if we have a clustered index. In this case the data is in sequence of the index key field as in figure 1.10. Now when we insert record 5 it must go into the first page because according to the existing index structure this page must contain all records from 1 up to, but not including, 6. However there is no room for record 5 so we have to split the data page into two pages as in figure 1.38.

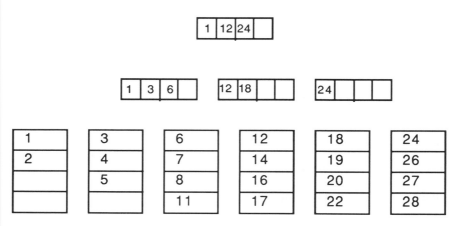

figure 1.38:   clustered B-tree page split

We now have a new data page which has to be indexed at the first intermediate level but there is no room so the node splitting continues until enough space is available to accept the new index pointer - the root node in this case. (If there was no room in the root node this would split creating a new level. Not too great a problem with clustered but this is a large overhead in the Sybase non-clustered index as the index pointers are different in the non-clustered intermediate level and the root level. Considerable activity is necessary to determine the intermediate record_id pointers.)

Again this node splitting can be minimised by a fillfactor which allows free space for expansion in each page. However as the data is the leaf level of the clustered index the fillfactor is applied to the data pages as well as the index pages. This will increase the size of the table which causes all multi-record retrievals to be slower. A 75% fillfactor increases the clustered data by 25% which increases all range enquiries by 25%. This is not to be ignored but normally the processing savings on insert/update are sufficient to justify it.

The clustered index with 75% fillfactor looks like figure 1.39.

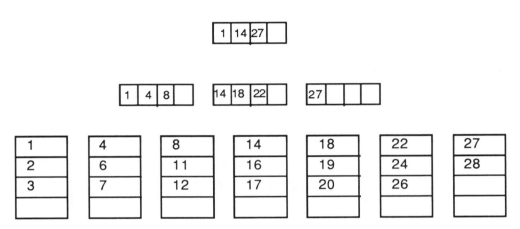

figure 1.39:   clustered B-tree with fillfactor

We can now insert another 25% of the table before we need to update any index. Even then the intermediate index node will not split until we have generated enough data page splits to fill the index page. This takes a high activity rate and clustered with a fillfactor is strongly advisable. But be careful of the increase in range retrieval.

Record deletions have no effect on the clustered index. As mentioned before there is no advantage in deleting sparse B-tree index entries - unless the page is deleted - it is only a pointer to the lowest value which is possible in the page. Sybase does not determine the existence of a record via a clustered index until it reaches the leaf level ie the data page.

Update to the clustered index is again actioned by delete followed by insert. As long as the data page does not split, any activity is contained in the data page level with no clustered index activity.

- locate record via index

- delete record shuffling up data in page

- insert record into page

The record is inserted into the same page because the data is in sequence and therefore, although Sybase has tried its best to move the record, it goes back into the same page.

Of course update may still cause page splitting so a reasonable choice of fillfactor is advisable.

1.6.4 Clustered plus non-clustered

This is a normal situation on a Sybase table: one clustered index and a number of non-clustered indexes. Figure 1.40 shows two indexes: clustered by name and non-clustered by numeric key. Both indexes have been created with 75% fillfactor.

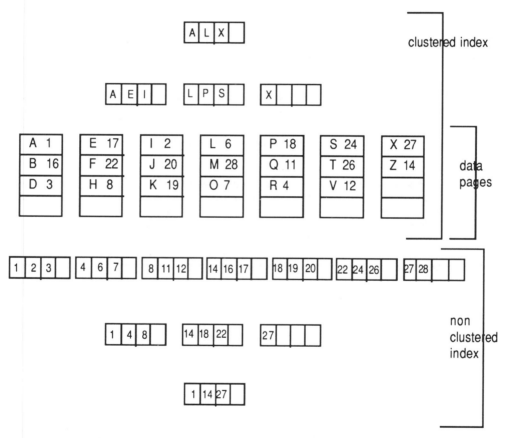

figure 1.40:   clustered and non-clustered indexes

Now when we insert a record we have the overhead of adding it to the data plus creating a new non-clustered index entry.

- locate clustered data page

- insert record

- locate leaf level non-clustered page

- insert index entry

If at any time there is no room in a page the appropriate node splitting will occur.

Deletion removes the record from the data page and updates the non-clustered index entry.

- locate clustered data page

- delete record shuffling data

- locate non-clustered leaf level index page

- delete index entry shuffling data

Update to a record is again expensive as it is equivalent to the above delete followed by the above insert.

- locate clustered index page

- delete record

- locate non-clustered leaf level index page

- delete index entry

- insert record to clustered data page

- insert non-clustered index entry

(Rereading the data and index pages in cache is trivial as it is a hash access to the buffer hash table. The pages are locked and not going anywhere. Well of course they could if there is a requirement for cache space but do *you* have a performance problem if a page you are updating is wrapped out of cache between the delete and the insert.)

This is only one non-clustered index. The overhead of several is additive. I normally find in Sybase that 4 non-clustered indexes on a table being updated needs attention from a performance viewpoint.

Now see how important a good fillfactor is on the data page by looking at the overhead of a data page split. If we add 2 records 'B' and 'C' into the first data page it has to split into two pages containing A, B, B and C, D which requires a new clustered index entry for the new page containing C and D. Fortunately there is enough room for this one new page pointer so there is no further node splitting in the clustered index. But the page split has now moved record D into a new page which has changed its record_id and so the non-clustered index needs updated for the new B and C and the moved D.

- locate clustered data page

- insert records

- split page

- update clustered intermediate level index node for new page

- locate non-clustered leaf page for new B

- insert new B leaf index entry

- locate non-clustered leaf page for new C

- insert new C leaf index entry

- locate non-clustered leaf page for D

- delete D leaf index entry

- insert new D leaf index entry

- log all changes

This is a large overhead (even without index node splitting) so try to avoid data page splitting on a clustered index.

1.7   Page splitting

Having emphasised that it should be avoided with a reasonable choice of fillfactor, let's look at how the page splits.

Index pages always split 50:50 and data pages normally split 50:50. There are 2 exceptions to the data page 50:50 split. The 50:50 split is quite simple as shown in figure 1.41, with half of the records going to a new page and half remaining in the current page.

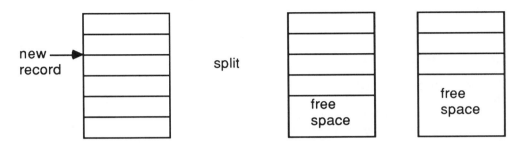

figure 1.41:   50:50 page split

The split is based on number of records and if this gives an uneven space split so that one page is almost full, the split may continue to a third page as shown in figure 1.42.

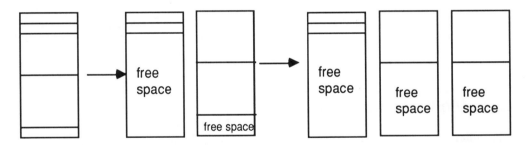

figure 1.42:   three-way split

Notice that the 50:50 split is migrating the table/index towards a 75% full page on average: 100:0 when full, 50:50 when split with an equal probability of every percentage in between. So it is worth starting at 75% with the system wide fillfactor set by sp_configure. If sufficiently active the table/index will migrate to 75% full pages, so why not start there so that range based enquiries do not vary as the fillfactor settles down. Of course if you have a very low activity table or a very high insert rate then override the system setting with an individual setting in create index.

There are two exceptions to the 50:50 data page split - index pages always split 50:50.

monotonic data

duplicate data

In these cases the page splits 100:0 to give an empty page for the new record. This is only on inserts of course: an update which causes a data page split will always split 50:50.

1.7.1 **Monotonic data**

Monotonic data is defined as data with a regularly increasing key such as 1, 2, 3, 4.... The increase does not need to be serial and a date/time key also qualifies as does 1, 3, 6, 7..... Such a key will be filling pages from top to bottom as if the structure was a heap structure with the next key being greater than the previous one and so going into the last page of the table. The server tries to recognise this and not split 50:50 because if it did split 50:50 the empty space would never be used. Instead it splits 100:0 by allocating a new, empty page for the monotonic growth.

Sybase does this if the new record is being added to the foot of the page and the last addition was also to the foot of the page. I have no detail on how Sybase determines this but the obvious method is by the row number in the offset table at the end of the page.

Of course Sybase will get it wrong sometimes but getting it wrong is not going to increase the incidence of page splitting, just delay it to the next record which hits the page left 100% full. In fact it may reduce the incidence slightly as almost empty pages will appear occasionally instead of being half full after a 50:50 split.

1.7.2 **Duplicate keys**

The other occasion of a 100:0 split is when a duplicate key is added. Again Sybase detects this if the new record is being added at the end of the page and the last record was added at the end of the page and was for the same key value. In this case Sybase again splits 100:0 but it is different to the monotonic split as the new page is reserved for the duplicate key value.

In the monotonic case the table continued to grow into the new page making maximum use of the free space in the new page irrespective of the key values. In the duplicate case the new page is reserved for the one key value which caused the split.

In the duplicate case it is not really a page split but a page overflow with the new page being linked to the original page as in figure 1.43.

To add a new record of key 'S' the index points to the original page and then the two overflow pages are scanned to locate the free space for the new record.

This suffers all of the problems of overflow chains when being processed, the principal one being that to locate a specific record the average scan time is half the number of pages in the overflow chain. So be careful if you cluster on a key field which contains replicates: it is fast for retrieval but you may see the updates hesitate occasionally when they happen to hit a long chain of duplicate values.

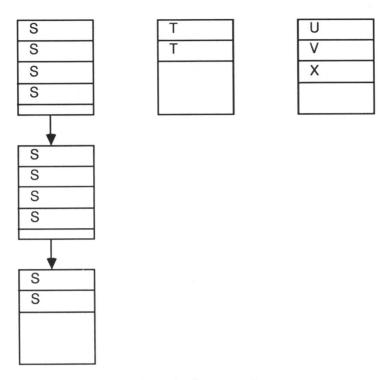

figure 1.43:   duplicate overflow

1.8 **Fragmentation**

Deletes from a table always leave holes of free space throughout the table. Sybase always shuffles the records in a page to ensure that the free space is at the end of each page, but if the key does not cause random insert hits on the pages this free space per page will be largely unused.

In a heap table, free space in a page is never reused. All inserts to a heap structure are always at the end of the table, so any deletes throughout the table leave free space which is unused.

In a clustered table the free space is reused as long as the key is chosen so that new records are inserted throughout the table and not concentrated on a group of pages or at the end of the table as in monotonic data.

However you must always be aware that there will be an element of free space throughout the table especially within the pages.

When a data page is completely emptied it is not returned to free space but is still part of the allocation to the table as it is still part of an 8 page extent. It is simply marked as deallocated by the extent structure bit map but still reserved for the table. Sybase does not return pages to free space until a complete extent of 8 pages is deallocated. Therefore when a request is made for a new data page Sybase will allocate one of the deallocated extent pages that it has currently reserved for the table. Not until there are no deallocated extent pages will Sybase request another extent from free space.

Index page maintenance is as for data page maintenance with one exception. When a transaction is traversing the index and it comes across an index page containing one index entry it will merge that index entry with an adjacent index page on the same level and delete the now empty page.

Note that Sybase does not initialise pages when they are returned to free space: they are initialised when retrieved from free space: so an insert/ update which requires a new extent will need to wait while Sybase initialises the 8 pages.

1.9 **Summary**

Most of the Unix relational databases are on a par when it comes to facilities and performance. Sybase addressed itself to a performance based, client/server architecture to provide a tangible difference to the other products. Such features as stored procedures and sparse B-tree indexing were new features aimed at performance, the former only now being achieved by Sybase's rivals and the latter still being unique. Dictionary based domain (rules, defaults) and referential (trigger) integrity coupled with a change to the standard locking scenario introduced a major advantage in the client/server world of database processing.

There are flaws in the overall picture - it would be strange if there were not - the most significant being a stoic adherence to page level locking and an annoying lack of performance in the implementation of triggers. This is not meant to imply that Sybase triggers are inefficient: they compare very favourably with the other vendor's implementations of rules/triggers, but that there are times when the trigger code is interpreted instead of being compiled, which gives a slower response time.

However it is not unreasonable to congratulate Sybase on achieving its first step in a high performance client/server architecture and we look with interest at the next stages in the development to consolidate this and use its open server architecture to solve some of the new problems introduced by client/server processing in a distributed database environment. The use of open servers functioning as clients and/or servers depending on the processing requirements and communicating by remote procedure calls which support two-phase commit, has Sybase well placed to take maximum advantage of their slight lead in this new computing environment.

And finally....

About seven years after leaving college, two ladies met by chance in the
High Street of a small town. They retired to a coffee shop to discuss what had
happened to them in the intervening years. One was very talkative and held the floor
non-stop for ten minutes talking about her husband, marriage, children, house and so
on.

Realising that she had hogged the conversation, she apologised and asked her
companion about her life.

"Well I'm married. In fact I've been married for five years, but I have no children. In
fact I'm still a virgin."

Seeing her friend's eyebrows rise, she continued:

"It must be difficult for you to understand. You see, I married a successful Sybase
salesman and all he does is sit at the end of the bed and tell me how good it is going to
be when I eventually get it!"

Chapter 2

Installing
and
starting
a server

This chapter describes how to install and start a server. The installation files - interfaces, RUNSERVER and errorlog - are described in detail and their role in connecting clients and using the server is explained.
The contents of the master device - master, model, tempdb - are described with the emphasis on the system tables in master.

O'Reilly's Second Law

When all else fails, read the instructions.

Commands covered in this chapter:

sybconfig (sybinstall/
                        vmsinstal)
startserver
showserver
shutdown

2.1   Introduction

Sybase uses the term System Administrator (SA) for the function which administers the database and its environment. This is known by most of us in the database world as the Database Administrator (DBA) and this is what Sybase means. However as this is a treatment of Sybase, I shall defer to their term of SA although, personally, it conjures up a much more global administration function than just the database. A minor point, but be careful, SA means database administration only.

How does one become the SA? Well usually by being in the wrong place at the wrong time because who in their right mind really wants to be the SA. Working all the unsociable hours because you cannot do what you want without stopping the operational system, and taking all the flak when something goes wrong, whether it's your fault or not.

In my case I was sitting in the office at 18:30 when the boss came out of his office. I thought that he had gone and I was just making up my flexitime. He says "Ah, John..." Now that's a cue for beating a hasty retreat when the boss approaches you like that. "We've just got TOTAL onto the system. I think it would a great idea for you to set it up and find out as much as you can about it." So I became the DBA. And I loved it: but it is a thankless task

Having been volunteered as the SA, how do you get into Sybase as the SA? You log in as "sa" with a null password. Immediately after installation the system is set up to recognise the SA as the user "sa" with a null password. As soon as you have logged in, change the password using sp_password. Sybase recognises the special user "sa" and allows this user access to everywhere with all read/write/execute rights. So if someone finds out your "sa" password (s)he can do considerable damage. Never disclose your "sa" password. If you are a single SA as opposed to an SA group then I'll explain later in chapter 4 how to grant temporary permissions to other users if they require access because you are not there.

If you are an experienced SA already then you will find Sybase lacking in the really helpful support facilities that the SA needs in an emergency. Like when you have a disk full problem...what has caused it? What databases are on the disk and what tables are on each database? This really should not be too unexpected since Sybase is only about 10 years old as an operational product and such facilities are only beginning to appear, mainly from third parties.

2.2   Installation

Before we can use the system we need to install it. If this is not your responsibility as the SA then make it so. At the very least look over the shoulder of the software installer and see what is happening. I'm sure that if you offer to do it there will be no problem.

Sybase is loaded from the tape (or whatever) as a SYBASE directory (the upper case is just for emphasis) which contains the sub-directories as shown in figure 2.1.

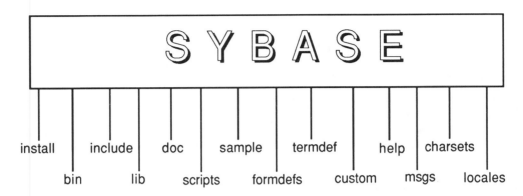

figure 2.1:   Sybase software directories

Briefly these contain:

install	Installation programs, readme files and server configuration files.
bin	Executables for the standard routines run from the operating system eg the bulk copy facility, bcp, the line input sql routine, isql, and the data server.
include	Header files for libraries.
lib	Host language libraries.
doc	On-line manual pages.
scripts	Various sql scripts used during the installation.
sample	Db-library and/or apt sample code.
formdefs	Forms to run data workbench (dwb) and/or apt.
termdef	Compiled terminal definition files for use by dwb and apt.
custom	Customise files for dwb users.
help	Help message text.
msgs	System messages eg login screen, copyright etc.

charsets   Character set translation and sort order files.

locales   Language specific files.

Typically this directory structure will be sub-directories of the home directory of the user SYBASE. If you are using another directory structure then it must be owned by the user SYBASE and the environment variable SYBASE must point to the base directory.


```
eg    setenv SYBASE /usr/u/sybase/directory

      DEFINE SYBASE [SYBASE.DIRECTORY]
```


(In all of the following discussions I shall assume Unix environments and refer to VMS only when there is a difference in the Sybase command.)

Once the vendor's software is on the disk then we need to install one or more database servers to support our data and processing environment. How many servers? One will do but you may find it easier to control if you have more than one server. Say one for the test databases and one for the operational databases. It's up to you. My personal preference is to have two servers: test and operational. I find it much easier to control access to each of them and I can play with the test server without disrupting the operational server. Even the SA needs somewhere to test new software and changes.

So how do we install a server?

To install a server, attach to the $SYBASE/install directory and issue the command:

sybconfig   (sybinstall for versions earlier than 4.8)

```
                      sybconfig
```


(In VMS you will need to log on as SYSTEM to have sufficient privileges to complete the installation and enter:


```
$    @SYS$UPDATE:VMSINSTAL SYBASE010 SYB_DEVICE
```


where SYB_DEVICE is the name of the device containing the SYBASE software.)

During the installation you will be asked a few pieces of information which you will need to decide in advance.

server name	default SYBASE, otherwise up to you
pathname	full pathname for server location

size of master device	raw partition in sectors	
	minimum	20480
	recommended	28672
	Unix file in M bytes	
	minimum	10
	recommended	14

query port number	the network port number that the client/server connection uses. Used port numbers will be in /etc/services which you need to keep up to date as it is not updated by the installation.
serial number	the Sybase site serial number.
default language/ sort order	depends on the version of the server and if you requested other than US/English.

The installation consists of a series of menus from which you select the type of installation.

sybconfig presents:

Select Sybase product to be installed

1   SQL Server
2   Open Client/C
3   Data Workbench
4   Report-Execute
5   APT-Execute
6   APT Workbench

Selecting 1 presents:

Please select type of install

1   Initialise software
2   Install a new server
3   Upgrade an existing server

r   return to previous menu
x   Exit to operating system

Selecting 1 requests the serial number and then sets the appropriate permissions on the files. Once this is done the same menu is displayed. Selecting 2 presents.

1   Raw disk partition
2   Regular Unix file

r   return to previous menu
x   Exit to operating system

Selecting 1 or 2 requests the pathname, master device size, server name, query port number and language information. Be careful when you create a raw partition for Sybase as it must not begin at track 0, cylinder 0. This stores the disk label and if Sybase is installed on a raw partition which includes it, Sybase will happily overwrite the disk label.

2.2.1 Installation files

If you accepted the default server name during installation then it is called SYBASE. This server has three important files:

$SYBASE/install/**errorlog**

$SYBASE/install/**RUNSERVER**

$SYBASE/**interfaces**

In VMS: $SYBASE_SYSTEM:[SYBASE.INSTALL]**errorlog**

$SYBASE_SYSTEM:[SYBASE.INSTALL]**RUNSERVER**

$SYBASE_SYSTEM:[SYBASE.INSTALL]**interfaces.**

Note the '.' at the end of the interfaces file name in VMS. This is necessary otherwise the name defaults to interfaces.lis.

If the installation failed then you are probably logged in as the wrong user. The sybase/install directory is owned by SYBASE and you may need to be logged in as SYBASE to install a server. There are many other reasons for the installation to fail, such as devices not owned by SYBASE, wrong kernel booted (ie supplied by Sybase),

such as devices not owned by SYBASE, wrong kernel booted (ie supplied by Sybase), master device size wrong, insufficient swap space, network port number in use ... but do not panic, these are documented in the installation guide or the troubleshooting guide and are easily corrected.

If you have started a second server or chosen a name other than the default (say test) then this server has three important files:

$SYBASE/install/**errorlog_test**

$SYBASE/install/**RUN_test**

$SYBASE/**interfaces**

In other words each server has its own errorlog file, its own RUNSERVER file and shares an interfaces file. Note that the RUNSERVER file name is in uppercase...not important in VMS but a nuisance in Unix.

The client accessing software and the server use these files to determine where the server is in the network and where the databases used by the server are on the disks. The interfaces file specifies the server network information and the RUNSERVER file specifies the server disk information.

Connection from a client is via a runtime variable DSQUERY which specifies the name of the server which the client is using.

```
             setenv DSQUERY test

In VMS:      define DSQUERY test
```

Again these variables are in upper case and the setting of the variables in Unix depends on the Unix shell you are using:

```
eg    Bourne shell

         DSQUERY=test
         export DSQUERY
```

Setting this instructs the client application that the server being used is "test". This points the client at the relevant entries in the interfaces file which indicate the network node that the server resides on and the port numbers to be used for the connection. Our dual SYBASE and test servers could have an interfaces file of:

```
#
SYBASE
        query tcp sun-ether fred 2001
        master tcp sun-ether fred 2001
        console tcp sun-ether fred 2002

#
test
        query tcp sun-ether fred 9996
        master tcp sun-ether fred 9996
        console tcp sun-ether fred 9997
```

Query is the port number used by clients connecting to the server to transmit and execute SQL queries. Master is the port number on which the server "listens" for input from the clients. Console is the port number that the server uses to perform tape back-ups.

Sun-ether is the network type and fred is the network host name. So both of our servers are on the same network node.

Having the location of the server, the RUNSERVER file tells the server where the master device and the errorlog are located. We now have everything that we need with the client connected to the appropriate server which has the location of the system tables in the master device and the file in which it can log messages and errors. These are obligatory for a functioning server although the console terminal will be used by the server for the error and warning messages if you accidentally delete the erroglog. Note that if you do delete the errorlog to free some space, it is not immediately available but is reclaimed only when the server has been shutdown.

Let's look at the contents of interfaces and RUNSERVER in a little more detail by considering a client - dwb - connecting to the server "test" located on the network node glenlivet. There is another server - sales - on the network node lagavulin.

interfaces

```
#
test
        query tcp sun-ether glenlivet 1025
        master tcp sun-ether glenlivet 1025
        console tcp sun-ether glenlivet 1026
#
sales
        query tcp sun-ether lagavulin 3000
        master tcp sun-ether lagavulin 3000
        console tcp sun-ether lagavulin 3001
```

```
RUN_test
    #! /bin/csh -f
    #  server name: test
    #  dslisten port:1025
    #  master name: /dev/rsd3d
    #  master size: 51200

    setenv DSLISTEN test

    $SYBASE/bin/dataserver
    -d/dev/rsd3d
    -e$SYBASE/install/errorlog_test
```

The size in RUNSERVER is in pages (2K usually) although the installation requests the size in sectors (512 bytes) when using a raw partition.

The client software with DSQUERY set to "test" locates the interfaces entry for "test". It always knows where this is as it is in the directory pointed to by the SYBASE variable. The entries for "test" in the interfaces file indicate the node on the network on which the "test" server resides and the port number which is used for the client-server communication. The RUN_test file for this server then completes the loop, specifying the location of the master device and errorlog_test file. The RUN_test file also contains the server DSLISTEN variable which corresponds to the client DSQUERY variable. Note that the port number in the RUNSERVER file is for documentation only and startserver does not check it.

So to connect to the default server:

```
        setenv SYBASE ~sybase

        setenv DSQUERY SYBASE
```

To connect to a non-default server:

```
        setenv SYBASE $SYBASE/test
        (a different directory containing the interfaces
          file for the test server)

        setenv DSQUERY test
```

When you have a multiple server configuration with servers on each node then there will be an interfaces file on each network node. This will have been created independently on each network node. When new servers are created on the same node of the network the entries are appended to the interfaces file. However when a new node has a server defined on it, the interfaces file on the new node is independent of the other nodes and contains only the server(s) on that node. For Open Server operation in a Sybase environment it is necessary to have each interfaces file contain every server on the network. This is not done automatically by Sybase and you will need to create a master interfaces file using a text editor to include references to every inter-communicating server in the network, and copy it to each node. So even if you do not have a network at the moment, plan ahead by using unique server names on the separate machines and identical interface files on each machine.

2.2.2 Master device

As part of the installation the master device is created. The disk location for this is requested during installation and it contains three databases: master, model and tempdb as shown in figure 2.2.

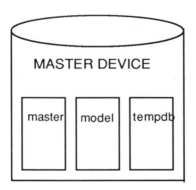

figure 2.2:   server initialisation

master: This is the database which contains the system tables - called the system catalog by Sybase. These tables are a complete definition of the databases, tables and other objects used by the server.

model: This is the template database which is used by the create database command. A copy of the contents of model is loaded into each new database during the create database. The size of model is also taken as the default size of the new database. The default size of the database, if no size is given in the create command, is the larger of model and a

no size is given in the create command, is the larger of model and a configuration variable - set using sp_configure. The default configuration setting is 2 M bytes. So the default, default size is 2 M bytes.

tempdb: This is the server working storage. Any command which uses temporary working storage uses tempdb. No other area is used for working storage. Of course if the requirement is small then cache will be used but it is still an allocation from tempdb.

The size of the master is determined by the need for temporary storage but, as a minimum 14 M bytes is needed to hold the three databases: master, model and tempdb. The size of the master device is requested during the install and is given in megabytes if the device is a disk file or in sectors if the device is a raw partition. (Raw partitions are recommended for Unix to ensure 100% recoverability. I shall cover this in detail in chapter 3 although I have already mentioned to avoid the disk label.) The master device will default to 10 M bytes but do not accept this and use the recommended 14 M bytes.

The system tables in the master database will grow as the system grows - number of objects being more important than data size in this case. There is no standard size but about 4 M bytes will usually be required for this database.

Model will contain little of any size and the default size of 2 M bytes is usually sufficient for model.

Therefore tempdb is the dominant database when deciding space for the master device. A decision is not necessary at this point and the 14 M bytes will ensure sufficient space for installation. The master device may be extended later once the tempdb requirements are better understood. (We shall discuss this in more detail when we look at space allocation in chapter 3.)

Model is useful to the SA when there is a set of definitions which needs to be globally shared: for example standard rules and defaults which each new database must contain. By defining these in model they are automatically created in each new database. They must be copied to existing databases which I shall deal with in chapter 5.

So the installation of a server creates a master device containing 3 databases and three files as shown in figure 2.2.

2.2.3 Console program

To enable the "dump" and "load" commands to use tape drives, the console program has to be running. To start the console program:

```
$sybase/bin/console
```

2.3 Starting and shutting down the server

Having installed a server - and it takes less time than it took for me to explain it - although you need a little preplanning mainly on network names and port numbers, it is not yet functioning and has to be started. (Recent releases of the install using sybconfig leave the server running.) This is done quite simply by attaching to $sybase/install and entering the command:

```
startserver
```

There is a 50:50 chance at this point that it will not work of course. This is always because you are logged into Unix as the wrong user. Remember that the install directories are owned by SYBASE so log in as SYBASE to start the server if you have a problem.

The startserver as above starts the default server SYBASE. To start another server use the -f option:

```
startserver -f RUN_test
```

The full syntax of the command is:

startserver

```
startserver -f runserver_file_name   -m
```

where: -f runserver_file_name   is used to start a non-default server
            -m   is used to run in single user SA mode
                                        (usually to rebuild the master device after
                                        a failure)

VMS:
```
startserver /server=servername /masterrecover
```

So a typical startserver execution will be:

Unix

```
cd $SYBASE/install
startserver
```

VMS

```
set default $SYBASE_SYSTEM:[.install]
startserver
```

This will display any action taken to recover incomplete transactions from the previous shutdown. As well as displaying these as the server is started, the messages are also recorded in the errorlog. If you have an automatic start-up routine it is always worthwhile to check the errorlog after the start, just in case. A point worth noting is that the errorlog is always appended to and will eventually fill up the disk on which it is placed, unless you take some clean-up action. Allowing the errorlog to fill up will cause performance problems as all messages will be sent to the console terminal. Any automatic start-up is a good place to rename the old errorlog before the server restarts. Don't delete it without copying it first as you may need it for audit purposes.

To see which servers are currently active use the showserver command:

showserver

```
showserver
```

user	pid	%cpu	%mem	sz	rss	tt	stat	time
sybase	1234	0.0	0.7	112	88	01	I	0:00
				/usr/sybase/bin/dataserver				
				-d/dev/rxy1d				
				-e/usr/sybase/install/errorlog_test				
sybase	1235	0.0	20.2	3512	3168	01	I	0:06
				/usr/sybase/bin/dataserver				
				-d/dev/rxy2d				
				-e/usr/sybase/install/errorlog				

Apart from telling which servers are active this tells us where the master device and the errorlog are. As the output does not show you the name of the server this is often the easiest clue to the name of the server - default uses errorlog, a named server uses errorlog_name.

The VMS output does not give you the errorlog name so you need to use the process_id - pid - and match this to the object name which is the name in the interfaces file.

```
ncp> show known objects
ncp> exit
```

To stop an active server use the shutdown command from isql:

shutdown

```
shutdown [with nowait]
```

The nowait option shuts the server down immediately without waiting for any of the currently executing processes to complete, so any restart after this shutdown will recover each database. Normal shutdown does the following:

> disables all logins except "sa"
> prevents existing users running any more commands
> waits for currently executing commands to complete
> performs checkpoints in each database
> causes the SQL server process to exit

Remember at this point that we have just installed the server so the "sa" password is null. Do not hesitate. Login into isql as "sa" and change the password. And do not forget your "sa" password because you will not be able to get into the server as "sa" without killing the Unix process, deleting the server and reinstalling - which reassigns a null password to "sa".

Stopping a server is easy enough and you will need to do it regularly but occasionally you will want to delete a server completely - to remove an old test or training server. To delete the server you need to remove all traces of it from the system and it is not done automatically. You need to:

> delete the RUNSERVER file
> delete the errorlog file
> delete the master device!!!! (if an operating system file)
> edit the interfaces file to remove the server entry

In other words delete everything that the install creates.

2.4   **System tables**

Now that we have installed and started the server, let's discuss the system tables which
are in the master database. These are all that we have at the moment as we have not yet
created any databases or tables of our own. So most of the tables will be empty and the
system catalog will contain only system information. Any system catalog contains a
record of itself, otherwise it does not conform to the relational model.

There is a set of system catalog tables which resides on the master database and not on
any other. These tables describe the global server components.

syscharsets	Information about the available character sets or sort orders.
sysconfigures	Tunable server parameters such as recovery interval, available memory, number of user connections.
sysdatabases	Information about every database on the server such as owner, recovery information.
sysdevices	Information about available space for databases and dumps. If a device is not in this table it cannot be used by the server.
sysengines	One row for each SQL Server engine currently on-line.
syslanguages	The languages known to the server.
syslogins	All valid SQL server account logins.
sysmessages	All SQL message text.
sysremotelogins	Defines the remote account logins.
sysservers	Defines the remote servers.
sysusages	Information on the allocation of databases to physical space.
syscurconfigs	The current server parameters.
syslocks	The current active locks.
sysprocesses	The current server processes.

The last three master tables - syscurconfigs, syslocks, sysprocesses - are dynamic tables which are built when the user requests to see the contents. They are not retained on disk but created when the information is requested by the user.

There is a second set of system tables which is database specific and therefore resides on each database. As the master database is a database in its own right, it also has a set of these tables.

sysalternates	Defines the aliases for a user in the database.
syscolumns	Defines each column used in tables in the database.
syscomments	The text comments for procedures, triggers, views and rules.
sysdepends	Defines dependency relationships between objects in the database eg a table referenced in a trigger.
sysindexes	Defines the disk space used by tables and indexes in the database.
syskeys	Contains the definitions of the primary, foreign and common keys.
syslogs	The transaction log.
sysobjects	Defines each object in the database.
sysprocedures	The compiled stored procedures.
sysprotects	Defines what each user can do.
syssegments	Defines the segments declared for the logical mapping of objects to devices.
systypes	Defines the user datatypes in the database.
sysusermessages	The user defined messages which are used in procedures.
sysusers	Defines who can use the database.

These tables make up the Sybase system catalog and to function properly as an SA you must have a detailed understanding and familiarity with the content of each of these tables. To understand why a procedure like:

```
create proc objects @type varchar(2)
as
begin
      select name from sysobjects
            where type = @type
end
return
```

is important and necessary, and to further understand its shortcomings are fundamental
requirements of any good SA. To get you to this level of knowledge I shall explain
each system table in detail as we use the commands which create entries in them. Of
course there are Sybase system procedures which display the contents of the system
tables and in general these are quite sufficient. However there are a few instances where
the system procedures are insufficient - like the above list of object types in a database.
In these cases you need to create your own procedures and to do that you need to
understand the system catalog tables. Even if you do not create your own procedures
you still need a detailed understanding of the catalog. Chapter 3 discusses some user
commands to extract useful information from the system tables.

Sybase do not make it easy. Sometimes the joins between the system tables are not as
obvious as the schemas in the vendor's documentation make them appear to be. The
principal examples of this are the joins between sysusages and syssegments where the
join is via the field segmap which is a bit map of the segment allocation and between
syssegments and sysdevices where the join is on the first database page number of the
segment being between the low and high numbers of the device. Not only that but it
makes you look good if you have all of these special commands at your disposal. And
if you have been in the job of SA for long, you know that you need an edge most of the
time.

Figure 2.3 is a schema diagram of the system tables present only in master and figure
2.4 of the system tables present in any database (including master). There are foreign
key joins between some of the tables in the separate schema diagrams such as SUID
from syslogins to sysusers, but I have not shown them to keep the diagrams simpler.

Appendix A gives a list of the system tables with descriptions of the fields and indexes.

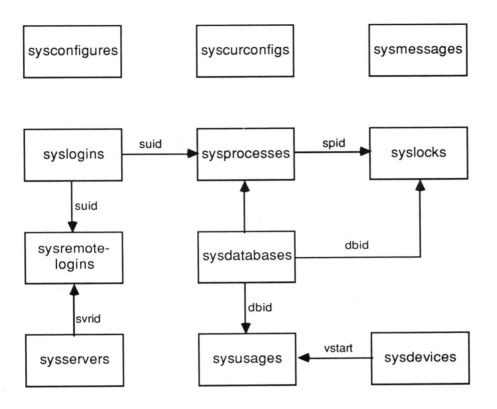

figure 2.3:   master only system table schema

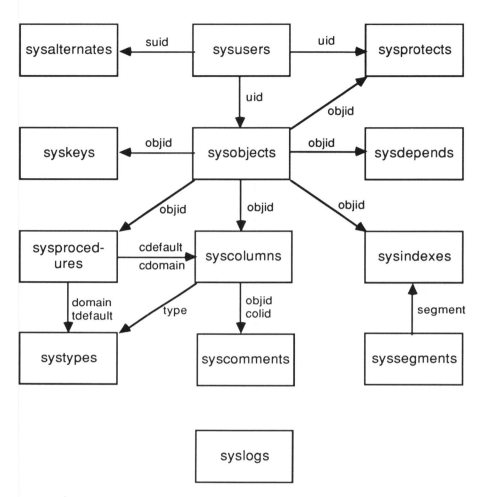

figure 2.4:   all databases system table schema

2.5   **Summary**

Installation of Sybase is a simple exercise with a little advance planning of server name, master device size and network information.

The installation creates the files:

interfaces	defines server network information
RUNSERVER	defines server disk layout
errorlog	records all messages

and the databases

master	contains the system catalog
model	create database template
tempdb	working storage

Starting and stopping the server uses the commands

startserver	starts the server defined in the RUNSERVER file
shutdown	run from isql to stop the current server

Since 4.0.1 the major version 4 releases have been about internationalisation features, although much work has also been done on the back-up server and multi-processing.

4.2	International language capabilities.
4.8	Multi-processing, multi-byte character sets.
4.9	Maintenance release.

2.6   Questions and research

1 You have been called in to someone else's installation and asked to take over the SA role. Fortunately the "sa" password is null. How do you find out as much as you can about the Sybase installation.

And finally....

The year was 1974. The IT industry was desperately trying to convince everyone that computers were the things to help you run your business successfully in modern times.

The IRA, however, were not impressed and planted a bomb at ICL's Bridge House offices in Putney. The bomb duly went off but thankfully no-one was hurt.

An ICL spokesman sought to play down the incident by cheerfully announcing

"...there was little damage because there are no computers in the building."

Chapter 3

Allocating space and creating databases

This chapter describes the initialisation of disk space and its allocation to databases and logs including disk mirroring and use of the default device. Creation and expansion of databases and logs is covered with a treatment of how to estimate the necessary sizes.
The logical segmentation of the space is described to demonstrate how database objects may be placed on separate devices.

O'Reilly's Third Law

Inside every small database there is a big one bursting to be set free.

Commands covered in this chapter:

> **disk init**
> **disk mirror**
> **disk unmirror**
> **disk remirror**
> **create database**
> **alter database**
> **drop database**

System procedures covered in this chapter:

> **sp_diskdefault**
> **sp_helpdevice**
> **sp_spaceused**
> **sp_logdevice**
> **sp_dboption**
> **sp_addsegment**
> **sp_dropsegment**
> **sp_placeobject**
> **sp_helpdb**
> **sp_helpsegment**

3.1   Introduction

Sybase allocates space in several steps:

> physical allocation
> logical segmentation
> database creation

The physical initialisation reserves areas of the actual disk drives for the server. Sybase calls these devices. These devices are then logically divided into segments to allow object placement. The databases are created on the pre-allocated devices and the objects of the databases are created on the logical segments belonging to these devices. This placement of objects into segments of a database which occupies specific disk areas, allows complete control over disk usage both for space and disk access utilisation.

3.2   Disk initialisation

Sybase allocates disk space to a server. The physical disk drives of your installation are initialised as Sybase devices and are available for the server to which you are logged on at the time you issue the initialise command. Sybase has no practical limit to the amount of space that you may allocate to a server, although there are limits to the number of devices per server and segments per database, and in practice you will tend to be hardware restricted. In general, however, you will plan your disk allocation according to your database requirements and therefore may I recommend a simple disk initialisation of one or a few devices per physical disk drive. If your databases are large enough or you can share several into one device then one device per physical disk drive is good enough. However there are excellent reasons for smaller devices for logs, the master device and for small, secure databases.

So we could have an initialisation as shown in figure 3.1 which shows two physical disks, one with two devices and one with one device.

Sybase unfortunately interchanges the words device and disk in all of its literature. Wherever you see the term disk in Sybase literature it means a Sybase device ie a physical allocation of disk space which belongs to a server and resides on a physical disk drive as an operating system file or a raw partition. I shall always use the word device except in the command syntax where disk is used.

Note that the Sybase allocation of disk space is a physical allocation which takes up disk space as an operating system file or a raw partition. (Unix actually creates a sparse file and does not grab the space until you request it in a create database command. So you may not have what you think you have if other systems are contending for the physical space. Be careful.)

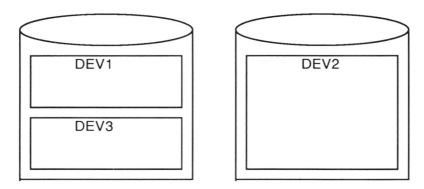

figure 3.1:   device initialisation

It is essential in Unix that you make the operational logs and master devices as raw partitions and give careful consideration to making the operational databases raw partitions as well. As raw partitions Sybase has complete control over cache management and when the Sybase cache manager writes a page to disk it is physically output to the disk. If you use Unix files then, when the Sybase cache manager writes a page to disk, the Unix file manager intercepts this request and if Unix has room in its cache the write does not go to disk at that time but waits until the Unix cache manager needs space or until the periodic flush exercise. So when a system failure occurs Sybase cannot guarantee 100% that it can recover a Unix file because of the Unix operating system intervention in the cache management. The server cannot always recover because the Unix cache may not write the pages in the order that they were written by the server. If a data page is written before a corresponding log page and there is a failure between the writes: recovery is impossible. Possibly not a serious problem for test and development databases but not to be recommended for logs, master and production databases.

To initialise device space issue the disk init command:

disk init

```
disk init
      name = "logical_name",
      physname = "physical_name",
      vdevno = device_number,
      size = number_of_pages
      [, vstart = virtual_address]
      [, cntrltype = controller_number]
      [, contiguous]
```

where:

name	The name of the device in all references within Sybase.
physname	The name of the operating system file or raw partition. In Unix the operating system file must not already exist. The SYBASE account must have read/write access to the directory containing the raw partition and file creation privilege to the directory which will contain the operating system file.
vdevno	A unique device number from 1 up to a configurable maximum. sp_helpdevice shows the device numbers already used and sp_configure shows the maximum. Device number 0 is reserved for the master device and the maximum is 255 devices per server.
size	The size of the device in Sybase pages (generally 2K).
vstart	The virtual address of the start of the device. Do NOT touch this parameter, Sybase will allocate it automatically.
cntrltype	A type number which identifies the device type: disk or tape. Do NOT set this for disks. The server sets it automatically.
contiguous	Used with VMS disk files only, to ensure contiguous space on the disk. The device will not be created if enough contiguous space is not available.

```
disk init
      name = 'test_dev',
      physname = '/dev/rsd3d',
      vdevno = 10, size = 204800
```

This creates a disk device called test_dev as a raw partition with a size of 400 M bytes. If you make a mistake in this command such as specifying an already existing disk file the errorlog contains the error message. If disk init fails while setting up the disk space it can leave you with problems. In Unix there is a reasonable chance that the file will remain in existence and you will need to delete the file to reissue the same command. Also under Unix the server may have registered the virtual device number and you may not be able to reuse this number until you have rebooted the server. Under VMS the logical_name may be still in use and not reusable until you have restarted the server.

Every device that you create uses up 34 K real memory (64 K with open server), so don't get carried away: the simpler the better.

A slight digression before we talk any more about devices to paint the overall physical picture of a server environment.

Figure 3.2 illustrates the basic relationships between the objects which define the server space allocation.

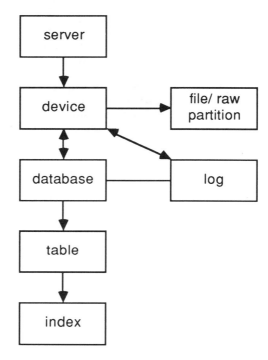

figure 3.2:   physical relationships

There is an additional logical segmentation of devices which I shall deal with later in this chapter.

The server has many devices and a device belongs to one and only one server. This is true of database devices only as dump devices may be shared by several servers.

A device may have many databases and a database may be spread across many devices.

Each database has one log and the log belongs to one database but may be on one or more devices which may also be data devices. However a data device is always a data device which may contain a log. A log device is reserved solely for logs. You may redesignate a data device as a log device: however you will be unable to write data pages to the device and reads will cause warning messages to be written to the errorlog.

There is no system procedure to reverse this accidental designation and you need to update the system tables by resetting the segmap in sysusages. This requires "allow update" access to the system tables and is not a good idea. Try not to make this mistake. (Recovering the data without updating sysusages is discussed in section 3.12.)

Each database may have many tables and each table many indexes with an index being defined on one table and a table being defined on one database. I have diagrammed this rather simply as it is a logical relationship where a given table or index name may be present in several databases although they are separate objects which are fully qualified by the database name. In other words, the primary key to an index is database_name.table_name.index_name. Allocation of tables and indexes is further defined by logical segments which I explain later. (In fact the primary key to an object also contains the owner name, as I explain in chapter 4: database_name.owner_name.object_name.)

3.3 Device mirroring

The mapping of devices to operating system files or raw partitions is shown as one to many but this is not a true one to many relationship as a device is mapped to a file or partition on a one to one basis. The many aspect is caused by the ability to mirror a device to maintain a physical up-to-date copy of the device's contents. Thus a device is mapped to one partition or file, which may be mirrored, and each file or partition can contain only one device or the mirror of the device.

Devices are mirrored with the disk mirror command:

disk mirror

```
disk mirror
    name = "logical_name",
    mirror = "physical_name"
    [, writes = {serial  |  noserial}]
    [, reads = {mirrored  |  nomirrored}]
    [, contiguous]
```

where

name   Logical name of the device to be mirrored as defined in the "disk init" command.

mirror   Physical file or raw partition name of the mirror device.

writes   Specifies whether the writes to the devices are serial in that the primary finishes before the secondary device starts or parallel which permits the writes to take place at the same time. Default is serial.

reads

Mirrored reads allow the server to optimise data reads by choosing the fastest response from the mirrored combination for an SQL select. Default is mirrored.

contiguous

Allocates contiguous disk space for VMS as with disk init.

```
disk mirror
        name = "disk_mirr1",
        mirror = "/mirr/rsd4m"
```

Note that Sybase mirroring is on a device basis and that device to database mapping is many to many. So to retain a physical mirror of a database you must mirror every device that the database is allocated to and this may cause portions of other databases to be mirrored if a device is being shared.

Ideal candidates for mirroring are the master device and the log device(s). If you lose the master device, the server crashes and no work can take place. So mirror it to ensure that a single failure does not bring the system down. Have a "waitfor mirrorexit" to ensure early warning when one of the mirrors fails. The failure is recorded in the errorlog.

Similarly the log device(s) should be mirrored. Each database has a log which should be on a separate device from the database for recovery reasons (see chapter 5). The logs may share one log device although this may create rather a bottleneck on disk activity. No matter the configuration, mirror the log device(s). A log device failure means that the database is unusable, so again, to protect from a single failure bringing the system down, mirror the log device(s).

In an ideal world every device would be mirrored for redundancy purposes - which is applied by some fault tolerant systems. If data fault tolerance is essential then you must mirror the data devices. This can benefit retrieval but will degrade updates. Sybase issues both read requests and uses the result returned first to respond and ignores the second result. If one of the disks is heavily loaded by non-Sybase activity this may provide a perceived improvement in the response time. (I say may because nothing is certain in performance and such factors as other activity on the physical disk and cache usage will impact on the throughput.)

Updates, of course, are degraded as the write has to take place to two devices. The choices are in series or in parallel. Serial writes take place to the primary device and, once that has been committed, to the mirrored device. Parallel writes take place at the same time to both devices. Note that only the transaction commits take place to disk during the database transaction, all of the data page updates take place in cache and the cache manager or checkpoint decides when the page will be written to disk. So the majority of the update is logical and does not take place during the transaction lifetime and has no effect on the individual transaction response time (unless the system is disk bound when any increase in disk activity will have a detrimental effect). But do not ignore the overhead: it is twice as many writes which must be absorbed by the overall disk capacity. And remember that it is the device which is mirrored so any page updates - including indexes - are mirrored.

My personal preference is to mirror the master device(s) and the log devices but consider data mirroring very carefully. When the master device is mirrored, it may be a good idea to reduce the mirroring load by moving tempdb to another disk which is not mirrored. Failure of a non-mirrored tempdb is not such a serious problem as it may seem, as not all transactions will fail when tempdb is not available.

Sybase data mirroring is an overhead and there are alternatives which you should consider: such as mirroring at the hardware level, eg Digital's disk shadowing, or processing the transaction log dumps against a database dump to maintain an up-to-date database dump as stand by.

3.3.1 Mirroring the master device

Mirroring the master device is an excellent idea but is not done in a uniform manner by Sybase.

VMS is the simple one as you are asked during the installation if you want to mirror the master device and to supply the device location. This automatically updates the RUNSERVER file. The entry of the master device mirror must be present in RUNSERVER to start the server when the mirrored master is being used.

For Unix or if you do not have the information at installation time - and usually you do not because you are not sure of the size of tempdb - then you can mirror the master device with a simple disk mirror command. Unfortunately this is not a special execution of the disk mirror command - an option would be nice - and so it does not update the RUNSERVER file. You have to do this yourself using an editor. This requires you to add the -r entry to indicate the physical name of the mirror device.

```
#!    /bin/csh -f
#     Server name:production
#     dslisten port: 1025
#     master name:/dev/rc1d0

setenv DSLISTEN production

exec  /sybase/bin/dataserver
      -d/usr/master.dat
      -r/usr/master.mir
      -e/sybase/install/errorlog_production
```

3.3.2 Unmirroring and remirroring

Devices may be unmirrored, temporarily or permanently using the disk unmirror command.

disk   unmirror

```
disk unmirror
    name = "logical_name"
    [,side = {primary | secondary}]
    [,mode = {retain | remove}]
```

where

name   The logical name of the device as defined in disk mirror.

side   Specifies which one of the pair - primary or secondary - to unmirror. The default is secondary.

mode   Specifies if the unmirroring is permanent or temporary. The default is temporary (retain).

```
disk unmirror
    name = "disk1", side = primary
```

If unmirrored temporarily, the device may be remirrored using the disk remirror command.

disk   remirror

```
disk remirror
    name = "logical_name"
```

where

name   The logical name of the device as defined in disk mirror.

```
disk remirror name = "disk1"
```

When the "disk mirror" command is issued, Sybase writes a copy of the primary device contents onto the mirror device. Thereafter updates take place identically to both devices to maintain a hot standby copy of the device. When one of the devices is not available (either planned unmirroring or unplanned crash: there is no difference to the mirrored device), Sybase recognises that one device is unavailable and continues in degraded mode making the updates to the single device. No log or "catch-up" file is maintained by Sybase while one device is down. When the failed device is reintroduced by the "disk remirror" command, Sybase takes a fresh copy of the current device contents onto the device just reintroduced.

So be careful when you reintroduce a mirrored device after a failure or planned unmirroring. Sybase will copy the device contents which will significantly impact on disk throughput. So do not reintroduce mirror devices during the busiest period of the day. You may have to, of course, to reestablish fault tolerance but it is a significant overhead in Sybase which, as an SA, you may defer by taking a deliberate decision to wait a little until the system is quieter. You'll be able to tell if the SA has done this. (S)he will be sitting with fingers, arms, legs and anything else crossed hoping that the unmirrored device does not fail. If this is too much of a risk to you, do not take it: suffer the performance overhead to let you relax.

3.4 Default device

When no specific placement is made in the create database command, the database must be placed somewhere and a default device is defined to be used when no device is specified.

Default devices are specified, by the SA only, using the system procedure sp_diskdefault:

sp_diskdefault

```
        sp_diskdefault logical_name, option
```

where

option   defaulton or defaultoff

Once a device has been created it may be defined as a default device.

```
        disk init name = 'disk_1',
                physname = '/usr/disk.dat'

        sp_diskdefault disk_1, defaulton
```

Any number of devices may be defined as default devices. In this case the space is allocated on an alphabetical basis: the server fills the devices up one by one, moving onto the next available default device in alphabetic sequence.

Even if a device has been used as a default it may be removed from the defaults at any time.

```
sp_diskdefault master, defaultoff
```

Existing allocations are not affected by removing a device from the defaults: the device is simply not reused for default allocation.

The initialisation makes the master device a default device. It is highly recommended that you change this to avoid user objects accidentally being allocated to the master device.

3.5   Database creation

Now that we have the devices we can create our databases using the create database command. This is the command which reserves the disk space exclusively for the database.

create   database

```
create database db_name
      [on device_name = size
            [, device_name = size]...]
      [log on device_name = size
            [, device_name = size]...]
      [FOR LOAD]
```

where

db_name   Server unique database name.

device_name   A device as created by "disk init".

size   The database size in M bytes.

FOR LOAD   A fast option which must be used only when creating a database
                     for loading a dump. This option does not initialise the database
                     space as initialisation is done by the load database. When a
                     database fails it often has be dropped and recreated before the
                     load. The FOR LOAD option ensures that the page initialisation
                     is not duplicated. **Do not use this option without load
                     database.**

```
create database test_db

create database systest_db
          on diska = 5,
          diskb = 4, diskc = 2

create database prod_db
          on diska = 20
          log on log_dev = 6
```

The create database command obtains and initialises the required amount of disk space from the device. If not all of the requested space is available the result depends on how much space can be obtained. If the minimum database size cannot be allocated, the command fails. If the minimum is available, as much as possible is allocated and a warning message output. Minimum database size defaults to a configuration variable (set with sp_configure) or to the size of the model database in the master device: whichever is the greater. Model defaults to 2 M bytes and this is about the minimum database size that you need to do any useful work as the system catalog information loaded in at create time takes up about 1 M byte.

The create database command uses model as a template in the creation. In doing this it locks model until the create is complete. Therefore create database is a single thread command ie only one at a time.

Create database creates two distinct portions to the database: one for the data and one for the log. There are three combinations to placement of each portion.

Both data and log on the same device by default.


```
      create database fred
```

or   ```create database fred on dev1 = 6```

or   ```create database fred on default = 5```

This creates both the data and log of the database on the same device: the first on the default device with default size, the second on the device dev1 with 6 M bytes and the third on the default device with 5 M bytes. With the default option for the log we have no control over how big the log can grow: it may use up the complete device.

Both data and log on the same device explicitly.

```
        create database fred
                on dev1 = 4
                log on dev1 = 2
```

or   ```
        create database fred
                on default = 3
                log on default = 1
```

No difference from the first one as for placement and space usage but because we have a separate log - even though it is on the same device - we have more control over it as it cannot now grow beyond the size we specified.

**Data and log on separate devices.**

```
        create database fred
                on default = 60
                log on dev2 = 12
```

or   ```
        create database fred
                on dev3 = 40
                log on dev4 = 12
```

This option of data and log on separate devices is the recommended option for all production systems as it gives you maximum control over size, placement and recovery.

You do, of course, need a reasonable number of disks before data and log separation gives you much disk performance improvement. If you have a simple one disk system then there is little advantage in separate devices for log and data for performance reasons. Each device which you create requires a connection to the server which reserves 34 K bytes of memory. In a one disk system I would suggest two devices with a choice of placement as shown in figure 3.3.

The first configuration has one device for the master and the other device for data and log. This suffers a little as the allocation of pages in the data device will be mixed between the data and the log, which can affect the log read/write times as the log pages are not sequential. Also - and possibly more importantly - if you lose a single device you have lost both data and log with no chance of complete roll forward from a dump.

The second configuration has the master and log on the same device. This allows full recovery from a device failure and increases the sequential nature of the page allocation to the log. However it may create a disk access bottleneck as tempdb and the log are sharing the same device. But if this is significant it will be significant on a one disk system no matter where tempdb and the log are located. (On a multiple disk system it is not normally a good idea to put a user database log on the master device.)

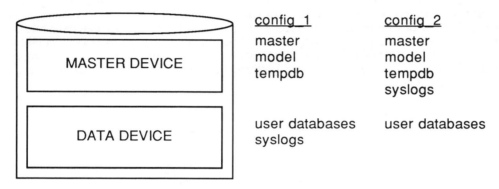

	config_1	config_2
MASTER DEVICE	master model tempdb	master model tempdb syslogs
DATA DEVICE	user databases syslogs	user databases

figure 3.3:   single disk configuration

My recommendation in a one disk system is one device for master and log and one device for the data.

Even in a shared data/log device it is advisable to explicitly state the size of the data and log as:

```
create database fred
        on default = 20
        log on default = 4
```

This means that the log cannot grow beyond 4 M bytes and if you get a device full problem you know whether the data or log has caused the problem and can take the appropriate corrective action. If you have not explicitly created a size for the log it will grow to the maximum available in the device and when a device full message occurs, you will not be sure whether the data or log has got too big.

Why bother which one has got too big? Well, if the data has expanded to use up all of the device allocation, you need to decide whether some application specific action such as archiving is necessary or whether extra space is required. If the log has got too big then you need to consider if it needs to be cleared out more often or whether extra space is needed. Having no knowledge of what has caused the problem gives you less control, which is a bad idea for the SA.

More importantly the separate declaration of the log space places the log on a separate segment on the device which allows much more control on dumping and recovery by permitting the use of the "no truncate" option of "dump transaction". The separate size declaration, even on the same device, allows the recovery system to treat the log as a separate object. I would always advise this.

In a larger disk configuration you can increase your control by placing the log on a separate device. You can construct any combination from one log device per database to one shared log device for all databases. The latter is still one log per database but all logs are placed on the same physical device. Each database has its own syslogs table: there is no global log table although they may all share the same device. This sharing of the log device may create a disk access bottleneck, so be wary of putting all of the logs on the same log device.

```
create database fred1
       on dev1 = 20
       log on dev8 = 4

create database fred2
       on dev2 = 10
       log on dev8 = 1

create database fred3
       on dev1 = 15
       log on dev8 = 2
```

We now have additional control in that we can place the log on a separate disk from the data to optimise disk head movement; we can mirror the log device(s) for fault tolerance and we have total control of size and dumping of the log.

Do not go overboard on this although. As much as it is the ideal and, in my opinion, essential for production databases, it does not need to be applied to everything. Test, training, development databases often do not need this level of sophistication and a simple data and log on the same device will be sufficient.

```
create database prog_test
       on test_dev = 100
```

A database configuration setting of "truncate log on checkpoint" (see section 3.14 on sp_dboption later in this chapter) will ignore the log by clearing it out regularly without dumping it. This leaves the test database "unrecoverable" except to the previous dump so, if you adopt this scenario, make sure that you dump the database regularly and that everyone using the database is aware of the amount of work that they may need to reinput. Note that the "unrecoverable" nature applies only to a media failure ie loss of the database which requires a roll forward from the previous dump. Any rollback situation or restart after a system failure should still work.

Small, slowly changing production databases also lend themselves to this approach. If you only do a handful of updates to a database between dumps, then there is little reason to dump the log, simply dump the database in which case the log does not need to be on a separate device. In this case truncate the transaction log to clear it out before dumping the database as it will save time in the database dump. (See chapter 5 for the "dump tran" options.)

So a separate log device for most production databases, but each case on its merit. As a rule of thumb on size, Sybase recommend that it is advisable to have a separate log to issue dump transaction if the database is greater than 4 M bytes. I find this figure strange as it's not the database size which is crucial but the combination of size and update activity between dumps. It all depends on how long you can afford the on-line system to be down. It will take about 1 hour to load each 300 M bytes of the dumped database and then you have to roll forward from the transaction logs. So structure your dump scenario based on how long you have to recover.

The size that you request for the data and log is initialised by the create database command and is reserved totally for that database. No one else can use that disk space and you cannot release unused space once it has been reserved by the initial create command. You can expand the space allocation, but you cannot reduce it. So it is reasonable to determine your space requirements as accurately as possible before you issue the create command. This really is crucial in space allocation for the SA. You cannot reduce the space allocated to a database except by bcp out, drop database, recreate to reduced size and bcp in. **NOT a good idea.**

3.6   Data size calculation

You can do this at various levels of sophistication depending on how detailed you want the calculation to be. No matter how detailed you calculate sizes the approach is to estimate the size of each table; add these together and make an allowance for indexes and free space.

At the simplest level I calculate as:

size of table = number of records * average record size

size of database = sum of table sizes

data space allocation = size of database * 3

(If you think that a "fudge" factor of 3 is high, remember that we have not allowed for indexes and free space in the actual calculation.)

By comparison the detailed calculation is:

average record size =   sum of average field sizes
                                + 2 byte fixed overhead
                                + 4 byte variable overhead
                                + 1 byte overhead for each variable field

(see chapter 1 for an explanation of the record layout)

records per page = page size * 0.75 / average record size

(assuming an initial packing density of 75% and rounding up to the nearest integer)

table size = number of records / records per page

size of database = sum of table sizes

data space allocation = size of database * 2
                          (We have allowed for free space but not indexes.)

Of course you will put the detailed calculation into a stored procedure and simply enter the appropriate parameter values. But I normally consider that the margin of error in such basic figures as number of records is so large that the simple rough calculation is sufficient.

A comparison of the calculations using a 150 byte record with 1,000,000 records in the table is:

Rough calculation

    size of table   = 150 * 1000000 bytes
                   = 75,000 pages   (2 K pages)

    data space allocation = 75,000 * 3 = 225,000 pages

Detailed calculation

    records per page   = 2000 * 0.75 / 150
                        = 10

    table size   = 1000000 / 10
                   = 100,000 pages

    data space allocation = 100,000 * 2 = 200,000 pages

Irrespective of how you do the calculation, you must do it. I know that you can expand the allocated space later, but getting it as close as you can is important to the initial choices in object placement.

I have left the index sizes out of the initial calculations as the final index choices will not be known until you are finalising the physical design and the initial allocation is often earlier than that. If you are able to delay your choice on disk space until you have finalised the physical design then you can make more accurate index calculations.

3.7   Index size calculation

The number of pages taken up by an index is so dependent on the size of the index key that the large ones are always worth calculating during the physical design stage.

Let's take the 1,000,000 record, 100,000 page table and a 10 byte fixed length field which is to be indexed. The various index overheads are explained in chapter 1.

clustered

$$\text{index entries per page} = \text{page size} * 0.75 / \text{index entry size}$$
$$= 2000 * 0.75 / 15$$
$$= 100$$

first level number of pages $= 100000 / 100$
                                 $= 1000$
second level number of pages $= 1000 / 100$
                                 $= 10$
root level $= 10 / 100$
                                 $= 1$

number of pages for the clustered index $= 1011$

(The clustered index has index entries for each page in the table ie 100000 pages)

Non-clustered

leaf level entries per page $= 2000 * 0.75 / 17$
                                      $= 88$
intermediate level entries per page $= 2000 * 0.75 / 21$
                                      $= 71$

leaf level pages $= 1000000 / 88$

$$
\begin{aligned}
&= 11363 \\
\text{first intermediate level pages} \quad &= 11363 \;/\; 71 \\
&= 160 \\
\text{second intermediate level pages} \quad &= 160 \;/\; 71 \\
&= 3 \\
\text{root level} \quad &= 3 \;/\; 100 \\
&= 1 \\[6pt]
\text{non-clustered index number of pages} \quad &= 11427
\end{aligned}
$$

So the space requirements for indexes are not insignificant and once you know which fields will be in the indexes, you must calculate the sizes.

These figures are reasonably typical for indexes and a rough rule of thumb is:

clustered index:	1% of data size
nonclustered index:	15% of data size

3.8 Free space

The database obviously needs free space for data expansion and a growth factor should be made in the initial calculations. However there is always a need for an amount of free space in the database for such aspects as index creation. Although index creation uses work space there is also a need for free space in the database itself.

When creating a clustered index the data records are sorted into sequence of the key values. This means that the data records move into new pages to achieve the new sequence. The new data table is written before the old table is deleted and so at least enough free space to take the full new version of the table is required to create a clustered index. Most of the Sybase literature requests that you make allowance of 120% of the table size as free space to create a clustered index on a table. However I would suggest that you allow more in the order of 150 - 200% of the table as free space.

This is significant as it must be available all of the time and can be considerable. A 600 M byte database with a 200 M byte table will need an extra 400 M bytes simply to cater for the creation of a clustered index on the large table. You may think that you could temporarily expand the database just to create enough space to do the index creation and then release it, but this is not possible. Any expansion of the database space remains a permanent assignment as with the initial assignment of space. So a good idea but not possible.

You need enough free space to take 2 times the size of the largest table in your database and it must always be free, or you must make it free immediately before the creation and then it remains allocated to the database. If this is a real problem, an alternative is to bcp out to a disk on another system and reload with the clustered index in place. Drop any non-clustered indexes for the reload and rebuild them once the data is reloaded. I'm not recommending this: it's only if you have a serious space problem.

3.9 **Log size calculation**

How long is a piece of string? (Twice the length from the beginning to the centre.) Initial rule of thumb used by most SAs is 20% of the data size. But it depends on the activity and the frequency with which you dump and clear out the log. Sybase operates a changes log which usually means that inserts and deletes use up most room in the log as they are effectively copies of the record. So a high activity insert rate may require a larger log than an update intensive system. If you have a large table in the database then a major update to that table will require a log of 2-3 times the size of the table.

However be careful here as Sybase updates are actioned as a delete followed by an insert - without exception. Therefore it is only for updates in place that the log entry is a simple changes entry of the altered bytes in the page. If Sybase does not update in place then the log entries for an update are the delete from the old page and an insert to the new page.

The rules for Sybase not updating in place are:

- update of a variable field

- update of a field which allows null

- update of an indexed field

- update of more than one record in the table by the transaction

- update of a table which has an update trigger

So be careful, most Sybase updates will cause the update not to be done in place but to move the record and therefore there will be more log entries than you expected. Always assume that a Sybase update is not done in place and estimate log space appropriately.

3.10 Monitoring space usage

Sybase does not provide much in the way of space monitoring tools. The system procedure sp_spaceused is all that is on offer and this provides:

sp_spaceused

db name	db size	reserved	data	index size	unused
fred	40 M	16320 K	12480 K	3680 K	160 K

This uses sysusages to determine the amount of used space in the database and sysindexes to determine the space used by each object: table and index.

database_size   amount of space requested in the create and alter commands

reserved   amount of space currently reserved for use

data   amount of space being used by data

index_size   amount of space being used by indexes

unused   amount of reserved space not currently in use

When an object requests more space Sybase allocates an extent of 8 pages ie 16 K bytes. So an object will have space reserved for it but not currently containing information. The allocated extent is reserved exclusively for the object and not available to any other object. The object will use the extent pages until there is no more room in the extent when it will request another extent. (This is a reasonably efficient use of space as the pages in the extent are always allocated to the object if there is any data in them. Pages which become empty remain allocated as part of the extent and are used first by the object before it requests another extent from the free space.)

So, in the extreme, a one record table with 3 non-clustered indexes will have space allocated to 4 objects: data + 3 indexes and will be reserving 4 * 8 extents ie 64 K bytes.

Figure 3.4 illustrates the unused and free space situation.

The unused space is reserved for each object which requested it. The free space is available for new objects or more space for existing objects. Free space is database size - reserved.

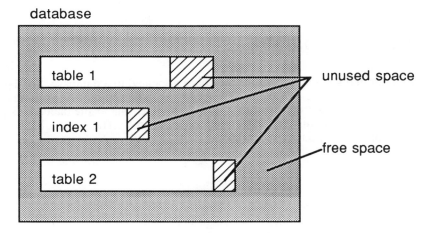

figure 3.4:   space allocation

sp_spaceused can also be used on a table.

```
sp_spaceused fred_tab
```

name	rows	reserved	data	index_size	unused
fred_tab	20	32 K	10 K	2 K	20 K

A couple of quick calculations will save you some time and some headaches when a create fails. Each new object requires an extent of free space ie 16 K. Execute sp_spaceused on the database to make sure that there is at least this amount of free space before running a create table. (Of course if you are this close to full you are in trouble anyway.)

More importantly if you are building a clustered index on a table do a sp_spaceused on the table to check the table size and on the database to check the free space. If there is not twice the table size as free space think carefully about increasing the database size before building the clustered index. And if you do not have the table size free, then the clustered index build will fail.

Even Sybase do not rave about some of the results from this system procedure - prior to v4.8 - with negative sizes not unusual and you may find it more advantageous to write your own routines from the system tables for the various levels of space usage. However the problems are with the figures in the system tables - especially sysindexes - so rewriting the system procedure will not benefit you dramatically. Although a routine to give you free space immediately is a good idea - see questions and answers to this chapter.

3.11 **Expanding databases**

As already mentioned you cannot reduce the space allocated to a database. So planning is important, but even the best of plans will need to be adjusted as data volumes grow beyond even your most generous estimates. And remember that as the data tables grow, the free space required for clustered index creation must grow. The space allocated may be increased using the alter database command.

alter   database

```
alter database db_name
         [on device_name = size
         [,on device_name = size]...]
         [FOR LOAD]
```

The size and device allocation are similar to the create database command. The FOR LOAD option is used after "create database FOR LOAD' when recreating a database for loading from a dump. (Both create and alter are necessary to redefine the database allocation exactly as at the dump. This is explained in detail in section 5.5.1.)

```
alter database fred
```

This allocates the default database size on the default device.

```
alter database fred on default = 20
```

This allocates an additional 20 M bytes on the default device.

```
alter database fred on dev1 = 15
```

This allocates an additional 15 M bytes on the device dev1.

```
alter database fred on dev1 = 5
alter database fred on dev2 = 10
alter database fred on default = 5
```

This expands the database fred by 20 M bytes into three devices.

A worrying problem is for tempdb to fill up during a large query. Do not panic when this happens: it may just be an unfortunate combination of tempdb requirements which will not happen again. Such occurrences are often infrequent and may be avoided once known. If you are sure that you need extra space then simply expand tempdb:

```
alter database tempdb on dev5 = 40
```

but once you have done this you cannot get it back. If disk space is reasonably scarce do not be panicked into expanding tempdb: consider it carefully and take your time.

A more important reason for expanding tempdb is for disk placement. You want tempdb to be by itself on a device which does not share the disk with any other disk intensive device - like the log device. (Note my previous exception in a one disk system. There are <u>always</u> exceptions.) You cannot remove the default 2 M bytes of tempdb from master but you can expand it into a larger device located on a low activity disk. As the devices are used in alphabetic sequence a good choice of name will cause the new device to be used first for tempdb storage. If you get into really serious temporary space problems, such as a large "order by", you will need to increase tempdb. If you really need to get this space back you can remove the entries from sysusages and restart the server. You will need to enable "allow updates" and remove all device fragments. And **be careful**.

Note that a database cannot consist of more than 32 device fragments and that a single request for space may be satisfied by multiple device fragments. This will only occur when the use of create/drop database has been excessive. Sysusages shows you the device fragmentation.

3.12 **Expanding the log**

There is no direct command for expanding the log. (I do not know why not as the Sybase recommendation is for separate log and database objects: but there isn't.) Instead the alter database command is used to expand the database onto a new device and then this device is reserved for the log only. This reservation is done using the system procedure sp_logdevice.

sp_logdevice

```
sp_logdevice db_name,device_name

alter database fred on log_dev2 = 15

sp_logdevice fred, log_dev2
```

This increases the log of the database fred by 15 M bytes on the device log_dev2.

If there is free space on the device containing the log, the sp_logdevice is not required as the device is already a log device and an alter database by itself will increase the log on the current device.

Interestingly the alter database on a separate device creates an allocation which is available for use by both data and log. The sp_logdevice then exclusively reserves the device for the log. Be careful here as sp_logdevice takes no notice of any existing use of the device and will change a device previously used for data into a log only device. This can be a nuisance as there is no command to change a log device into a data (or shared) device. This means that the device is no longer used for new data and all reads to data pages on this device will cause warnings to be written to the errorlog. To recover the data pages from the log device, recreate the clustered index containing the pages on the log device (you can get the indid from the warning messages).

3.13   **Database deletion**

A database is deleted using the drop database command:

drop   database

```
drop database db_name [, db_name...]

drop database fred_db
```

This deletes the database and all of its objects, deallocates and frees the storage allocation and removes all references to the database from the system tables. This is an SA/dbo command and must be run from master. The database being dropped must not be in use by a user (including the SA) or the command will fail.

Sometimes the database is in a damaged state and this command does not have sufficient power to delete the damaged database. In this case the consistency checker (dbcc) must be used to delete the damaged database:

```
dbcc dbrepair (fred_db, dropdb)
```

3.14 **Database environment**

There is a set of database environment options for a database which allows customising of what may be done in each database. These options are set using sp_dboption.

sp_dboption

```
sp_dboption        "db_name",
                   "option",
                   {true | false}
```

where option is:

dbo use only
: Makes the database single user for use by the dbo (SA) only. This is useful for the SA after a restore to allow him/her to check a few things before letting the rest of the users into the database.

read only
: Makes the database read only.

select into/bulk copy
: If this is not set then neither of these commands may be carried out in the database. This is not a particularly good setting to have on a production database but often worth having on a test/development database to allow ad hoc creation of tables. Any use of select into or bulk copy invalidates the transaction log based recovery and any dump transaction command will fail. So use with caution on production databases which must be recovered from transaction dumps and transaction logs.

single user
: As for "dbo use only" but this time the user may be anyone. From your viewpoint as SA this is not a relevant option as you will use "dbo use only" but be careful even of this if there are multiple users aliased as the dbo in a test environment.

truncate log on chkpt
: At each checkpoint this setting clears out the transaction log by deleting completed transactions from the log. Use of this means that the database cannot be recovered from the transaction log as the log is not dumped by this option. So use this only when you are confident that lost input is not a problem eg in a training database.

sp_dboption is an SA or dbo only command and must be executed from master. Once issued the settings do not take effect until you have issued a checkpoint in the database.

```
use master
go
sp_dboption      "fred",
                 "select into/bulk copy",
                 true
go
sp_dboption      "fred",
                 "truncate log on chkpt",
                 true
go
use fred
go
checkpoint
go
```

It is not possible to use this command on master but if you want system wide settings eg all databases as read only, then you could make the settings on model and they will be copied in the create database command.

3.15 **Segments**

Having physically allocated the space available on each database we now define logical segments on the devices so that we can specify the placement of the objects (tables and indexes) that we create in each database. Prior to v4.8 Sybase allows only 32 segments per database including the default segment. This is not a serious restriction as a segment may span devices but in a very large database with many disk drives it makes you think about the segment allocation a little. From V4.8 this has been increased to 192 segments per database which should be sufficient for anyone.

At initial creation of the database three segments are created automatically:

system segment: for the system tables

default segment: for the data and indexes

log segment: for the database log

These are used by default by the server when allocating space unless there is a specific segment allocation.

```
create database fred
        on dev1 = 5,
        on dev2 = 1
        log on dev3 = 8
```

will give a default segment allocation as shown in figure 3.5.

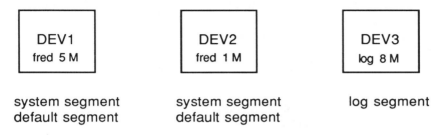

figure 3.5:   default segment allocation

As we create tables and indexes on this database they will be allocated to dev1 until it fills up and then to dev2 (alphabetic sequence).

What we are aiming for is the smoothing of the disk activity on each device (in reality on each physical disk but I shall assume a device per disk just to make the discussion easier). To do this we need to place objects on specific devices. We do not do this directly onto the device but create named segments on the devices and place the objects in the segments.

Creating segments is done with the system procedure sp_addsegment.

sp_addsegment

```
        sp_addsegment segment_name, device_name
```

To create segments for our database fred in figure 3.5:

```
        sp_addsegment seg_a, dev1

        sp_addsegment seg_b, dev2
```

Which gives a segment allocation as shown in figure 3.6.

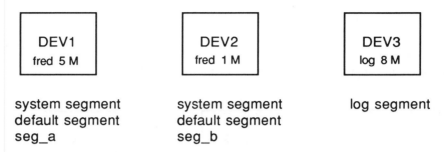

figure 3.6:   named segment allocation

We can now create tables and indexes on these named segments, by adding the segment name to the create statement, to ensure that they are allocated to a specific device.

```
create index ind_1 on tab_1(col_1) on seg_b
```

Unfortunately we have not reserved dev2 exclusively for seg_b as it still has the initial allocations of the system segment and the default segment. Any objects allocated to the default segment will use dev2 when the space on dev1 is full. Remember that devices are used in alphabetic sequence so it was only chance that dev1 was used first: it may be the device that you want reserved that is first in the allocation sequence.

To ensure that a device is reserved only for those objects that we specifically allocate to it, we also need to drop the initial system and default segment allocations. Dropping segments is done using the system procedure sp_dropsegment.

sp_dropsegment

```
sp_dropsegment  segment_name,
                device_name
```

So to reserve dev2 for seg_b we need to drop:

```
sp_dropsegment "system", dev2

sp_dropsegment "default", dev2
```

We now have a segment allocation as shown in figure 3.7 and complete control over the use of dev2.

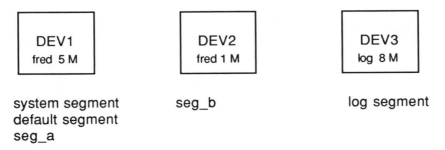

DEV1	**DEV2**	**DEV3**
fred 5 M	fred 1 M	log 8 M

system segment   seg_b   log segment
default segment
seg_a

figure 3.7:   exclusive segment allocation

To summarise the steps and do another example.

1   Create the database on specific devices.

```
create database fred
        on dev1 = 10,
        on dev2 = 8
        log on dev3 = 5
```

2   Create segments on the data devices to allow controlled placement of objects.

```
sp_addsegment seg_a, dev1
sp_addsegment seg_b, dev2
```

3   Remove the default segments from all devices on which you require exclusive control for placement and remove the system segment from all but one device. The removal of the system segment is not mandatory.

```
sp_dropsegment "default", dev1
sp_dropsegment "default", dev2
sp_dropsegment "system", dev2
```

You can drop all of the default segments as long as you always name a segment on the create command. But leave one system segment: the system catalog tables for the database need to go somewhere. Of course with the system tables allowed on only one device be careful that this device does not fill up.

Now let's create a database on 2 devices, log on a third; extend the database to a third device; create 2 segments on one device and 1 segment on the others; reserve the 2 segment device for our exclusive allocation.

1   Create the database.

```
create database fred
        on dev_a = 10,
        on dev_b = 8
        log on log_dev = 4
```

2   Extend the database.

```
alter database fred on dev_c = 6
```

3   Create the named segments.

```
sp_addsegment myseg_1, dev_a
sp_addsegment myseg_2, dev_a
sp_addsegment myseg_3, dev_b
sp_addsegment myseg_4, dev_c
```

4   Reserve dev_a.

```
sp_dropsegment "default", dev_a
sp_dropsegment "system", dev_a
```

We now have exclusive control of dev_a for allocation of objects and controlled placement on dev_b and dev_c although dev_b and dev_c will also contain the system tables and any objects that we do not specifically place on a segment.

So the commands:

```
create table tab_1 on myseg_1

create index ind_1 on tab_1(col_1) on myseg_3

create table tab_2 on myseg_1

create table tab_3

create index ind_2 on tab_2(col_1) on myseg_4
```

```
create index ind_3 on tab_3(col_1)

create table tab_4 on myseg_2
```

will give an allocation as shown in figure 3.8.

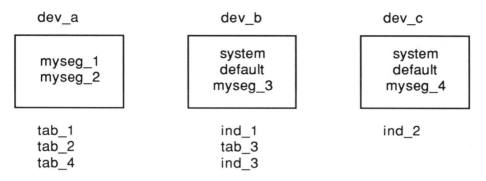

figure 3.8:   object allocation

Remember that the clustered index and the data of the table are the same object although they are created in separate commands. Therefore the clustered index and the table may not be on different devices. Sybase will allow you to create the clustered index on a segment that is on a different device than the table but will migrate the data records to the index device on index creation. You might think that this is crazy but if the devices are on different physical disks it may speed up the clustered index creation by introducing parallel disk activity into the process. This is minimal although because the new device will be used only for the write at the end of the process, but it cannot be slower. (Famous last words!)

The above example used an alter database to get the database onto dev_c. When alter database is used to expand a database onto a new device the system and default segments are created as normal. When the device is already in use by the database the existing segments are used.

3.16 Object on more than 1 device

So far we have looked at how to place objects on specific disks to even out the disk activity. The logical extension of this is to spread an individual object over two or more disks so that disk access is shared across the disks.

This uses the system procedure sp_placeobject:

sp_placeobject

```
        sp_placeobject seg_name, object_name
```

The approach is to define a segment that covers the devices:

```
        sp_addsegment dual, diska

        sp_addsegment dual, diskb
```

and inform the server that the object has to use this segment:

```
        sp_placeobject dual, tab_1
```

in which case the server will allocate free space alternatively from diska and diskb as it needs it. Note that as space allocation is in extents of 8 pages the placement of records will not be spread on a record by record basis but on an 8 page group basis. And this will start to break down once individual pages are emptied as these are reallocated before a new extent is requested. This is a little pessimistic as Sybase does try to allocate neighbouring pages when space is required, but it cannot do this all of the time.

Because of this lack of control over which disk an individual record is placed on, I personally have very little time for this approach. Splitting the allocation of records in a table across more than one disk is normally required to increase parallel disk activity which requires control over which records go on which disk. This is not possible with the Sybase approach and I would suggest splitting the table into several and placing each portion on a different segment on a different disk. This allows you program control of record placement by table_name which gives the required parallelism. (But it requires a union to get the data back together: so consider your options - especially as union is not supported until version 4.2 and even then cannot be included in views.)

3.17 System tables

There are 5 system tables which contain information on space allocation.

> sysdevices
> sysdatabases
> sysusages
> syssegments
> sysindexes

The following is a summary of the commands which update them and the system procedures which extract information from them for reference purposes.

Table	system procedure	commands
sysdevices	sp_helpdevice	disk init
	sp_addumpdevice	disk mirror
		disk unmirror
		disk remirror
sysdatabases	sp_helpdb	create database
	sp_changedbowner	drop database
	sp_dboption	
sysusages	sp_helpdb	create database
	sp_logdevice	alter database
	sp_addsegment	drop database
	sp_extendsegment	
syssegments	sp_helpsegment	
	sp_addsegment	
	sp_dropsegment	
sysindexes	sp_spaceused	create table
		create index

Let's have a detailed look at each table.

3.17.1 sysdevices

One row for each device with the information:

select * from sysdevices

low	high	status	type	name	phyname	mirrorname
16777216	16875022	3	0	data	/dev/rsd3e	null
0	20000	16	2	diskdump	/dev/null	null
33554432	33603638	2	0	logs	/dev/rsd3f	null
0	10239	3	0	master	the_master_device	null
0	610	16	0	tapedump1	/dev/rmt4	null
0	20000	16	2	tapedump2	/dev/rst0	null

where

name   The logical name and primary key.

phyname   File/raw partition name of the device.

mirrorname   File/raw partition name of the mirror device.

status
2	database disk
3	default database disk
16	dump device (tape or disk)
24	tape dump with noskip (no label checking)
32	serial writes
64	device mirrored
128	mirroring temporarily disabled
512	mirroring active

cntrltype
0	database disk
2	disk or tape streaming dump device
3-8	tape dump device

This is created by disk init, updated by the disk mirroring commands and displayed by sp_helpdevice.

sp_helpdevice

device name	physical name	description	status	cntrltype	device number	low	high
log	/log.dir/log.dat						
		special, physical disk, 4 MB					
			2	0	5	83886080	83888127

```
master     /sybase/master.dat
                special, default disk, physical disk, 30 MB
                             3       0       0       0        15359

diskdump /dev/null  disk,    16      2       0       0        20000
                    device

tapedump1 /dev/rmt4
                tape, 19 MB, dump device
                            16       3       0       0         610

tapedump2 /dev/rst0
                disk, dump device
                            16       2       0       0        20000

proddisk  /prod.dir/prod.dat
                special, MIRROR ENABLED, default disk, mirrored
                on /mirr.dir/mirr.dat, serial writes, reads mirrored,
                physical disk, 12 MB
                           738       0      10   167772160 167772671
```

The installation creates the devices: master, diskdump, tapedump1 and tapedump2. The dump devices are covered in chapter 5 on recovery but it is always better to name your own disk dump devices - diskdump is unusable as a dump device.

Information on a specific device is shown with:

```
        sp_helpdevice device_name
```

The system procedure sp_helpdevice is quite sufficient to show what is in sysdevices. This is usually true of the system procedures but there is often some useful information missing.

In the case of sysdevices there is little extra that can be displayed outside of sp_helpdevice except for which disk devices are database devices and which are dump devices. This separation is sometimes useful to the SA and is easily achieved by:

```
select name, phyname, mirrorname,
       status, size = high - low + 1
       from sysdevices where cntrltype = 0
```

which will show the database devices (and similarly for dump devices with cntrltype = 2 or 3).

name	phyname	mirrorname	status	size
data	/dev/rsd3e	null	3	97807
logs	/dev/rsd3f	null	2	49207
master	the_master_device	null	3	10240

Note that mirroring a device alters the status so use the cntrltype to check for database/dump devices, not the status.

Another useful output from sysdevices is the total database space:

```
select total_disk_usage = sum(high - low + 1)
        from sysdevices where cntrltype = 0
```

total_disk_usage

      157254

Note that the output is in pages ie 2 K bytes.

3.17.2 sysdatabases

One row for each database containing the information:

select * from sysdatabases

name	dbid	suid	mode	status	version	logptr	crdate dumptrdate
master	1	1	0	0	1	1289	Jan 1 1990 12:00 am Apr 2 1992 8:00 pm
model	3	1	0	0	1	46	Jan 1 1990 12:00 am Mar 30 1992 9:00 pm
pubs	5	1	0	0	1	47	Mar 30 1992 9:30 pm Apr 4 1992 11:00 pm
tempdb	2	1	0	0	1	45	Jan 1 1990 12:00 am Mar 30 1992 8:30 pm
fred	4	1	0	0	1	1030	Mar 30 1992 9:00 pm Apr 4 1992 10:00 pm

where

dbid   The unique database id allocated by the create database command.

suid   The unique server id of the database owner.

mode   An internal lock set during database create.

status   Indicates the settings of sp_dboption and also if the database needs to be
                recovered.

                The binary control bit settings are:

0x04	select into/bulk copy
0x08	truncate log on checkpoint
0x10	no checkpoint on recovery
0x20	crashed while loading database
0x100	database is suspect: will need to dropwith dbcc dbrepair
0x400	read only
0x800	dbo use only
0x1000	single user only
0x4000	database name has changed

version   The version of SQL server running when the database was created.

logptr   A pointer to the transaction log.

The system procedure sp_helpdb interprets this data and picks up the database size
from sysusages.

sp_helpdb

name	db_size	owner	dbid	created	status
master	2	sa	1	Jan 1 1990 12:00 am	no options set
model	2	sa	3	Jan 1 1990 12:00 am	no options set
tempdb	20	sa	2	Jan 1 1990 12:00 am	select into/bulk copy
pubs	2	sa	5	Mar 30 1992 1:00 pm	no options set
fred	40	sa	4	Mar 30 1992 2:00 pm	no options set

3.17.3 **sysusages**

One row for each distinct space allocation to a database containing the information:

*select * from sysusages*

dbid	segmap	lstart	size	vstart
1	7	0	1024	4
2	7	0	1024	2564
3	7	0	10240	1540
4	7	0	1024	3588
5	7	0	10240	50331648
5	7	10240	10240	10266314

where

segmap   A bit for each segment which includes this device allocation.

lstart   The first logical database page number.

size   The size in pages of this allocation.

vstart   A virtual disk address which points to the physical disk that the allocation is on. Vstart lies in one of the high/low pairs on sysdevices indicating which device the allocation is on.

This is rather useless and you need to make the join to sysdevices to pick up the device name. sp_helpdb with the database name does this quite adequately.

sp_helpdb   fred

name	db_size	owner	dbid	created	status
fred	40	sa	4	Mar 30 1992 11:00 pm	no options set

device_fragments	size	usage
dev_1	20 MB	data and log
dev_2	20 MB	data and log

So sp_helpdb can assist in answering non-specific questions such as:

which devices are for data
          sp_helpdb on each database and note device names

allocated space per device
>sp_helpdb on each database and sum the figures

free space per device
>take the above sum away from the total device allocation

But none of these are particularly friendly and there is no help in the simple requests such as what databases are on a specific device.

3.17.4 sysindexes

One row for each object in the database containing - amongst other data - the actual space used by the object. For the moment I shall ignore all but the space allocation data and the segment number field. If the table has a clustered index then this indicates the size of the table otherwise the table has an entry in sysindexes.

The following is the v4.2 layout, sysindexes layout has changed from V4.8 - see 3.18.4.

select name, dpages, reserved, used, rows, segment from sysindexes

name	dpages	reserved	used	rows	segment
tab_1	20	24	0	360	12
ind_1	5	8	0	0	25

where

dpages   The number of pages used by the object.

reserved   The number of pages reserved for the object.

used   The number of pages used by the clustered index.

rows   The number of rows in the table

segment   The number of the segment to be used next for space allocation.

This is the only table which gives the actual space usage by objects and unfortunately - prior to v4.8 - it is sometimes not the most accurate ie wrong. Dpages can sometimes have a negative value and select count(*) from table can give a different result than rows. The table is updated dynamically for inserts and deletes but it does get out of step and an update from dbcc is often advisable. The most common problem is after dropping an index, although I have found similar problems with other page based deletion commands such as truncate.

From v4.8 Sybase have improved the quality of information in sysindexes and I have found no fault with sp_spaceused.

3.17.5 syssegments

One row for each segment mapping the segment name to the segment number.

select * from syssegments

segment	name	status
0	system	0
1	default	1
2	log segment	0
3	myseg_1	0

where

status	1 indicates a default segment

The system procedure sp_helpsegment displays the syssegments information with no difference from a select *.

sp_helpsegment

segment	name	status
0	system	0
1	default	1
2	log segment	0
3	myseg_1	0

However sp_helpsegment is more useful with a specific segment name as input when it displays the devices and objects related to the segment.

sp_helpsegment   system

segment	name	status
0	system	0

table_name	name	indid
sysalternates	sysalternates	1

syscolumns	syscolumns	1
syscomments	syscomments	1
etc	etc	etc

where

indid	0	table
	1	clustered
	2-254	non-clustered
	255	text

Further information on segments is available using sp_helpdb with the database name when it displays the device fragments and the associated segments.

sp_helpdb   fred

name	db_size	owner	dbid	created	status
fred	5 MB	sa	4	Mar 30 1992 1:00 pm	no options set

device_fragments	size	usage
dev_1	1 MB	data only
dev_2	2 MB	data only
dev_3	2 MB	data only

device	segment
dev_1	myseg_1
dev_1	myseg_2
dev_2	system
dev_2	default
dev_3	myseg_3

Useful but note again that there is nothing which goes the other way round to give segments on a device.

That's the standard output, now let's look at some extra commands on these system tables to extract the missing information.

3.18 Some useful extracts from the system tables

3.18.1 Which databases and who created them

```
select d.dbid, d.name, l.name
    from sysdatabases d, syslogins l
    where d.suid = l.suid
    order by d.name
```

This information is available from sp_help but this does not give the dbid which is often useful to the SA.

3.18.2 Which databases and how big

```
select d.name, d.dbid,
    "size in MB" = sum(u.size) * 2048 / 1048576
    from sysdatabases d, sysusages u
    where d.dbid = u.dbid
    group by d.name, d.dbid
```

If you want to be more precise, the page size can be obtained from spt_values.

3.18.3 Which databases are on a device and how much is allocated to them.

```
select u.dbid, db.name, u.size
    from sysusages u, sysdevices d, sysdatabases db
    where d.cntrltype = 0
    and u.vstart between d.low and d.high
    and d.name = 'device_name'
    and db.dbid = u.dbid
    order by u.dbid
    compute sum(u.size) by u.dbid
    compute sum(u.size)
```

Or a simple sum(size) group by u.dbid, db.name.

3.18.4 **List of tables and sizes**

```
select o.name, i.dpages, i.rows
     from sysindexes i, sysobjects o
     where indid in (0, 1)
     and o.id = i.id
     and o.type = "U"
     order by o.name
     compute sum(i.dpages), sum(i.rows)
```

This has changed from version 4.8.This is a problem with such home grown routines: Sybase may change the system table structures without any notification.

```
select      o.name,
            dpgs=data_pgs(i.id, doampg),
            rows=rowcnt(doampg)
     from sysindexes i, sysobjects o
     where indid in (0, 1)
     and o.id = i.id
     and o.type = "U"
     order by o.name
     compute sum(data_pgs(i.id, doampg)),
             sum(rowcnt(doampg))
```

There are many more, some of which I have asked as questions to this chapter and I hope that it emphasises the need to know your way around the system tables. Look at the Sybase system procedures to see how the system tables interact and create your own simple procedures to give you this level of information on the layout of your server. Then name them as "sp_" system procedures and put them in master so that they are globally available to you.

3.19 **Summary**

The disk init command allocates physical space on the disk storage for the server. The create database command then reserves space on these devices for exclusive use by the named database. Create database reserves space for both data and log with these being allocated on the same device or on separate devices. Separate allocation of the log to its own device is recommended.

Tables and indexes created in a database then use the devices to which the database is allocated in alphabetic sequence. This default object placement may be overridden by defining named segments on the devices. These segments have no physical space allocated within the device and are limited only by the device size.

Placement of a table or index on a specific disk is done by creating a device on the disks; creating the database on this device; creating a segment on this device and creating the table or index on this segment.

3.20 Questions and research

1 Having just installed and started a server - the default SYBASE - make a note of the commands you need to execute to create a table on one disk with its non-clustered index on another disk.

2 As an illustration of how weak Sybase is in really useful SA commands try to use the system tables - not stored procedures - to determine the following.

 devices on the system

 size of each device

 free space per database/device

 list of indexes with sizes

 simple column structure of a table

 simple list of indexes belonging to a table.

And finally....

A mathematician, a physicist and a computer salesman were challenged to measure the height of a cathedral tower.

To help them each was given a barometer and a stop watch.

When asked to present their method and result the mathematician said that he calculated the height to be 80.64m. His method was to go to the top of the tower, drop the barometer and use the stopwatch to measure the time until it smashed on the ground.

The physicist had no need of the stopwatch. He measured the barometric pressure at ground level and then at the top of the tower and by careful calculation found the height to be 82.35m.

The computer salesman had no hesitation in giving his answer of 81.33m which astounded the judges as it was absolutely correct.

When asked for his method, he was at first reticent but finally revealed that he had sought out the cathedral verger who gave him the height in exchange for the stopwatch and the barometer.

Chapter 4

Logins
users
and
privileges

This chapter discusses the setting of the appropriate names, ids and passwords to enable login to the server and use of databases once login is achieved. The granting and revoking of command and access privileges to the users in the databases is then described.

O'Reilly's Fourth Law

Blessed is the end user who expects nothing, for (s)he will not be disappointed.

Commands covered in this chapter:

    grant
    revoke
    setuser

System procedures covered in this chapter:

    sp_changedbowner
    sp_addlogin
    sp_password
    sp_defaultdb
    sp_droplogin
    sp_adduser
    sp_addalias
    sp_addgroup
    sp_changegroup
    sp_dropgroup
    sp_helpuser
    sp_helpgroup
    sp_who
    sp_helprotect
    sp_addserver
    sp_addremotelogin
    sp_remoteoption
    sp_serveroption
    sp_helpserver
    sp_helpremotelogin

4.1   **Introduction**

We now have databases defined - with or without the various tables, indexes etc - but so far we are the only user who may login to the server and use these databases.

We need to create logins (accounts) for people to get to the server and then user names in each database for them to use the databases. You make this as simple or complicated as you wish but you need to define two stages: a login to the server and a user name in each database that the login requires access to.

As we are dealing with the database access the assumption is that each person who has to be given access to the server already has an operating system login and password. The normal approach here is to retain these as the login and password to the server. The server will default to the operating system login and a null password when a client tool such isql or dwb is used. So life is easier if you use the operating system logins. This login only attaches to the server and no database access is assumed, so there are few security problems.

Once allowed access to the server a separate user name must be defined in each database that you wish the login to have access to. Again the simple approach is to retain the same name but there are various grouping and aliasing facilities to make life a little easier for the SA when defining users in databases.

So each person who needs access to the server has to be defined as a login in master and then as a user in each database to which access is allowed as shown in figure 4.1.

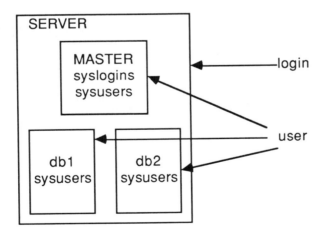

figure 4.1:   server and database access

The login to the server is defined in master and creates entries in syslogins. Each login is identified with a unique server wide identifier - server_id SUID.

To use a database - including master - each user is defined in the database which creates an entry in sysusers in the respective database. Each user is identified in each database with a database unique identifier - user_id UID.

login

- permission to attach to the server
- entry in syslogins
- no default access to any user database
- identified by SUID
- also called "account" by Sybase

user

- permission to use a database
- entry in sysusers
- access to home database only
- identified by UID
- two special cases: groups and aliases

4.2 Classes of user

There are 3 classes of user in Sybase: SA, dbo, user. The SA has absolute rights everywhere. (S)he can go everywhere and do anything. The database owner (dbo) is as powerful as the SA but only in the database which (s)he owns. The regular user is controlled completely by the SA or the dbo and can do only what (s)he is allowed to do by the more privileged SA and dbo.

Database ownership is automatically given to the person who creates the database. I would recommend that this is the SA and if you adhere to that, you will want to pass ownership of some of the databases to other users. This is done with the system procedure sp_changedbowner.

sp_changedbowner

```
sp_changedbowner login_name

use fred
go
sp_changedbowner prog_1
go
```

This can be used to give some users create database rights. I believe that the SA has more control by doing all database creation and conferring database ownership to a few users. I prefer to retain ownership by the SA and, if necessary, alias specific users as dbo (see 4.4.1). This gives less problems during recovery as sa/dbo is always SUID of 1.

4.3 Logins

Logins are created in master using the system procedure sp_addlogin.

sp_addlogin

```
sp_addlogin login_name
            [, password]
            [, default_db]
```

Only the SA may create logins and you must be in the master database.

```
isql -Usa -Pwhatever

use master
go
sp_addlogin fred
go
```

The default password for each login is null. This is not a bad idea but should not be allowed to last for long as most logins will be obvious eg names, so you need to create the culture of users setting and changing their passwords at regular intervals.

To change their own password a user uses the system procedure sp_password.

sp_password

```
sp_password old_pw, new_pw  [, login_name]

sp_password mac, scot
```

Only the SA can use the login_name to change another user's password. To set a password to null use the string NULL without quotes. If you have to change a user's password but do not know the old password, as SA you may input NULL for the old password and no checking is done.

The default_db is the database that the login to the server will attach you to. The default for this is master so from the SA's point of view it is important to create logins with the default database defined so that users are not left in master. Most users will not remember to issue a "use database" command so always set the default database for the login. All users have read access to master to allow the system to check the login_name against syslogins and to read system procedures, so if you do not specify a default database users will be left sitting in master after login.

An entry for each login is made in syslogins. The password column is not encrypted but select permission is not allowed on this field to anyone but the SA. There are also no system procedures to read syslogins.

SUID/UIDs are unique throughout the server and each database respectively, and are allocated sequentially in syslogins and sysusers. If a login/user is dropped the SUID/UID is not reused unless it is the last used number. Therefore there is no guarantee that the same login/user on different servers/databases will have the same SUID/UID. This is important in privilege checking which is done by id and not name. Checking is done on UID in each database with the SUID being mapped in each database to the UID. Do not assume that servers with identical login_names and user_names will be the same internally. The only exception to this is the SA who is always SUID number 1.

4.3.1 Changing the default database

The default database to which the user is attached may be set in sp_addlogin or separately changed using the system procedure sp_defaultdb.

sp_defaultdb

```
sp_defaultdb login_name, db_name

sp_defaultdb user_1, fred
```

This may be executed by the SA to change anyone's default database or by the user to change his/her own default database. This means that the user may set his/her default to master. There is no audit, check or report on this so keep a close check on syslogins to see what is going on. (In my opinion the users have no need to change their default database and I would deny them execute permission on sp_defaultdb.) I know that they can always issue "use master" to gain access to the master database, but at least it closes one route.

There is also no check that the user is allowed to use the database which has been set as their default - which is the same when the login is created. You need this unchecked database access situation as the logical steps are to create the login and default database attachment before you define the user in the database.

Why not just drop the login and add it again to redefine the default database? Because the SUID will change and all the privilege checking will be wrong.

4.3.2 **Dropping a login**

When a login is no longer required - the person has left the company - it should be dropped using the system procedure sp_droplogin.

sp_droplogin

```
sp_droplogin login_name

use master
go
sp_droplogin user_1
go
```

This may be executed by the SA only.

Dropping a login does not automatically do any clean-up such as dropping all user names related to the SUID or checking to see if the SUID owns any objects. No checks are performed: the login is dropped from syslogins.

So if you wish to destroy all record/influence of the user you need to drop all user names from the relevant databases and all owned objects. There are two important points to this:

- Only allow objects to be created by the SA or the dbo.

- When a person leaves the company, drop the login to bar them from any external access to the server, create a new login for any staff replacement and alias the new login to the old user in the database. (This is covered later when we discuss database users.) This prevents unauthorised access but minimises the changes that have to be made at the privilege level.

If you drop a login by accident, you have caused yourself work. Adding the login back means that the new login is not recognised as the same person as the SUID has changed and you will have to change the ownership of any objects owned by the original user by dropping and recreating. This is an excellent reason for using groups as we shall see later.

4.4   **Users**

Login gives you the right to use the server and to be attached to a database, but gives you no rights to do anything in the database. To work in a database the login_name is mapped to a user_name in the database. The server unique SUID is mapped to a database unique UID. This mapping must be done in every database in which the user wishes to work.

The login to user mapping is done using the system procedure sp_adduser and creates an entry in sysusers.

sp_adduser

```
sp_adduser login_name
           [, user_name]
           [, group_name]
```

Make sure that you are in the correct database before you add the user.

```
use production
go
sp_adduser fred
go
```

This maps the login fred to the user_name fred in the production database.

```
use test
go
sp_adduser fred, controller
go
```

This maps the login fred to the user_name controller in the test database. This is useful if one person carries out a specific function as the login may be changed as the person changes but the user_name may remain the same in the database so all privilege checking is unchanged. This is a one to one mapping and if several logins carry out the same function the alias feature is needed.

A special user_name of **guest** is used as a default to allow anyone to access a database. This is not created automatically in the database but must be added like any other user.

```
sp_adduser "guest"
```

This means that anyone who can login to the server will have access to a database which has a guest user defined. The server first checks to see if there is an entry in sysusers. If there is no entry for the SUID but there is a guest entry you will be treated as a guest in the database with all the privileges attached to the guest UID. (This is not recommended in production systems but I personally find it useful in a training database used to train new staff when I do not know the logins which will require access to the database.)

Guest users have a UID of 2 and SUID of -1 as there is no one to one mapping of SUID to UID for guest users. The dbo or SA is always UID of 1. So create all objects in a database as SA or dbo. Then the UID does not change and the privilege checks are easier. In production databases create objects as the SA - you want complete control over the production systems anyway. In test and development databases when designers and programmers want freedom over what objects they create and when they are created, alias everyone to the dbo. This has a more important reason as all objects are identified by a composite primary key of object_name and UID on sysobjects. So if the programmers are all different UIDs the procedures, tables, indexes that they create are owned by them and not automatically available to other designers/programmers in the database. If everyone appears to be the dbo there is no problem as everyone has access to everything in the database.

4.4.1 Aliases

We do not need to call the user in the database the same name as the login to the server. However the user_name parameter in sp_adduser is a one to one mapping of login to user. If we wish several logins to be known as the same user in the database - as above for the dbo - then we need to use aliases. These are defined by the system procedure sp_addalias.

sp_addalias

```
sp_addalias login_name, user_name

sp_addalias user_1, dbo
```

If login_name is already defined as a user in the database it cannot be aliased to another user_name. Any one login may have only one user_name in the database, so being both a user and aliased to another user is not allowed. You cannot alias anyone to "sa".

As mentioned before this is most useful in a development database when all developers may be aliased to the dbo which is easiest to maintain and causes least problems.

Why not just give all developers the same login?

It has the same effect but is a little different from a control viewpoint. An alias allows you to login to the server uniquely and gives the SA much better control over who has access to the server. The same login has the same SUID which has the same UID and so the SA is not only unable to keep people out of the server but cannot tell which individual is causing any trouble.

If different logins are aliased to the one user_name in the database then you are yourself on the server and so the SA controls who gets to the server on an individual basis as well as having the SUID available in the database to write to an audit trail if someone misbehaves.

Aliases are recorded in the system table sysalternates. Yes I know that the name is different. In general the system procedure is singular and it updates the plural table name. So sp_addlogin updates syslogins...except for sp_addalias which updates sysalternates.

4.4.2 Uses of aliases

Aliases are useful to the SA in two ways.

The first is that they make life easy in a test/development database as previously mentioned by having everyone looking like the dbo and therefore ownership of all objects is the same, no matter who creates them.

If I have the SA being the dbo in test_db and I alias fred to be the dbo in test_db, the system table entries are:

```
use test_db
go
sp_addalias fred, dbo
go
```

syslogins

name	SUID
sa	1
fred	20

sysusers

name	SUID	UID
dbo	1	1

sysalternates

SUID	ASUID
20	1

Note that the checking sequence to see if a login is a valid user in a database is sysusers for SUID, sysalternates for SUID, sysusers for guest. So use of aliases is a small overhead.

The second use of aliases for the SA is in moving databases from one server to another. Because we can never guarantee that logins have the same SUID on different servers we cannot move a database to another server and expect people to be able to login and use the databases. Because the SUIDs will have changed all of the object ownership and privilege checking will be different and many routines will fail to execute. By aliasing everyone to the dbo all objects are owned by the dbo who is always UID 1 and therefore there is no change to the ownership when the database is moved. I would not recommend this for production databases as you will not wish regular users to have dbo rights in a production database, but it is extremely useful for non-production databases.

I would like to stress that the easiest object ownership scenario is to have the SA create all of the production databases and objects in them and alias everyone who uses development and test databases to dbo. This does give the SA a lot of work in the production databases but you really do want this level of control anyway, so do it.

4.4.3 Dropping users

Depending on how they have been set up, user names are dropped using the system procedure sp_dropuser or sp_dropalias.

sp_dropuser

```
sp_dropuser user_name
```

sp_dropalias

```
sp_dropalias login_name
```

Note the use of the login_name when dropping an alias. An aliased user is not known by a unique user_name as there may be several logins aliased to the one user_name. But the SUID which is mapped to the common UID is unique, so dropping of an alias is by login_name.

You cannot drop a user who owns objects in the database: you need to drop all of the objects first.

4.5   Groups

Groups have nothing to do with allowing access to the server or a database but are simply a means to facilitate assigning privileges to users. Each user may have privileges granted and revoked to the user_name or users may be grouped together and the privileges granted and revoked to the group_name. Privilege setting to groups is easier for the SA and the checking is slightly less of an overhead as the system tables are smaller.

Groups are added to sysusers using the system procedure sp_addgroup.

sp_addgroup

```
sp_addgroup group_name
```

The group_name is unique in the database and is added to sysusers with a UID greater than 16383. There is a default group of "public" which is UID of 0. Groups look like users as far as the system tables and privilege mechanisms are concerned.

Having added a group, users in the database are attached to it either when the user is added with sp_adduser or by moving them out of the default public group into the named group using the system procedure sp_changegroup.

```
sp_adduser  fred, fred, programmer
```

or

sp_changegroup

```
sp_changegroup group_name, user_name

sp_changegroup programmer, fred
```

Notice that there is no default setting of the second parameter of sp_adduser. If you set the group_name when you add the user you must repeat the user_name in the second parameter of sp_adduser.

A user may be attached to only one named group and the group_name must exist before users are attached to it. In fact everyone is always in public no matter how you attach them to a group so each user may be in public and one named group.

```
sp_adduser fred, fred, analyst
go
sp_adduser john
go
sp_changegroup programmer, john
go
```

Fred is in the group analyst, john is in the group programmer and both of them are in the group public.

4.5.1 Dropping groups

A group_name is dropped from the database using the system procedure sp_dropgroup.

sp_dropgroup

```
sp_dropgroup  group_name
```

A group may not be dropped if there are any users currently attached. To drop a group while the users are still active in the database you need to change the users back to public - I know that they are already in public: it is only to remove them from the named group - and then drop the empty group.

```
sp_changegroup "public", fred
go
sp_dropgroup programmer
go
```

Note that public is a reserved word and must be enclosed in quotes.

4.6 System tables

There are 3 system tables - syslogins, sysusers, sysalternates - associated with logins and users.

4.6.1 syslogins

One row for each login to the server containing the information.

select * from syslogins

suid	status	accdate	totcpu	totio	spacel	timeli
1	1	Mar 30 1992 11:00 am	0	0	0	0
2	0	Mar 30 1992 11:00 am	0	0	0	0
3	0	Mar 30 1992 11:00 am	0	0	0	0
4	0	Mar 30 1992 11:00 am	0	0	0	0
5	0	Mar 30 1992 11:00 am	0	0	0	0

result	dbname	name	password
0	master	sa	john
0	master	probe	null
0	sales	clerk	sales
0	test	prog	null
0	manufact	store	bin

There are no system procedures to display this table and "select *" is available only to the "sa" as the password field is protected from access by any other user. The password is not encrypted so be careful when you display this table. Status, totcpu, totio, spacelimit, timelimit and resultlimit are all reserved columns by Sybase and I have no information on them - although they are reasonably obvious.

4.6.2 sysusers

One row for each user and group in the database containing the information.

select * from sysusers

suid	uid	gid		nameenviron
-2	0	0	public	null
-1	2	0	guest	null
1	1	0	dbo	null
2	3	0	probe	null
18	4	16384	fred	null
-2	16384	0	programmer	null

where

suid   The unique server_id: sa is always 1

probe is always 2
public is always -2
guest is always -1

Guest and public may have many logins attached to them so a special SUID is allocated.
Probe is a system login/user which is used by the two-phase commit processing. Do NOT drop it if using two-phase commit, but if not using two-phase commit, you might as well drop it as you will come to no harm.

uid   The user_id unique in this database.   sa/dbo is always 1
                                                                   guest is always 2
                                                                   public is always 0
                                                                   groups are always
                                                                   greater than 16383

gid   The group_id unique in this database. Groups are treated like users with UID/gid > 16383 and have a row in sysusers. There is no separate system table for groups.

environ   Again reserved by Sybase and I have no information on this column.

The data in sysusers is displayed with the system procedure sp_helpuser.

sp_helpuser

users name	Id in gp	group name	login name	default db
dbo	1	public	sa	master
guest	2	public	null	null
probe	3	public	probe	master
fred	4	programmer	fred	sales_test

The group information on sysusers is displayed using the system procedure sp_helpgroup.

sp_helpgroup

group name	group id
programmer	16384
public	0

Information on the users in a group is displayed with sp_helpgroup and a specific group_name.

sp_helpgroup   programmer

group name	group id	users in group	user id
programmer	16384	fred	11
programmer	16384	john	14

4.6.3 Built-in functions

There is a set of built-in functions which displays login, user and database identification.

suser_id(user_name)	returns SUID
suser_name(SUID)	returns login_name
user_id(user_name)	returns UID
user_name(UID)	returns user_name
db_name(db_id)	returns database_name
db_id(db_name)	returns database_id

```
select suser_id(fred)

select suser_name()
```

The null argument returns the current login, user or database identification.

4.6.4 sysalternates

One row for SUID and alternate SUID combination.

*select * from sysalternates*

suid	altsuid
1	12
6	8
6	10
6	9

This is really only a link table and is meaningless by itself. sp_helpuser on a specific user_name displays the aliased users.

sp_helpuser   dbo

user_name	ID_in_db	group_name	login_name	default_db
dbo	1	public	sa	master

Users aliased to user
login_name
fred
john
jill

Note that an aliased user may not exist as an individual user in sysusers and therefore we lose all individual knowledge of the aliased users.

```
use sales_db
go
sp_adduser programmer
go
sp_addalias fred, programmer
go

sp_helpuser fred                    says fred does not exist

sp_helpuser programmer              will show fred as alias
```

However the system procedure sp_who works on the suid so fred will show on the output.

```
sp_adduser programmer                    ·
go
sp_addalias fred, programmer
go

sp_helpuser fred                    says fred does not exist

sp_helpuser programmer              will show fred as alias
```

However the system procedure sp_who works on the suid so fred will show on the output.

sp_who

spid	status	loginame	hostname	blk	dbname	cmd
6	runnable	fred	glenlivet	0	sales_test	select

4.6.5 System table summary

table	procedures	commands
syslogins	sp_addlogin	none
	sp_droplogin	
	sp_password	
	sp_defaultdb	
sysusers	sp_helpuser	none
	sp_helpgroup	
	sp_adduser	
	sp_dropuser	
	sp_addgroup	
	sp_dropgroup	
	sp_changegroup	
sysalternates	sp_helpuser	none
	sp_addalias	
	sp_dropalias	

4.7 Privileges

Assigning privileges is a simple matter using two commands - grant and revoke - with privileges being assigned to the execution of commands - create, drop etc - and to the access of objects - select, update etc. These privileges may be assigned to users, groups and/or public.

In addition Sybase has an object hierarchy which limits the amount of privilege checking and can provide significant access limitations eg all access via stored procedures with no direct execution of the select command.

The users/groups to which privileges may be assigned also have a hierarchy in which the privileges are checked as shown in figure 4.2.

The privileges are checked in this sequence, so users are checked before groups before public. This means that if a user has access to an object and you add the user to a group which has no access to the object, the user still retains access to the object. This is a standard means of having a group setting with individual user exceptions.

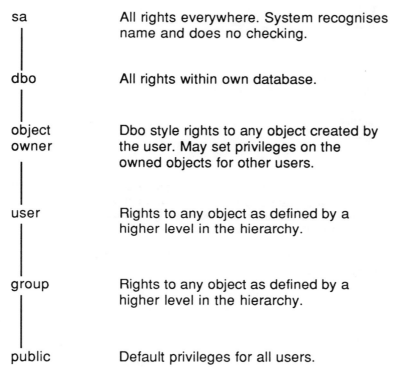

sa	All rights everywhere. System recognises name and does no checking.
dbo	All rights within own database.
object owner	Dbo style rights to any object created by the user. May set privileges on the owned objects for other users.
user	Rights to any object as defined by a higher level in the hierarchy.
group	Rights to any object as defined by a higher level in the hierarchy.
public	Default privileges for all users.

figure 4.2:   user privilege hierarchy

4.7.1 Command privileges

The SA may grant command privileges within a database. This is unusual within a production system where you simply want the user to be able to operate the production system from the client applications, but will be required in a test/development database. The simplest settings are as stated before: alias everyone in the test/development databases to the dbo and they will have all rights in those databases.

Some commands may not be transferred to other users.

SA only
disk init
disk reinit
disk refit
disk mirror
disk unmirror
disk remirror

        kill
        reconfigure

SA/dbo only
        checkpoint
        dbcc
        load database
        setuser
        grant
        revoke

Of the remaining transferable commands "create database" may be transferred by the
SA only. Note that if you grant this privilege to another user the command updates
sysdatabases in master so the user will need to be defined in master with update
capability on the system tables. Not a good idea!

The default command privileges are summarised as follows with an indication whether
or not they may be transferred.

sa	tr		dbo	tr
create database	Y		checkpoint	N
disk commands	Y		create default	Y
kill	N		create procedure	Y
reconfigure	N		create rule	Y
shutdown	N		create table	Y
			create view	Y
			dbcc	N
object owner	tr		dump database	Y
drop object	N		grant	N
grant on object	N		load database	N
			revoke	N
			setuser	N
table owner	tr		user/public	tr
create index	N		begin transaction	N/A
create trigger	N		commit transaction	N/A
delete	Y		print	N/A
insert	Y		raiserror	N/A
select	Y		rollback transaction	N/A
truncate	N		save transaction	N/A
update	Y		set	N/A
update statistics	N			

(User/public has no-one to transfer privilege to.)

Command privileges are set using the grant and revoke commands.

grant/revoke

```
grant {all | command_list} to name_list

revoke {all | command_list} from name_list
```

The name_list may be public or any valid user_name or group_name in sysusers.

```
grant create proc to public
go
grant all to fred, programmers
go
revoke create table, create view from john
go
```

Clearly the use of groups makes this an easier task for the SA and much easier to maintain.

4.7.2 Object privileges

The owner of an object has the ability to modify the schema of an object which means commands such as alter, create, drop. These schema modification privileges may not be transferred to other users by the object owner: only by the SA or dbo. Other users in the database are granted or revoked privileges on the data in the object by the SA, dbo or object owner to allow them to select, delete, insert etc on the object.

The SA may set privileges on any object for anyone anywhere.

The dbo may set privileges on any object for anyone in the database.

The object owner may set privileges on the object to any user of the object for access to the data only.

Object privileges are set using the same grant and revoke as for command privileges with an additional "on clause" to specify the object.

grant/revoke

```
grant action_list    on object_name[(column_list)]
                     to user_list
```

```
revoke action_list   on object_name[(column_list)]
                     from user_list
```

where

action_list	select
	insert
	update
	delete
	execute
	all
object_name	table_name
	view_name
	procedure_name
user_list	user_name
	group_name
	public

If you allow named users to create objects in a database then the dbo of the database - who did not create the object and is just another user - does not get automatic privileges on the object. However the dbo cannot be barred from any object in the database as the dbo may issue the setuser command to look like any user in the database.

setuser

```
setuser  [user_name]
```

Use a null user_name to get back to yourself.

```
setuser
```

Care is required in the sequence of grant and revoke both to avoid mistakes and to save you input effort.

To revoke privilege from one user in a group:

```
grant create proc to programmer
go
revoke create proc from fred
go
```

Even though fred is in the group programmer, he has no create proc capability because of the checking hierarchy which checks the user first. Also, if you issue more than one privilege (grant and/or revoke) against a user/group the last one issued is the one which is active.

Similarly to exclude one column from a group or user:

```
grant select on tab_1 to programmer
go
revoke select on tab_1(col_1) from programmer
go
```

This is a standard approach: to bar one, grant to all and revoke from the one.

4.7.3 Privilege hierarchy of objects

Procedures/triggers use views and tables, and views use tables all of which may have different privileges set on them. However the privileges of the contained objects are not checked when the procedure/trigger/view is created, only when they are executed. The amount of checking when the object is executed depends on the ownership of each object in the hierarchy.

The hierarchy of object privileges in Sybase allows you to restrict users to a particular level of access such as view access to tables. This is very useful. If I want to ensure that all users access data via stored procedures I can:

```
grant execute on proc_1 to public
go
revoke select on tab_1 from public
go
```

This ensures that everyone can execute the procedure proc_1 which selects from the table tab_1 but cannot directly use the select command on tab_1.

The hierarchy is shown in figure 4.3.

If the ownership of the objects in a hierarchy is the same Sybase does not recheck the privileges but uses the privileges at the entry point. So executing a procedure which uses a view which uses a table will not cause the privileges on the view or the table to be checked if the ownership of the view and the table is the same as the procedure. So keep all production database objects owned by the SA and all test/development database objects owned by the dbo.

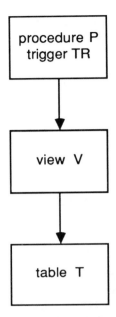

figure 4.3:   object privilege hierarchy

Consider the ownership hierarchies of figure 4.4. We have no problem with procedure P, view V, table T.

```
grant execute on P to public
go
grant select on V to public
go
revoke select on T from public
go
```

This means that access to table T is available via procedure P or view V but not directly on table T.

However:

```
grant execute on A to public
go
grant select on X to public
```

```
go
revoke select on B from public
go
```

means that nobody can access table B (except sa who has access everywhere). Entry at the view is allowed but the change in ownership at the table rechecks the privileges which bars access. Entry at the procedure level is allowed, change of ownership at the view causes the privileges to be rechecked but still allowed. However the next change of ownership at the table causes privileges to be checked again and access is not allowed.

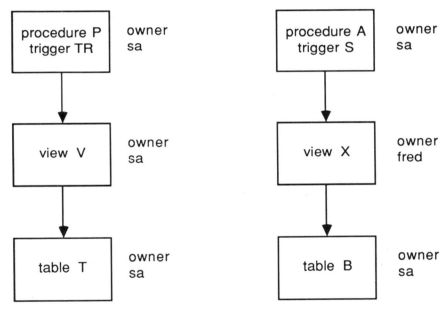

figure 4.4:   example privilege hierarchies

The privileges are checked at the entry level and not rechecked for any dependent or referenced objects unless the object ownership changes from the level above. Keep the ownership chains simple: SA in production and dbo everywhere else. This is particularly relevant in views and must not be forgotten when triggers are defined on tables.

Consider the table and view:

```
create table emp_tab as
      (emp_id int, name varchar(30))
go
revoke select on emp_tab from public
go

create view employee as
      select emp_id, name from emp_tab
            where emp_id = user_id()
go
grant select on employee to public
go
```

If the owner of the view and the table are the same then everyone can use the view. If the owner of the view and the table are different then no-one can use the view.

Triggers act as any other object in the hierarchy but you need to be a little careful as not everyone can create triggers. Only the owner of the table may create a trigger on the table. This helps of course in the privilege hierarchy but you need to be careful that the trigger does not access a table owned by someone else as the privileges will be rechecked and the trigger fail which causes the invoking command to fail.

```
user_2
      create tab_2 as (ctrl int)
      go

user_1
      create table tab_1 as (a int, b int)
      go
      grant insert on tab_1 to public
      go
      create trigger trig_1 on tab_1 for insert as
      begin
            update user2.tab_2 set ctrl = ctrl + 1
      end
      return
      go
```

An insert on tab_1 will fail unless update access is allowed on tab_2 to the users inserting on tab_1.

So keep ownership simple.

4.8   **Access to system procedures**

System procedures are globally available and reside in master. Therefore users have global access privileges to system procedures which means that any user has privilege to execute a system procedure in all databases or in no databases.

Because the system procedures reside in master you need to revoke access in master which requires the user to be defined as a user in master for privilege to be revoked. This is not a good idea. All users need read access to master to check syslogins and to read the system procedures but this is done by a guest user in master. (Do not delete guest from master or nobody will be able to login.)

It is an easy task to deny access to a system procedure from all users because all users whether named in the database or not are members of public. So denying access on a global basis is easily done by revoking access to public in master.

```
use master
go
revoke execute on sp_configure from public
go
```

This ensures that nobody - except the SA - can execute sp_configure, unless you have granted them specific access as a user or group since users and groups are checked before public.

4.9   **System tables**

4.9.1   **sysprotects**

Grant and revoke update sysprotects. This table is kept as small as possible by revoke actually deleting existing grant entries. So if you grant access to fred there is a sysprotects entry. If you revoke this access the grant entry is deleted and the revoke entry inserted.

*select * from sysprotects*

id	uid	action	protecttype	columns
240001234	0	193	205	01
240001234	2	193	205	01
240001234	2	195	205	null
240001234	2	196	205	null
240001234	2	197	205	01

where

id   Unique id in database of the object on which the privilege is set.

action   The action on which the privilege is set.

select	193
insert	195
delete	196
update	197
execute	224
create database	203
create default	233
create proc	222
create rule	236
create table	198
create view	207
dump database	228
dump transaction	235

protecttype   205 - grant
                      206 - revoke

columns   A bit map of the columns of the object on which the privilege is set. Bit 0 indicates all columns, a 1 in the appropriate bit means that the permission applies to that column.

Privileges on a specific object are displayed using the system procedure sp_helprotect.

sp_helprotect   tab_1

type	action	user	column
grant	delete	fred	all
grant	insert	fred	all
grant	update	fred	all
grant	select	fred	all
grant	select	public	all

Privileges on a specific user may also be displayed using the system procedure sp_helprotect.

sp_helprotect   fred

type	action	object	column
grant	delete	tab_1	all
grant	update	tab_1	all
grant	insert	tab_1	all
grant	select	tab_1	all

4.10 **Managing remote access**

The preceding logins and users allow use of databases on the local server. In a networked configuration Sybase allows access to procedures on remote servers ie servers on other network nodes. The initial configuration for this is defined using sp_configure and is described in chapter 8. Having enabled remote access, we need to set up the servers in the network and the logins to allow access to a remote server.

The sequence of events is:

> sp_configure: to enable remote access
> sp_addserver: to add the servers
> sp_addremotelogin: to add the logins

```
sp_configure "remote access", on
go
```

Having set remote access on with sp_configure we need to define the servers which are involved in remote access using the system procedure sp_addserver.

sp_addserver

```
sp_addserver server_name [, local]

sp_addserver glenlivet, local
go
sp_addserver tomintoul
go
```

Every server taking part in the remote access must have every other server defined as remote and itself as local. Consider three servers: glenlivet, aberlour and tomintoul:

glenlivet

```
sp_addserver glenlivet, local
go
sp_addserver aberlour
go
sp_addserver tomintoul
go
```

aberlour

```
sp_addserver aberlour, local
go
sp_addserver glenlivet
go
sp_addserver tomintoul
go
```

tomintoul

```
sp_addserver tomintoul, local
go
sp_addserver aberlour
go
sp_addserver glenlivet
go
```

Note that each server must also have all of the servers defined in the interfaces file. This is not done automatically and you will need to edit the individual interfaces files or create one with all servers in it and copy it around: the latter being a more reasonable approach once the network configuration is settled.

Having defined the servers in the network, the login ids which will be checked when a remote call is executed are defined using the system procedure sp_addremotelogin. These are defined on each called server ie the remote servers.

sp_addremotelogin

```
sp_addremotelogin server_name
                [, local_login]
                [, remote_login]
```

where: server_name   the server name on which the remote logins are being defined ie the server you are currently working in.

local_login   the login name on the called server ie the server
                               you are currently working in.

remote_login   the login name on the calling server ie the login
                               you are mapping to local_login.

Each server must have the standard logins/users defined using sp_addlogin and sp_adduser. The sp_addremotelogin simply defines the mapping of the remote logins to the local logins. This mapping may be done in one of three ways.

1 Use the remote login as the local login.

```
sp_addremotelogin tomintoul
```

This is not a particularly sensible option as it requires an exact match of ids and names between the servers which is not easy to maintain as described earlier in chapter 4.

2 All remote logins to a single local login.

```
sp_addremotelogin tomintoul, fred_rem
```

This is a common approach as it requires least work by the SA and it is not too unreasonable to treat all remote logins as the same for security and privilege checking. It does of course lose the strict audit control of who is doing what, for which you need the third option.

3 A one-to-one remote to local mapping.

```
sp_addremotelogin tomintoul, john, john_rem
```

4.10.1 Password checking

When a remote login is made to a local server, the default is to request password verification. This may be overridden for specific remote logins using the system procedure sp_remoteoption to treat the remote login as "trusted" and not request password verification.

sp_remoteoption

```
sp_remoteoption          remote_server,
                         login_name,
                         remote_login,
                         option,
                         {true | false}
```

where

remote_server   The remote server name.

login_name   The login on the local server.

remote_login   The login on the remote server.

option   "trusted": currently the only option. The default is false ie
                       password verification.

```
sp_remoteoption tomintoul, sa, sa,
                "trusted", true
```

In general it is easiest for the one login to have the same password on every server -
isql insists on this - and you need to be a little careful when changing password. It is
best to change the password on all remote servers - with an rpc - before you change it
on the local server.

```
exec tomintoul.fred.dbo.sp_password null, jk
go
exec aberlour.fred.dbo.sp_password null, jk
go
exec sp_password null, jk
go
```

4.10.2 Timeout

The site connection handler automatically drops any physical connections which have
not had a logical connection for over one minute. To avoid this happening the
"timeouts" option of the system procedure sp_serveroption may be set on to maintain
all connections until one of the servers is shutdown. When the server is restarted, the
option remains true and the site connection handler automatically reestablishes a
connection when a remote procedure call is made.

sp_serveroption

```
sp_serveroption      server_name,
                     option,
                     {true | false}
```

where

option   "timeouts": currently the only option. Default is false which disconnects
              physical connections after one minute of no logical connection.

```
sp_serveroption aberlour, "timeouts", true
```

4.10.3 Procedure calls

If the servers have been set up as above then stored procedure calls may be executed
from one server to another simply by qualifying the procedure with the server name.

```
exec  glenlivet.malt_db.dbo.show_prices
```

This is the only method in current Sybase versions of remote access to other servers.
Only the procedure name may be qualified with the server name. It is not possible to
write a single SQL command where the tables reside on different servers ie it is not
possible to qualify a table name with the server name.

So:

```
SELECT c.name, o.ord_no
    FROM glenlivet.cust_db.dbo.customer c,
         aberlour.order_db.dbo.orders o
    WHERE c.cust_no = o.cust_no
```

is **not** a valid command.

This means that commands must be fully executed on a single server - although the data
may come from multiple databases per server. This is a distinct restriction to full
distribution of data in Sybase. (This is being solved in the new Omni gateway server
which should be released before this book.)

4.10.4 **System tables**

sysservers

sp_addserver updates sysservers in master.

*select * from sysservers*

srvid	srvstatus	srvname	srvnetname
0	0	glenlivet	glenlivet
1	0	aberlour	aberlour
2	0	tomintoul	tomintoul

This is simply displayed using the system procedure sp_helpserver.

       sp_helpserver

                 sp_helpserver [server_name]

sp_helpserver

name	network_name	status	id
glenlivet	glenlivet	timeouts	0
tomintoul	tomintoul	timeouts	2
aberlour	aberlour	timeouts	1

where 0 is the local server

sp_helpserver   glenlivet

name	network_name	status	id
glenlivet	glenlivet	timeouts	0

sysremotelogins

sp_addremotelogin updates the system table sysremotelogins in master.

*select * from sysremotelogins*

remoteserverid	remoteusername	svid	status
1	NULL	-1	0

This is displayed using the system procedure sp_helpremotelogin.

sp_helpremotelogin

```
sp_helpremotelogin
        [remote_server [, remote_name]]
```

sp_helpremotelogin   tomintoul

server	remote user name	local user name	options
tomintoul	john	fred	

4.11 **Summary**

Access is allowed to the server by adding a login to the server using sp_addlogin. This login is unique to the server and does no more than allow password protected access and, optionally, attach the user to a database. Although attached to a database by the login, the user has no access rights in this database until a user name is defined in the database using sp_adduser. To use several databases a user name must be defined in each of the databases. The login name need not match with the user names and the relationship need not be one-to-one as several logins may be aliased to one user name. This is particularly useful in a test/development environment where all logins may be aliased to the dbo.

Once defined as a user in a database a set of command and/or object privileges may be set up for each user using the grant and revoke commands. This privilege definition may be made easier by forming the users into groups using sp_addgroup and defining the privileges against the groups.

Sybase has two privilege hierarchies: users and objects. The user hierarchy defines the sequence of checking - user, group, public - which is useful to allow individual user exceptions to take precedence. Thus a single user in a group may be given special privileges as the user is checked before the group. The object hierarchy reduces the amount of checking that has to be carried out by not rechecking privileges if the object ownership does not change. Thus the privileges on a table in a procedure will not be rechecked when the procedure is executed, if the procedure and the table are owned by the same user. This object hierarchy militates strongly for keeping the object ownership chains simple.

Access between servers using remote procedure calls requires the servers to have the remote access configuration option set using the system procedure sp_configure as described in chapter 8. Access between the servers is then achieved by defining the servers in the network using sp_addserver and by defining logins from the remote servers using sp_addremotelogin.

4.12 **Questions and research**

1   Create two logins to the server and make them users in the database.

Alias one of the logins to the other user.

Create a group and assign both users to this group.

Check each step with the appropriate system procedures.

2   Create a third login with privilege to create a table.

Login as this user, create a table and revoke all access from everyone.

Drop the user's login and determine how non-SA users may access the table.

3   Suddenly the phone rings. Nobody can login to the server. You can as "sa" and you find that syslogins contains all the login names that are having trouble logging in with the correct passwords. What is wrong?

And finally....

What's the difference between a car salesman and a computer salesman?

A car salesman knows when he is lying!

"How could you swindle people who trust you?" the computer salesman was asked.

"How can you swindle people who do not trust you?" he replied.

"It's going to be a real battle of wits," warned the computer salesman.

"How brave of you to go unarmed," said his manager.

A man walked out of a room where a computer salesman was making a presentation. Someone asked him if the salesman had finished his speech.

"Yes he finished his speech shortly after he started, he just hasn't finished talking yet."

Chapter 5

Backup
and
recovery

This chapter discusses the recovery mechanism and the dump and restore commands and procedures. The transaction management is discussed first to describe the transaction log entries and the actions taken to recover from media and system failures. The commands and procedures necessary to enable this are then described with a special mention of the master database and a full system rebuild.

O'Reilly's Fifth Law

A bad sector disk error only occurs after you have done several hours of work without a back-up.

Commands covered in this chapter:

begin tran
rollback tran
commit tran
checkpoint
dump database
dump transaction
load database
load transaction
buildmaster
disk reinit
disk refit
isql
defncopy
bcp

System procedures covered in this chapter:

sp_configure
sp_addumpdevice
sp_dropdevice

5.1 **Introduction**

There are two aspects to backup and recovery: the management of the transaction to enable recovery and the procedures to carry out the recovery. The transaction management involves copying the effects of each transaction to a log so that the transactions may be repeated or any erroneous actions may be removed. The backup procedures involve the commands to dump and restore the database and the transaction log, and the recovery processing to repeat the transactions against the data.

There are several options to repeat the transactions: from application specific code which reprocesses the transactions to application independent automatic software to rewrite data updates to the database. It is the latter that we are interested in: how Sybase actions transaction management and recovery to provide a transparent ability to recover a database after a failure.

There are also two types of failure that the recovery management and procedures must be able to deal with: system failure where the currently executing transactions have not completed properly but the data on the database is intact and media failure where the database has been damaged and is no longer usable.

Sybase supports fully automatic recovery using a transaction log containing images of the data updates and checkpoints to synchronise the flushing of cache to disk. This by itself permits recovery from system failure by rolling back the before images of the uncompleted transactions. With the addition of a database dump and transaction log dumps, recovery may be made from a media failure by rolling forward the after images of completed transactions from the last database dump.

Sybase provides 100% recovery from a failure up to the last completed transaction. This requires all transaction records to be dumped which may be difficult if the media failure loses the only copy of the current disk log - but such combinations of sloppy system administration and capricious acts of God are beyond any vendor's foresight.

So far I have been loose with the terminology and lacking in definition so let's define a few terms.

system failure
An event which requires one or more executing transactions to go back to their start point. The event may range from a loss of data cache to an application error. The important aspect of a system failure is that the database is intact and not damaged or corrupted.

media failure
An event which causes the database to be damaged and unusable.

database dump
A copy of the database at a point in time.

transaction dump
A copy of the current transaction log. This dump will normally clear out the completed transaction information once the dump has completed.

rollback
A recovery process which recovers from a system failure by reversing the effects of uncompleted transactions on the database.

roll forward
A recovery process which recovers from a media failure by posting the completed transactions in the transaction log dumps to the database dump.

before image
A logical description of the information on the log which reflects the position of the relevant record immediately before it is updated by the transaction.

after image
A logical description of the information on the log which reflects the position of the relevant record immediately after it has been updated by the transaction.

5.2   Transaction management

Sybase operates a changes log which means it records only the changes to each data page made by the transaction. The insert and delete are easy to visualise as they need to record the complete record in the log. The update is not as simple as **all** Sybase updates are actioned as a delete followed by an insert. Therefore there are two log entries for an update: the insert change and the delete change.

5.2.1 Transaction

A transaction is a single unit of work as regards modification to the database. It has a finite start and end point and may contain one or more commands against one or more databases. A single, stand-alone command is automatically a transaction in Sybase. If you wish several such commands to be treated as a single transaction you must enclose the commands in a transaction block.

```
update tab_1 set col_1 = 15

begin transaction
     insert into tab_2 (1, 5, 10)
     insert into tab_2 (2, 8, 10)
     update tab_3 set ctrl = ctrl + 2
          where key_col = 999
commit transaction
```

The above shows two transactions: a stand-alone update and a multiple insert and update. The single statement transaction has an implicit begin/commit. For clarity I shall continue the discussion by always showing the begin/commit block. The transaction management always records a begin and commit entry on the log so it helps to show them in the discussion.

So:

```
begin tran
      update tab_1 set x = 15
commit tran
```

and

```
update tab_1 set x = 15
```

are executed and logged identically.

A transaction may have two outcomes: it may complete correctly with a **commit** or it may meet a condition which requires it to go back to the beginning with a **rollback**. The rollback situation may occur as an abort because of external system failure or may be deliberately requested by the transaction because of an error condition.

```
begin tran
      declare @var_1 int
      update tab_2 set entry = entry + 1
      select @var_1 = count(*) from tab_1
      if @var_1 = 0
      begin
            print 'no records'
            rollback tran
            return
      end
commit tran
```

The above transaction checks to see if there are records on the table: if not it rolls the transaction back reversing the update at the beginning of the transaction. (I know that it's a daft place to put the update: it's only an example.)

The purpose of fixing the start and end of the transaction is to ensure that the effects of the transaction may be repeated or reversed if there is a failure. A transaction is an "atomic" event which means that there is no in-between state with a transaction. It is all or nothing: either it happens or it does not.

```
begin tran
     update tab_1 set x = 15
          where p_key = 123
     update tab_2 set y = 20
          where p_key = 687
     update tab_3 set a = 157
          where p_key = 10
commit tran
```

During the transaction none of the updates are made to the database and none of the updated pages are available to other transactions once each update has started. Each update takes an exclusive lock on the data page in cache and this is retained until the commit so that no other transaction can have access to the page until the updating transaction has completed. (We shall look at this in more detail in chapter 6 on locking but quite simply we must lock until the commit as we have no guarantee that the transaction will not rollback and restore updated values back to their original state. Therefore once XLOCKed, no other transaction gets to the data until the locking transaction has completed - commit or rollback.)

Each update makes an entry in the transaction log and at the commit the log is flushed to disk before the data updates are written to disk. The log write is a force write to disk to guarantee that it gets there immediately, but the data writes are logical and are made under the control of the cache manager. Therefore in normal circumstances the only disk writes during the transaction are the forced log writes, as the data page updates occur whenever the cache manager (or checkpoint) requires them to. This will normally not be within the transaction boundary.

This sequence of events ensures that every completed transaction is logged to disk irrespective of what happens in cache. Therefore if recovery is required the disk log may be used to rollback or roll forward depending on the action of the transaction.

The sequence of events is:

> log a BEGIN TRAN record
>
> for every modification to a page
>   log the modification
>   modify the page in cache
>
> log the COMMIT/ROLLBACK TRAN record
>
> flush the log to disk
>
> release the locks on the cache pages

Remember that in Unix the only guarantee that a write reaches the disk immediately is when the device is defined as a raw partition, to prevent the Unix cache manager intercepting the write request. So if you want to be able to guarantee 100% recovery make sure that you create the log device(s) as raw partitions. From a simple performance aspect, it avoids data being cached twice which is a rather inefficient use of physical memory.

The log information is written to the system table syslogs which is a heap storage structure with no index. Therefore all log records are written to the last page of syslogs and as each database has its own syslogs this is a single user interaction which makes it the fastest possible method of getting data into a table. It also has no "hot spot" contention as it is a single system process which writes to the log. The log entries are classified as data rows by Sybase but they do not have the same structure as shown in figure 5.1.

log header	record log

figure 5.1:   log record layout

log header

a 12 byte header containing
> row number
> log record type
> transaction_id
> length of row

record log

A variable number of bytes containing the modified data. The Sybase log is a logical log of what the change was and where it occurred. So a minimum of changed data with a page offset is recorded in the log record. This functions as both a before image (BI) for rollback and an after image (AI) for roll forward.

Because the records in syslogs are not like other data rows you will not get readable output from a select statement. Although regular "select count(*) from syslogs" will give you a good idea of how the log is growing, the recommended method of getting an accurate log size is dbcc:

```
dbcc checktable(syslogs)
```

Do not use sp_spaceused on syslogs prior to v4.8 as it is completely inaccurate unless you have just checkpointed the database. From v4.8 the output seems OK but I still prefer dbcc checktable.

The various log records for a transaction are related by the transaction_id which is the record_id of the begin tran log record.

Note that all page modifications are logged which includes not only the data pages but any associated index updates.

Consider the tables:

```
create tab_1 ( a int, b int, c int )

create index ind_1 on tab_1(a)

create index ind_2 on tab_1(c, b)
```

The insert:

```
insert into tab_1 (1, 2, 3)
```

will create the log records:

> begin tran
>
> index page ind_1
>
> index page ind_2
>
> data page tab_1
>
> commit tran

Of course if the index updates caused node splitting there would be other index log records.

These log records are then used by the recovery mechanism to recover the database from a failure.

5.3 **Recovery**

Consider the transaction of figure 5.2 which inserts three records with the appropriate data log records.

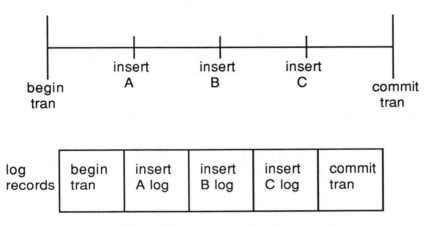

figure 5.2:   transaction log records

5.3.1 **Media failure**

If we have a media failure and require to restore the effect of this transaction we simply redo the logs of the inserts ie post the page changes to the appropriate page offsets. This roll forward is the recovery used when there has been a media failure which has lost the current version of the database. In logical terms we post the after images of the changes from the transaction log. In this case a previous database dump is reloaded and the committed transactions from the transaction log reposted to this dump. This brings the dump up to the state of the last completed transaction written to the log.

5.3.2 **System failure**

When a system failure occurs the transactions currently executing cannot complete and any information in cache may be lost. Because the transaction has not completed we do not know what stage the transaction has reached and therefore what effect the transaction has had on the data. The safest thing is to roll the transaction back to the start, restoring the database to its state prior to the start of the transaction, as if it had not taken place.

When a system failure occurs the rollback procedure is invoked for each currently executing transaction and the log records posted to the database to restore it to its state prior to the start of the transaction. In logical terms we post the before image of the changes from the transaction log.

The combination of dumps and log records allow roll forward from a media failure which has corrupted the database or rollback from a system failure which has not damaged the database but which has lost the currently executing transactions. An interesting problem is what to do when cache is lost as the log records for the current transactions were in cache - which is no longer available - and so rollback cannot be affected. The problem is already solved by the fact that we do not write updates to disk during the lifetime of the transaction but leave them in cache. Therefore if a transaction fails before committing it has had no effect on the database and therefore nothing needs to be done. Why bother with before images then? We shall see in a moment.

5.3.3 **Deferred updating**

A problem can occur when a long running transaction updates so many pages that the cache manager will have problems. The simple update command

```
UPDATE CUSTOMER SET X = X + 5
```

will change every page in the CUSTOMER table which could easily be larger than data cache. This is normally handled by not actioning the updates immediately but deferring them to the commit time. **Deferred updating** writes the updates to the log instead of directly to the data record in the page and then rereads the log at commit time and actions the updates. Therefore the write of the log at commit is actioned and then the data pages updated and left under the control of the cache manager, ensuring full recoverability.

5.3.4 **Checkpoint**

At first glance everything appears OK but an important fact of the system failure is that the data cache is lost. And this can contain several of the data record updates which completed transactions have issued. Remember that at the commit point, the log is flushed from cache to disk but the data record updates are deliberately left in cache to be paged out as required by the cache manager. We do this to save physical disk access to improve performance. But unfortunately it complicates our recovery.

In the scenario shown in figure 5.3 the recovery system can only assume that no action is required for transactions 1 and 2 as they have been completed and written to disk. However, although the log records have been written to disk, the efficient cache management system has not yet identified all of the updates or before images of transactions 1 and 2 as needing to be paged out of cache yet. So the database does not accurately reflect the updated versions of transactions 1 and 2. In fact we do not know what the state of the database is as we do not know which pages have been written to disk.

So the recovery system needs a point in time at which it can be sure that all updated cache pages have been flushed to disk. This is called a **checkpoint.**

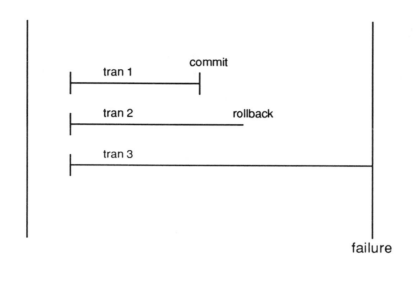

S 1	log 1	log 1	com 1	S 2	log 2	log 2	rbck 2

log

Figure 5.3: disk log at failure point

At a checkpoint the recovery manager quiesces the system by temporarily suspending all transactions, flushing the cache to disk, writing a record to the log and then allowing the suspended transactions to continue. When a system failure occurs now, the recovery routine knows that any updates before the last checkpoint entry in the log have been actioned and it need take action on only those transactions after the checkpoint.

If we consider the situation shown in figure 5.4 transactions 1 and 3 completed before the checkpoint and therefore no recovery action is necessary.

Transaction 2 committed after the checkpoint and therefore we are not sure if all the updates reached the disk, so we roll it forward after the checkpoint. Of course we may duplicate a write in doing this but it is strict overwrite, so better safe than sorry.

Transactions 5 and 6 started and ended after the checkpoint so the system will roll forward and rollback respectively.

Transaction 7 was executing at the time of failure so no action is required. Why not? Because nothing goes to disk until the commit or a checkpoint so there is nothing on disk for transaction 7.

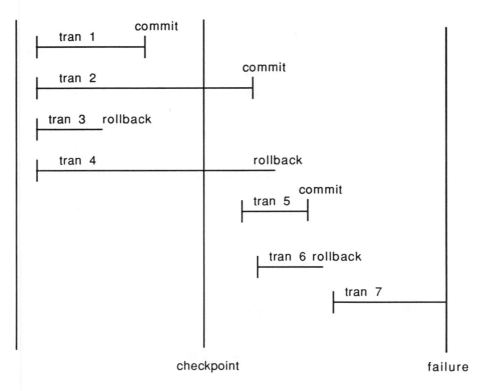

Figure 5.4: checkpoint recovery

Transaction 4 completed after the checkpoint but there is no guarantee that the posting initiated by the roll back reached the disk, so roll it back again. The complete transaction needs to be rolled back in this case because the rollback action occurred after the checkpoint so there is no guarantee that any of the original rolled back pages reached the disk. No data page updates go to disk directly: they all go via the cache manager.

Let's look at this one in a bit more detail as in figure 5.5.

The only guarantee that something is on disk is before the checkpoint which means that the only guarantee of the data on disk is the updated versions of A and B. Because the rollback portion of the transactions actioned after the checkpoint, all of the rollback pages may still be sitting in cache. So this transaction must be rolled back to the beginning and not just to the checkpoint.

The actual mechanics of recovery are a little more complicated than simply rolling forward or back based on relative position to the checkpoint record. Such a recovery scenario is valid only for a BI/AI style log which is not the case in Sybase. Therefore additional checks - mainly based on timestamp checks - are required for the relevant log records to determine if they should be actioned to disk.

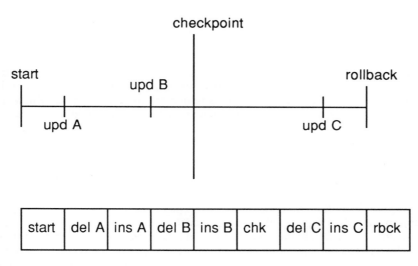

figure 5.5:   rollback over checkpoint

The checkpoint takes place at a regular interval as defined by the recovery interval set by sp_configure. The default interval is 5 minutes and the server uses this as the amount of time it should take to recover. After the server accumulates 5 minutes of data to recover a checkpoint is taken. Altering the recovery interval using sp_configure does not take place dynamically but requires a reboot of the server. The checkpoint process is invoked once a minute to check how much work is required to recover each database. If this is greater than the recovery interval, a checkpoint is initiated for the database. The calculation is based on the number of log records since the last checkpoint times 10 msecs.

Note that the recovery interval is not a maximum figure for recovery. If you create update transactions which run for hours then they will take a long time to rollback if they fail just before they are finished.

sp_configure is dealt with in detail in chapter 8 but the recovery interval is set as:

```
sp_configure "recovery interval", 3
go
```

The SA or dbo can issue a checkpoint at any time.

`checkpoint`

```
use fred_db
go
checkpoint
go
```

Prior to v4.8 the checkpoint disabled access to the database while executing - as explained earlier. From v4.8 users are allowed access to the database while the checkpoint executes. The only transactions which are frozen are those which are in the process of starting when the checkpoint executes. Therefore the overhead of the checkpoint has been reduced with only new transactions being delayed while the checkpoint executes.

5.3.5 Page locking

As the log record is the changed bytes in the page as an offset from the start of the page, this means that page level locking is crucial to the Sybase recovery. In a page with 2 records, if we delete the second and add a new record, the third record takes the place of the deleted one and now starts at the same offset as the record just deleted. As long as the page is locked while the deletion takes place, everything is OK because the actions are serial and so any recovery is serial in the same sequence. But if we allow the insert of the new record to take place before the delete completes - as in record level locking - a rollback of the delete will corrupt the data in the page as the deleted record will replace valid data.

This is similar to the standard uncommitted dependency problem of concurrency but the effect is different as we do not just lose data updates in a record but actually corrupt the page contents which is now attempting to start two records at the same offset in the page.

Sybase give many reasons for not implementing record level locking but this is one which they do not discuss often and it will make it difficult/costly to change from page level locking.

5.4   **Backup procedures**

The transaction log, checkpoint and rollback guarantee recovery and data integrity when there is a system failure which has not destroyed any data. We now need to have a set of procedures which will guarantee recovery and data integrity when there is a media failure which has destroyed data on the disk.

To do this we require a dump of the database at a point in time and a dump of the transaction log records since that point in time. The recovery mechanism can then reload the database dump and roll forward the completed transactions from the dump of the transaction log to restore the data in the database to the last completed transaction before the failure.

5.4.1   **Dump devices**

Before we can dump the database or the transaction log we need to create devices on which to write the dumps. Sybase has a default disk dump device but for some reason the physical device is a "null" device which is a bit bucket and can not be used to reload the dump. Why bother? Remember always to create specific disk dump devices as the dump to the default device, which looks as if it is dumping, is not usable.

Dump devices are defined using the system procedure sp_addumpdevice and create an entry in sysdevices in master.

```
sp_addumpdevice

        sp_addumpdevice "type",
                        "logical_name",
                        "physical_name",
                        cntrltype
                        [, {skip | noskip}]
                        [, tape_capacity]
```

where

type   Specifies if the dump device is "tape" or "disk".

cntrltype   2:   a byte streaming device such as disk or Unix cartridge
                     3-8: multi-volume tapes or VMS cartridge

skip/no skip   Specifies if the tape label should be checked or not.

tape_capacity   A value in M bytes to indicate multi-volume tapes for Unix. For dumps which require multiple tapes, the console program

prompts for a new tape when it reaches the specified
tape_capacity.

To define a tape dump device:

```
sp_addumpdevice "tape", "tape_1",
              "/dev/rmt4", 3, noskip, 100
```

To define a disk dump device:

```
sp_addumpdevice, "disk", "disk_1",
              "/usr/u/dump.dir/disk.dump", 2
```

To drop a dump device use the system procedure sp_dropdevice as for any device:

sp_dropdevice

```
sp_dropdevice "logical_name"
```

This simply removes the pointer to an operating system file, it does not delete the
physical file. You need to delete this from the operating system to free up the disk
space.

If you have more than one tape drive and you would like parallel dumps of separate
databases, you need to define the separate tape dump devices with unique controller
types.

```
sp_addumpdevice "tape", "tape_2",
            "/dev/rmt4", 3, 100
go
sp_addumpdevice "tape", "tape_3",
            "/dev/rmt5", 4, 100
go
```

5.4.2 **Dump database**

We can now use the dump device to dump the database and/or the transaction log. The database is dumped using the command dump database.

dump   database

```
dump database db_name to dump_dev_name

dump database fred to disk_dump_1
```

The dump is an on-line dump which means that it may be executed while users are using and updating the database. Clearly a dump of the database is a disk intensive activity so try not to do it during normal user activity. If you have a 24 hour, 7 day a week operation make sure that you dump during the low activity periods.

In addition to the overall increase in disk activity, the on-line dump has to maintain the integrity of the data which is being updated during the dump. It does this by taking a checkpoint at the start of the dump so that the dump and transaction log are synchronised and then dumps the pages in physical order from start to finish of the database space - multiple devices in alphabetical order. Transactions which are trying to update the database while it is being dumped are not allowed to do so immediately. If the page that the transaction is trying to update has been dumped, then the update is allowed. If the page has not been dumped then the transaction has to wait and the update request is put onto a queue. At a regular interval of every 'n' pages, the dump database checks to see if any transactions are waiting. If transactions are waiting the dump dumps the pages which the transactions are waiting to update which allows the transactions to continue.

The dump of the database is therefore a snapshot of the database at the time the dump started. As there may have been transactions running at the start of the dump - the checkpoint - there will be some incomplete transaction updates written to the dump and so you will see a recovery being done when the dump is reloaded to rollback the incomplete transactions at the checkpoint of the dump.

The Sybase dump is a logical dump which means that it dumps used pages only. So in a 100 M byte database if only 60 M bytes are used the dump is only of that 60 M bytes (These arbitrary figures interest you? You are an SA. Think problems when you see anything on databases. If there is a table of 30 M bytes in this database we are running close to not being able to create a clustered index because of the free space figure.) This may seem like a useful feature but it means that the restore of the dump is not writing every page of the database space. Therefore the unused pages which have not been overwritten by the restore must be initialised. This can take some time and is responsible for the long wait after the dump pages have been restored. Don't panic when the tape loads quickly and then waits for ages before the load finishes: it's only the unused pages being initialised.

This also means that you cannot reduce the size of a database using dump and load. In an active database there is no guarantee where the unused pages occur, so you cannot restore a dump onto a smaller database.

You can, of course, use the operating system disk back-up utilities to back-up every disk that the database resides on. You must dump the complete disk space but with a database using the majority of its disk space this is not a problem. Operating system back-ups need the database to be off-line but often the speed benefit can justify this.

My personal dump scenario is to dump the database to a disk device and then copy this to tape for grandfather - father - son security. This does, of course, require a lot of disk capacity and you need to control the process carefully. The Sybase dump is a complete overwrite to the dump device - no appending - so make sure that you have copied the previous dump to tape before you start the next one. (You could always dump to different disk devices but I do not like this.) More importantly, if you are dumping directly to tape do not get them mixed up, and overwrite the previous dump with the current one. If you have a failure during the dump you will have lost both current and previous dumps. Not a good idea!

Finally the dump device must be on the same server as the database. You cannot dump across the network to another server. You do not want to as it takes a long, long time in general. You can move the dump to another server and restore it on the other server to retain a copy of the database. This is possible as long as the servers are the same machine type eg Unix to Unix and VMS to VMS. How limited you are within the different hardware versions of the open systems, I do not know. Assume that it does not work until you have seen it happening. Do not believe Sybase or the hardware vendors until they have demonstrated it.

5.4.3 Dump database algorithm

1   Look up logical "device_name" in sysdevices.
2   Open database "db_name".
3   Acquire exclusive lock on syslogs.
4   Synchronise with checkpoint.
5   Open dump device - tape or diskette will be reopened for each volume.
6   Checkpoint the database to ensure that all dirty pages are flushed out to disk.
7   Synchronise with other users.
8   Write dump header to dump device.
9   Write pages for sysobjects and syscolumns to dump device.
10   Write out allocated pages to dump device, periodically checking the "write queue" to write pages out of sequence if another user waiting on the page.
11   Write dump trailer to dump device.
12   Close dump device - write end of file trailers at end of last volume for tape or diskette.
13   Re-synchronise with other users.
14   Release lock on syslogs.

15   Re-synchronise with checkpoint.
16   Close database "db_name".

5.4.4 Dump transaction

Dumping a large database frequently is a significant overhead: 300 M bytes is 150000 pages which is about 1-2 hours of disk activity simply to read the database and write the dump. So you do not want to dump the database too often. However you do not want to leave the system running for too long before taking some sort of security dump. If you dump the database every morning then the last thing that the user wants to hear when the system crashes at 16:00 hours is that you can bring back the database only as at the start of the day.

Sybase have put, and are putting, a lot of effort into improving the dump and load speed. From version 4.8 the dump speed has improved considerably - by a factor of 10 to dump G bytes in single figure hours - but I have no evidence that the load has progressed much beyond the 1 hour per 300 M bytes figure. It depends on the configuration but v4.8 will dump about 1.75 M bytes per second.

So we need to dump the transaction log regularly so that the possible unrecoverable period is minimised. Because the transaction log is smaller than the database it does not take as long to dump and it does not interfere with the transactions as it is unconcerned with the data pages. There is still a disk activity overhead but this is one that you will have to suffer. Keep the log and dump devices on physical disks which are not used by the rest of the system to avoid the increased disk activity having a direct effect on data access. And if peak activity is 10:00 to 11:00 dump the log at 09:30 and 11:30.

The transaction log is dumped using the dump transaction command.

```
dump    transaction

        dump transaction db_name to [dump_device]
            [{with truncate_only |
            with no_log |
            with no_truncate}]


        dump transaction test_db to tape_dev
```

I'll deal with the options in a moment.

So if we dump the database once a day at 06:00 we would dump the transaction log regularly during the day - say every 3 hours, or irregular intervals - depending on system activity. If we have a media failure during the day we reload the database dumps and each transaction log dump in sequence since the last database dump. Again my optimum scenario is to dump the log to a disk file and then copy this file to tape. As before with the database make sure that the disk file is copied before the next dump as the dump is a complete overwrite. With dumps to tape each dump needs a separate tape as you cannot have multiple dumps on the same physical tape, so make sure that you do not accidentally lose a current transaction dump. This has changed with version 4.8 to allow multiple dumps per tape.

Accidental transaction dump overwrite is more of a problem than overwriting a database dump as loss of one transaction dump means that the complete cycle since the last dump is useless. You cannot recover from the last dump database if one of the log dumps is missing or corrupt: the restore requires the log dumps in sequence with no gaps. So you do not have a recoverable database and need to do an immediate database dump. If you are lucky the system will not crash until this dump is finished. If you are lucky...

(Losing a database dump and going back to a previous dump is not such a disaster as long as you have all of the transaction dumps corresponding to the database dumps. You must keep both the log dumps and the database dumps in your cycle of dumps. A database dump is useless to the recovery system without the transaction log dumps.)

5.4.5 Dump options

The regular dump transaction:

```
dump transaction fred to dump_dev
```

dumps the complete transaction log, clears out all completed transactions and checkpoints the database. So regular transaction dumping keeps the log tidy and keeps its size down. This stops the log filling up which is an excellent reason for regular transaction dumps.

Dump transaction has three options which offer variations on this depending on the circumstances of the dump.

with truncate_only	This option does not dump the log to the dump device but simply clears out the log and takes a checkpoint. This is the option you use if you have a small database for which you are dumping the database only. Doing a dump transaction immediately before the dump database will make the database dump go faster because the log is nearly empty. You are not allowed to run a database without a log but, in this case, you are not interested in the contents of the log and do not intend to use the recovery system to restore from a log, so use this option to purge the log.

with no_log

You do not want to be in the position to have to use this option. This is the option to use when the log has filled up and there is no more space to continue working. When the log is full no more work can be done against the database and the system using the database stops. You need to dump the log to clear it out so that work may continue. The no_log option is able to clear the log and take a checkpoint of the database but does not produce a dump which is suitable for recovery.

with no_truncate

The regular dump transaction requires the database to be intact. Unfortunately when the database fails there will be a portion of the log still on disk but not dumped. The no_truncate option does not need the database to be intact and allows you to dump the current log of a damaged database. It does need the log to be on a separate device from the database and you must run it before you drop the faulty database. If this dump is successful - and there is no guarantee as you are in an error situation - you will be able to recover the database up to the last completed transaction. If the no_truncate dump is not successful then you will be able to recover only up to the last transaction in the previous transaction dump. Another reason for keeping the interval between transaction dumps as short as you can.

After using dump tran with the no_log or truncate_only options any subsequent changes cannot be used to recover from a media failure as a portion of the log has been discarded or has no dump checkpoint record. You **must** dump the database after using these options, so do not let the operational log fill up.

Some commands do not write page modifications to the log: high speed bulk copy, select into and truncate. In general a command which operates at the page level instead of the record level is not logged. A dump database is necessary after these commands. A dump transaction will fail and similarly any automatic dump script which contains a dump transaction will fail. Keep "select into" away from users in the operational databases as it will cause the regular dump transaction to fail. Not a good idea.

Create index is a special as far as recovery is concerned. Because the command causes a large number of modifications these are not logged: but the actual command is. This means that the recovery will rebuild the index. This can take a long time which you probably want to avoid during recovery. The Sybase load database is slow enough, do not prolong it with a big index rebuild. Dump the database after large index builds not because it cannot be recovered but because it takes a long time.

5.4.6 Dump transaction algorithm

1   Look up logical "device_name" in sysdevices.
2   Open database "db_name".
3   Check that log is on its own segment.
4   Check for "select into/bulk copy" or "trunc log on checkpoint".
5   Open dump device - note tape or diskette will be reopened for each   volume.
6   Start a transaction if not already in one.
7   Acquire exclusive lock on syslogs.
8   Checkpoint the database to ensure all dirty pages are flushed out to disk. This
      determines the truncation point and the dump point.
9   Write dump header to dump device.
10   Write out all log pages to the dump device, from the first page of the log to the
      dump point.
            If page is in inactive portion of the log, write a deallocation record for it.
            If page is the dump point, make a copy and modify it as necessary so it
            looks just as it did following the checkpoint (ie the checkpoint record is
            the last row on the page).
            If we are creating a transaction log dump (not truncate_only or no_log)
            write the page to the dump device.
11   Write dump trailer to dump device.
12   Close dump device - write end of file trailers at end of last volume for tape or
      diskette.
13   Update sysindexes information about the log.
14   Set up new first page of log.
15   Update in-memory structure that describes the database.
16   If a transaction was started, commit it.
17   Close database "db_name".

5.5   Restore procedures

5.5.1 Load database

When a media failure occurs the database is unusable and needs to be restored to its
current status from the database and transaction dumps. The first step is to load the
latest dump of the database using load database.

`load database`

```
        load database db_name from device_name

        load database fred from disk_dump_1
```

The database that is being restored with load database cannot be in use by any users.

This includes yourself so make sure that you are in master when you issue this command.

When a media failure occurs you may not be able to load the database from the dump because the database is marked as suspect by the server. In this case you need to drop the database and recreate it before you can run load database. However the standard drop database command may not execute because the database is marked as suspect and you may need to use dbcc dbrepair.

dbcc   dbrepair

```
dbcc dbrepair(db_name, dropdb)
```

Be careful when you recreate the database in this sequence as the database definition in the system tables must be as it was when the database was dumped. If the initial allocation was:

```
create database fred on dev_1 = 6
              logon dev_1 = 2
```

and then altered as:

```
alter database fred on dev_1 = 4
```

the allocation of the database will be as in figure 5.6.

Loading the logical page numbers of the initial allocation into the new allocation will give errors as log pages and data pages are being misplaced. This also applies to user defined segments on the database: so make sure that the definition of the recreated database matches the definition of the dump. An excellent reason for dumps of master and the relevant database after altering a database allocation of devices or segments.

Unfortunately Sybase does not tell you during the load that this mismatch of data and log pages is happening: to be fair it does not know without checking the allocations and the page contents. It is only reported when you run a dbcc checkalloc which is a real problem as the load is slow enough without having to run a dbcc checkalloc just to make sure that the allocations are correct. So make sure that any create before a load is the same allocation as the dump.

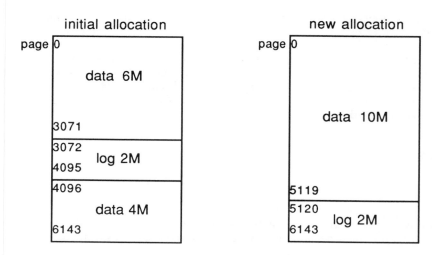

figure 5.6:   incorrect load allocations

5.5.2 **Load database algorithm**

1   Open database "db_name".
2   Verify that there are no other users and mark database "in load".
3   Look up logical "device_name" in sysdevices.
4   Open dump device.
5   Read dump header from dump device.
6   Mark sysdatabases row IN_LOAD. In case of a crash during load database, must redo it or drop the database.
7   Remove pages for this database from buffer cache.
8   Read all pages from dump device and write to database.
9   Read dump trailer from dump device.
10   Close dump device.
11   Remove stored procedures for this database from cache.
12   Rebuild descriptors.
13   Rebuild in-memory structure that describes database.
14   Run recovery.
15   Do version specific modifications.
16   For user database, mark all stored procedures as needing to be recompiled.
17   Zero all unallocated pages.
18   Set suid of dbo in sysusers to creator in sysdatabases.
19   Reset "in_load" from step 2 and IN_LOAD from step 6.
20   Allow other users into the database.
21   Close database "db_name".
22   If master database, kill SQL Server.

5.5.3 **Load transaction**

Having restored the latest dump of the database it will be out-of-date as it does not include all of the transactions which took place from the last dump database. This is unavoidable, of course, and is catered for by regular transaction log dumps which can then be recovered in sequence against the reloaded database. This is done with the load transaction command:

load   transaction

```
          load transaction db_name from device_name

          load transaction fred from log_dev_1
```

The transaction log dumps since the last database dump must be loaded in sequence against the loaded database with no gaps. Sybase helps as it checks the sequence of the reloaded transaction logs but it will not recover without all of the transactions logs: so do not lose one. Make sure that your operations staff label the tapes in such a manner that it is obvious which transaction dumps are linked with which database dumps and what the sequence of transaction dumps is.

Of course failure always occurs at the most awkward moment and you must make use of the "with no_truncate" option of the dump transaction command to ensure that you can restore up to the last completed transaction. A dump scenario of:

```
          dump database at 6:00 am
          dump transaction every two hours during on-line system
          dump database at 6:00 pm
          carry out overnight batch processing
```

will give you a distinct problem when the media failure occurs at 5:50 pm. There will be a valid database dump at 6:00 am with transaction dumps every two hours until 4:00 pm, but the period between 4:00 pm and 5:50 pm has not been dumped and therefore cannot be used in the recovery which will leave about 2 hours of transactions unrecovered. As discussed, the dump transaction has an option "with no_truncate" which does no checking with the database but simply dumps the current transaction log. This option of dump transaction is essential to ensure that recovery can be made up to the last completed transaction and should be the first thing that you do when a media failure occurs. The whole server is in an unstable condition - some of the disks are unusable - so do not get clever: dump transaction with no_truncate and then you can mess about to see if you can ascertain what is wrong.

So the sequence on media failure is:

```
dump transaction db_name
        to log_dev_dump with no_truncate

load database db_name from db_dump_device
load transaction db_name from log_dev_dump
repeat the load transaction
until all transaction logs restored
```

If the dump transaction with no_truncate is successful the database will be restored up to the last completed transaction. If the dump transaction with no_truncate fails - and you have no guarantee that it will work as the database is not intact - the database will be restored up to the end of the last regular transaction dump.

5.5.4 Load transaction algorithm

1   Open database "db_name".
2   Verify that there are no other users and mark database "in transition".
3   Look up logical "device_name" in sysdevices.
4   Open dump device.
5   Read dump header from dump device.
6   Verify that no rows have been added to syslogs since the last load.
7   Clear out descriptor and procedure caches.
8   Mark state in dbinfo as loading.
9   Update sequence number and state in sysindexes row and force out to disk.
10   Read all pages from dump device and write to database.
11   Change state in dbinfo to "in recovery".
12   Close dump device.
13   Change status from "in transition" to "not recovered" in in-memory structure that describes database.
14   Run recovery.
15   Flush all dirty pages out to disk.
16   Change state in dbinfo to "done loading".
17   Advance current sequence number to new one.
18   Change status from "not recovered" to "usable" in in-memory structure that describes database.
19   Close database "db_name".

5.6 Rebuilding the master database

There are many problems to an SA's life, not least the appearance of not seeming to do anything. As an ex-SA I believe that the best SA never appears to be doing anything because that means that the system is running OK. Just keep the terminal facing away from the centre of the office and have a function key that displays what looks like a stack dump.

However the real problem is when the system goes down because one of your required resources has failed. Obvious candidates are the log and the master database. At the very least have both of these mirrored so that a single failure does not stop the system. If a log fails then the database is unusable. Everybody writes to the log so if it is not available nobody can use that database. Don't panic. Fix the problem, create a log device, dump the database and back to normal. When you let the users back into the system is up to you, but you must dump the database as you do not have a recoverable situation until you have an up-to-date dump. The log has failed so you cannot recover completely from the previous dump. If you have been dumping the transaction log regularly then you will be able to roll forward to the end of the last dump of the log: but you will be unable to recover up to the last completed transaction.

At least in this situation the failure affects only one database and other users may still be working. But a failure of the master database stops everybody on the server, so make sure that you can recover the master database as quickly as possible. This is one area where you should be as prepared as possible. Keep users out of the master database so that it contains system tables only. This keeps it as tidy as possible with no user tables which keeps it as small as possible with faster dump and load times.

Keep an up-to-date dump of master. The most important times are after updates to sysdatabases, sysdevices and syslogins. At the very least have a separate log device for master so that you can dump transaction but as master is liable to be reasonably small my personal preference is to dump database after commands which update sysdatabases and sysdevices.

So dump master after:

create/alter/drop database	sysdatabases
add/drop devices	sysdevices
add/drop logins	syslogins

If you do not do this then the restored dump will not reflect the actual disk configuration and you will need to run rebuilding commands to update the system tables in master to reflect the current disk configuration. These take time and the whole system is down. Keep an up-to-date dump of master.

Even if you have an up-to-date dump the master database holds the system tables which define the complete configuration and therefore require a little special attention to recover. This is given by the special command buildmaster.

```
buildmaster -m
```

The buildmaster command is part of a regular install, the -m option simply reinitialises the master database leaving model and tempdb intact. The full syntax of buildmaster is:

`buildmaster`

	Unix	**VMS**
buildmaster	-d disk	/disk=name
	-c cntrltype	/cntrltype=value
	-s size	/size=value
	-r	/reconfigure
	-m	/master
		/contiguous

where

disk   The physical name of the device for the location of the master database.

cntrltype   Controller number for the master device. Defaults to 0. Leave it alone.

size   The master database size in pages.

-r   Rebuilds the master database with the default configuration parameters. When you are changing the configuration variables using sp_configure there is no check that you have not specified rubbish until you reboot the server, at which point it will not reboot. This option gets you out of trouble.

-m   Simply recreates the master database as described above.
            Does not change the configuration parameters.

You will be asked for device and size information:

```
buildmaster -m
```

device: /dev/rst1d

controller: 0   ALWAYS ENTER 0. Do not get clever.

size: in pages (be careful as the original install may have requested sectors)

Once the master database is initialised the buildmaster command kills the server. Start it up in single user mode to make sure that no other users can get near the system yet and reload your dump of master.

Make sure you alter your 'sa' password as the rebuild will have reset it to null and if your disk dump is on a named device you will have to add the disk dump device before you load master. The load of master will again kill the server so you can now start it for all of the users.

If you have an up-to-date dump:

```
dump database master to dump_dev
```

then the recovery of master is:

```
buildmaster -m
```

device: /dev/rst1d

controller: 0

size: 10000

```
cd /usr/sybase/install

startserver -m

isql -Usa
     sp_password
     go
     sp_addumpdevice "disk", "dump_dev",
                     "dump.dat1", 2
     go
     load database master from dump_dev
     go

startserver
```

If you have not been keeping an up-to-date dump of master then the dump that you have just restored will not reflect the devices, databases, logins that you have added since the last dump and you need to issue further commands to make master reflect the existing configuration. To update the system tables in master we need to run:

disk reinit	devices
disk refit	databases
scripts	logins

You cannot do disk init or create database as these initialise the disk areas as well as updating the system tables and so the above commands are required simply to update the system tables. Also there is no relogin command so you will need to rerun the isql script to re-add any logins and users. (Of course you do not have any users in master because you do not allow named users into master.) **All rebuilding from an out-of-date dump assumes that you know what you have to rebuild.**

When you have this rebuilding work to do, start the server in single user mode after the load database. Again you do not want users in the system when you are rebuilding the system tables.

5.6.1 **devices**

disk reinit

```
disk reinit
    name = logical_name,
    physname = physical_name,
    vdevno = virtual_device_no,
    size = number_of_pages
    [, vstart = virtual_address]
    [, cntrltype = controller_number]
```

The parameters are the same as for the disk init and the values **must** be the same as the original disk init. You must be in master to issue disk reinit.

```
disk reinit
    name = "sales",
    physname = "/usr/sales.dir/sales.dat"
    vdevno = 5,
    size = 8000
```

This recreates the entry in sysdevices without initialising the disk space.

5.6.2 **databases**

disk refit

```
disk refit
```

This is run from master and uses the rebuilt information in sysdevices and the current disk allocations to rebuild sysusages and sysdatabases.

Even running this on each database Sybase still recommend that you run the database consistency checker dbcc to check the allocations

```
dbcc checkalloc(fred_db)
```

and have a look at the relevant tables - sysdevices, sysdatabases, sysusages as mentioned above. Updating a reinitialised, refitted system which is not quite right can have disastrous results which are unrecoverable.

5.6.3 logins

I must confess that even I would not always dump the database after adding a login to master. But do record the new login in a script so that you can rerun the script after recovering master. Of course if you take this approach the user's password will revert to what it was originally. Make sure that you tell them this.

The latter comment of keeping scripts up-to-date applies to everything you do as SA. You are adjusting the system configuration with almost everything that you do so make sure that you can repeat it by recording it in a script. I know that this is extra work but do it: you do not want to have to think too much when the system has crashed. All you want to do is to press the button and watch an automatic recovery.

Keep a master script of your system configuration so that you can rebuild it at any time. Every change that you make - new login, new device, new database, increase to a database, new segment: everything - must be kept up-to-date in this script. This is not a substitute for regular dumps of master but an essential to allow you to rebuild the system configuration.

5.7 Logical system rebuild

Let's look at a full system rebuild in a little more detail.

Database dump and load are not always possible, for example when moving from one machine type to another or when recreating only part of the database. In such cases we need to go back to the beginning and reissue the appropriate create commands. It would be incredibly tedious, as well as drastically error prone, to manually reenter every command, so it is advisable to keep an isql script which contains the create commands for everything in the current database.

Being practical, it is much better to keep one script for each object set: devices, segments, databases, logins, users, tables, indexes, rules, defaults, permissions, procedures, triggers and views as it is much easier to control and maintain. And remember to keep the scripts up-to-date.

So what is a script file?

5.7.1 isql

A script file is an operating system file of the commands that you would execute in isql to create the various objects. It is included when entering isql from the operating system.

Unix

```
isql -Usa -Psa < db_create.sql
```

VMS

```
isql /user="sa" /pass="sa"
        /input=proc_create.sql
```

Get into the habit of using scripts for all of your SA creation commands and incorporate them into the overall system scripts as soon as possible. The full syntax of isql is:

isql

Unix	**VMS**
isql [-e] [-p] [-i] [-n]	/echo /statistics /noprompt
[-c cmdend]	/terminator = string
[-h headers]	
[-w col_width]	/colwidth = integer
[-s col_sep]	/colseparator = character
[-t timeout]	/timeout = integer
[-m error_level]	/errorlevel = integer
[-H host_name]	/hostname = host_name
[-U user_name]	/username = user_name
[-P pwd]	/password = password
[-I interface]	/interfaces = file_name
[-S server]	/server_name = server_name
< input_file_name	/input = file_name
> out_file_name	/output = file_name
	/rowsinpage = integer

where

-e   Echoes input.

-p	Prints statistics.
-i	Tags input and output with a process_id number.
-n	Removes the numbering and > prompt from input lines.
-c cmdend	Resets the command terminator. Default is 'go'.
-h headers	Specifies number of rows between column headings.
-w col_width	Sets the screen output width.
-s col_sep	Resets column separator. Default is space.
-t timeout	Specifies number of seconds before a command times out. Default is no timeout on commands and 60 seconds on login.
-m error_level	Specifies level below which no error message is displayed.
-H host_name	Specifies different host computer name.
-U user_name	User name.
-P pwd	Password.
-I interfaces	Specifies name and location of interfaces file to be used for connection.
-S server	Specifies name of server to connect to.

Points worth remembering in isql are:

- small batches, especially each create command in a batch by itself. I know that some of them do not need a separate batch but it saves some thinking if you put each create command in its own batch.

- **quit** or **exit** to exit.

- **reset** to discard incorrect batches of commands without running them.

- **execute** in front of stored procedures: only the first procedure in a batch executes without the key word, so make it a habit to always use the keyword especially in front of system procedures.

- do a **use database** as often as possible: no point in being in the wrong database and no harm in too many use databases. Remember to put it in its own batch.

always check to see if an object exists before using the create: the create will fail if the object already exists so check the appropriate system table before creating it (or do not create it if it exists already).

```
if exists (select * from sysobjects
    where name = 'upd_proc' and type = 'P')
    drop proc upd_proc
go
create proc upd_proc as
etc
```

Sybase has some installation scripts in $SYBASE/scripts which are reasonable examples, so have a look at them: eg installmaster, installmodel, installpubs.

5.7.2 defncopy

Scripts are essential for devices, segments, databases, tables, logins, users and permissions but there is an operating system command - defncopy - which copies the definitions of views, rules, defaults, procedures and triggers.

defncopy

	Unix	**VMS**
defncopy	-U name	/username = user_name
	-P pwd	/password = password
	[-S server]	/server_name = server_name
	[-I interfaces]	/interfaces = file_name
	out/in	
	file_name	
	db_name	
	object_name	
	[object_name...]	

where

out/in   Specifies the direction of the copy: out from database to operating system.

file_name   The operating system file_name.

As with any create, the objects created belong to the person executing the command, so use defncopy as SA or dbo.

Copy out:

```
defncopy -Usa -Psa out
        tabs_proc
        fred_db
        tab_1.proc
```

Copy in:

```
defncopy -Usa -Psa in
        tabs.proc
        fred_db
```

5.7.3 Bulk copy

Finally we need to load the data to the tables we have just recreated. When we cannot use load database the best method is to use bulk copy: bcp.

bcp

        bcp   table_name   in/out data_file

Unix	VMS
[-m max_errors]	/max_errors = integer
[-f format_file]	/format_file = file_name
[-e err_file]	/errorfile = file_name
[-F first_row]	/first_row = integer
[-L last_row]	/last_row = integer
[-b batch_size]	/batch_size = integer
[-n]	/native_default
[-c]	/character_default
[-t field_terminator]	/column_terminator = string
[-r row_terminator]	/row_terminator = string
[-i input_file]	/input = file_name
[-o output_file]	/output = file_name
[-U user_name]	/username = user_name
[-P pwd]	/password = password
[-I interfaces]	/interfaces = file_name
[-S server]	/server_name = server_name
[-v]	/version

where

in/out	The direction of the copy: in is from the data_file to the table.
data_file	The full path name of the input data.
-m max_errors	The maximum number of errors before the copy is aborted. The default is 10.
-f format_file	The path name of a stored set of responses to a previous run of bcp.
-e err_file	The file_name for any rows which were unable to be copied.
-F first_row	The number of the first row to copy. Default is 1.
-L last_row	The number of the last row to copy. Default is end of the file.
-b batch_size	The number of rows per batch for copy in. A checkpoint is taken after the batch_size.
-n	Performs the copy using the datatypes of the database columns.
-c	Performs the copy using character type as default with \t as field_terminator and \n as row_terminator.
-t field_terminator	Specifies the field_terminator.
-r row_terminator	Specifies the row_terminator.
-v	Reports the current version of bcp.

Bulk copy may be run from the operating system, data workbench or db_library. Data workbench is the easiest as you are protected from the parameters but not all of the options are available to you so I would recommend running bcp from the operating system.

Bulk copy runs in two modes: fast and slow. Fast copy runs when there are no indexes or triggers on the table and select into/bulk copy is set using sp_dboption. In this mode no rules fire, no triggers fire and the inserts are not logged. Defaults are assigned. As awkward as this can be with a separate integrity program needed to check domain and referential integrity and uniqueness of primary key, I would strongly recommend this method from a performance aspect. Slow bulk copy is exactly that: **slow**. You will have time to code the additional integrity program, test it extensively and run fast bulk copy in the time it takes slow bulk copy to run.

An exception to this is when the records are loaded in clustered index sequence to an existing clustered index: using the "with sorted key" qualifier. This can be fast. However you need to consider any effort to pre-sort the records, which may negate any savings. Try it.

To load a table:

> create table (using script)
>
> bcp data into table
>
> run uniqueness check
>
> create indexes
>
> run integrity checks

Specifying a batch size is highly recommended when loading data with bcp. Because fast mode bcp is not logged, it is not recoverable. However specifying a batch size forces a checkpoint after the specified number of records have been loaded. This gives an intermediate point to which the system can recover. More importantly, the checkpoint clears out the log. Even though fast bcp does not log the inserts, the page allocations are logged and a large bulk copy can cause more use of the log than you may expect. So always specify a batch size for this reason.

Remember that - even with checkpoints - bcp inserts are not logged in fast mode and therefore the full bulk copy is not recoverable: do a dump database after a fast bulk copy. Be careful when you have the "select into/bulk copy" option enabled. This allows the "select into" command to be executed in the database. This is a non-logged command ie the record updates are not written to the log, and therefore the database is not recoverable after a "select into". So it is extremely dangerous to leave this option enabled on a database.

In Unix running bcp will prompt you with the default field information from the database:

```
bcp fred_db.dbo.tab_1 out tab_out
```

enter the file storage type of field col_1 [char]:
enter prefix_length of field col_1 [0]:
enter length of field col_1 [12]:
enter field terminator [none]:

The possible responses are:

storage_type   Char to create or read an ASCII file. Char for varchar and binary
                      for varbinary, otherwise any datatype which is a valid
                      conversion. Timestamp data is treated as binary(8).

prefix_length   Indicates the length of the data field.
                      0   fixed length
                      1   variable length
                      2   binary/varbinary saved as char
                      4   text/image

length   Length for char/varchar. Maximum length of variable length
                      fields. Length * 2 for binary/varbinary saved as char.

field_terminator   Specifies the field_terminator - usually from
                      \t   tab
                      \n   newline
                      \r   carriage return
                      \0   null terminator
                      \\   backslash

(If you find that you have problems with numeric data conversions on input, use the -c
mode which will treat the input data as character and make the appropriate conversions
automatically.)

5.8   **Summary**

Sybase provides 100% recovery capability from both system and media failure. The syslogs system table contains a log of all changes made to the database with periodic checkpoints to flush data pages from cache to disk. This combination provides full recovery from a system failure by rollback of the before images of the data changes and full recovery from a media failure by roll forward of the data changes.

The roll forward to recover from a media failure also requires dumps of the database and the transaction log (syslogs). This is done with the dump/load database and transaction commands.

Recovery of the master database from a media failure is slightly more complicated with a buildmaster having to be issued before the database may be restored from the dump. If the dump of master is out-of-date regarding the device and database information the special commands disk reinit and disk refit must be executed to ensure the system tables reflect the physical configuration. Also any logins not restored from the dump must be added again to syslogins.

Finally, when previous dumps are not suitable eg when moving to different hardware, the isql scripts, defncopy and bcp commands must be used to rebuild the devices, databases, objects in the databases and the data.

And finally....

Training course instructor to student with eyes fixed in a manual: "What are you doing - learning something?"

Student: "No, I was listening to you."

Student: "Is a megabyte very much?"

Instructor: "Depends on whether you are entering data or writing a program to fit into it."

Instructor: "Could you please wake up that person to your left?"

Student: "You wake him up - you put him to sleep!"

Angry instructor describing his day: "Every time I got up to speak, some fool began to talk!"

Chapter 6

Multi-user
considerations

Concurrency
and
memory size

This chapter describes the Sybase approach to the important aspects of a multi-user environment such as concurrency and locking and the allocation of memory.

O'Reilly's Sixth Law

Any system which depends on human reliability is unreliable.

Commands covered in this chapter:

None

System procedures covered in this chapter:

sp_lock
sp_configure

6.1 Locking

Sybase's strategy on locking and concurrency is probably its weakest, and paradoxically potentially its strongest feature. Sybase locks at the page level and waits for contention on resources to go away. There are two resolutions to contention: when it is encountered the requesting transaction rolls back or the requesting transaction waits for the contention to be released. The waiting strategy adopted by Sybase causes several processing overheads in dealing with the queues which can build up and in resolving deadlocked transactions because transactions waiting for a locked resource may also have other resources locked.

Sybase locks at the page level as its lowest level of locking granularity. This goes back into the mists of time regarding the balance of locking granularity v processing overhead. Sybase stoically - or is it perhaps reverently - refuse to reconsider the results of old findings in the light of its other concurrency features and in the light of more powerful and faster hardware. In my opinion, Sybase's adherence to page level locking will leave it with an insurmountable bottleneck which will prevent it ever making again the level of performance improvement that it introduced to the relational market.

What Sybase seem not to realise, in adhering to page level locking, is that the original granularity solutions were based on ANSI standard locking strategies. Sybase default locking does not support the ANSI standard locking strategy of the SLOCK being retained until escalated to an XLOCK or until the transaction completes at the commit or rollback. Sybase retains the SLOCK on the page only for as long as the page is being read and then the SLOCK is released.

This type of optimistic locking strategy is essential in the client/server environment and gives Sybase a significant advantage over its rivals. Fortunately I believe that the client/server advantages far outweigh the page level disadvantage. However a move towards record level locking would remove a performance bottleneck from the architecture.

6.2 Server locking strategy

First of all let's have a look at the locking strategy at the server only, in isolation of the client, to allow us to concentrate on the lock settings and the concurrency control. Then we will have a look at the client activity which causes these locks to be set, to determine how to resolve any concurrency problems.

The traditional locking solution is shown in figure 6.1 where a multi-reader shared lock (SLOCK) is set when objects are read and a single user exclusive lock (XLOCK) is set when objects are updated (insert/update/ delete).

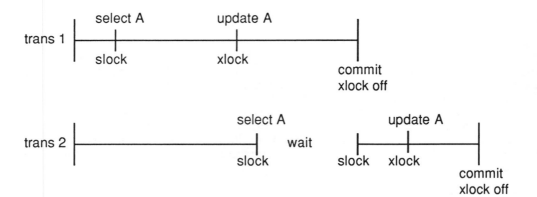

figure 6.1:   standard locking

If a read is made on an exclusively locked resource the read waits until the resource is free and continues with the released resource. (As mentioned above, the other solution to finding a locked resource is for the transaction to be rolled back immediately. Sybase does not use this approach. There are pros and cons to each approach - a detailed treatment being beyond this book - but it is essentially a balance of rollback overhead to queue overhead. In an ANSI standard locking environment I favour rollback on contention but in the optimistic approach of Sybase, I favour waiting for the lock to be released.)

All locks are retained until the end of the transaction - commit or rollback - to ensure a partially updated record is not released prematurely. The SLOCK is retained until it is escalated to an XLOCK in both of the transactions. If no XLOCK occurred the SLOCK is still retained until the end of the transaction. Retaining the XLOCK until the commit or rollback ensures 100% integrity of the updated data in that no transaction can obtain a partially updated record until the updating transaction has completed.

In most software there are two types of read lock - they don't always call them SLOCKs so it is difficult to keep the terminology consistent. The first type of read lock is used when the transaction wishes only to read the record and this is done by not setting any locks and ignoring existing locks. Data which is in the process of being updated may be read by the nolock transaction. It is up to the software to determine whether the value prior to the update (Oracle) or the current value (Ingres) is the one which is obtained. Clearly the latter approach leaves room for inconsistency if the update is subsequently rolled back. The second type of read lock is the ANSI standard, usually a different syntax of the select command - select for update - which retains the SLOCK until escalated to an XLOCK or the commit/rollback.

Unfortunately this type of concurrency control can cause deadlock contention between two transactions which are trying to update the same record as in figure 6.2.

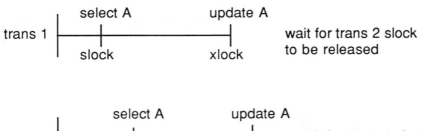

figure 6.2:   update deadlock

Most software will identify this deadlock and rollback one of the transactions to allow the other to complete.

Sybase eliminates this type of deadlock by not holding the SLOCK any longer than is necessary to read the page. This is shown in figure 6.3.

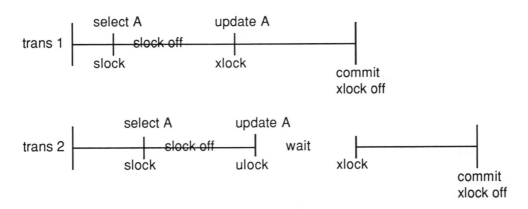

figure 6.3:   Sybase locking strategy

Now there is no SLOCK contention to deadlock the transactions and both can proceed to a correct conclusion. Sybase introduces a new lock, the update lock (ULOCK) as the first stage of the XLOCK to check if there is any contention before taking the XLOCK. If contention does exist and the transaction has to wait, it is the ULOCK which waits until the resource is free and is then escalated to an XLOCK.

Therefore the ULOCK has no existence outside of the XLOCK command and is immediately escalated to an XLOCK if there is no contention. The ULOCK is useful when examining locks with sp_lock as any ULOCKs are transactions waiting for other locks to be released to effect an update. This situation is often difficult to determine in other systems.

6.2.1 Deadlock

We still have the possibility of deadlock between transactions but only when they are contending for more than one resource as shown in figure 6.4.

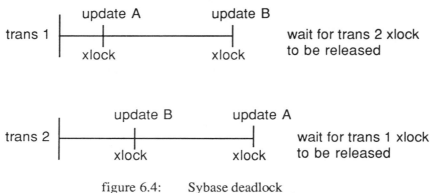

figure 6.4:   Sybase deadlock

Sybase detects this automatically and rolls back one of the transactions to allow the other to proceed. You have no control over which transaction is rolled back: Sybase decides on the basis of amount of work done.

6.2.2 Holdlock

The above locking strategy solves the two standard concurrency problems: no lost updates by XLOCKing pages and no uncommitted dependency by retaining the XLOCK until the transaction commits. This ensures that data cannot be corrupted by multiple, concurrent updates and that reads are not allowed while data is in a state of change during the update.

Therefore each record is guaranteed to be in a consistent state while it is being read. However a transaction which reads many records cannot guarantee that all of the records remain at the same state throughout the transaction. This means that the content of a record is as at the time the page is read and not necessarily as at the time the transaction started.

The simplest example of this read consistency or inconsistent analysis is shown in figure 6.5.

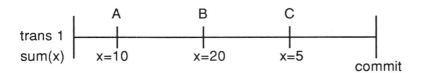

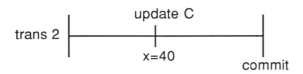

figure 6.5:   read consistency problems

When transaction 1 started, the sum of field x would have been 35 but transaction 3 stepped in before record C was read and the actual result of transaction 1 is 70. Full read consistency produces the result 35 ie the expected value at the start of the transaction.

Sybase does not support this automatically and it has to be made to happen by requesting a **holdlock** on the select command which retains the SLOCK until the end of the transaction ie commit or rollback.

```
select sum(x) from tab_1 holdlock
```

This places an SLOCK on the table at the beginning of the transaction which prevents update transactions changing any values until the SLOCK is released at the end of the transaction.

This is a real sledgehammer to crack a nut and I would never recommend the use of holdlock in any performance based system with a regular level of multi-user access. Locking a complete table is never a good idea. So although the facility is available, use it sparingly, with care, if at all. If you need read consistency think about an application softlock on the table which allows other readers and updates to the unimportant field(s) but bars updates to the field(s) on which read consistency is required. There is still significant contention but it is minimised by this approach.

6.2.3 Table locks

The above holdlock introduced the concept of locking at the table level. There are two types of table locks: **intent** locks and real locks.

The real locks are quite simple: SLOCK, XLOCK at the table level as opposed to the page level. The choice of page or table lock is determined by the optimiser. If the optimiser determines that a table scan is required then it will request a table lock instead of a page level lock on every page in the table. The only command that this does not apply to is the insert which never takes an initial table lock.

Table locks may also be set when a transaction takes more than 200 page locks on a single table. If a transaction is processing a table and takes more than 200 individual page locks eg an insert or an SLOCK with holdlock, then it will be escalated to a table lock and the page locks released. The figure of 200 is not configurable.

This escalation is facilitated by the other type of table lock: intent locks.

When a transaction takes a page lock it also takes an intent lock at the table level. So an SLOCK on a page sets a shared intent (IS) lock on the table and an XLOCK on a page sets an exclusive intent (IX) lock at the table level. ULOCKs do not get reflected at the table level as they are contention situations at the page level. The intent locks are not real locks and are simply used as semaphore settings by the contention system to facilitate table lock checking. As they are not real locks any number and mixture of intent locks can coexist.

If a transaction wishes to take an exclusive table lock then it would need to check if any page in the table has a current SLOCK or XLOCK. If a page has a current lock set then the table XLOCK would have to wait. To make the checking easier the table lock only checks against the intent locks at the table level as this contains the lock status of the pages of the table without knowing which pages are the subject of locks. Until the intent lock queue is clear on the table the table lock cannot be set.

The lock settings for the various commands are:

	table	page
insert	IX	X
update with index	IX	U, X
delete with index	IX	X
update without index	X	----
delete without index	X	----
select with index	IS	S
select with index and holdlock	IS	S
select without index	IS	S
select without index and holdlock	S	----

| create clustered index | X | ---- |
| create non-clustered index | S | ---- |

6.2.4 **Demand locking**

A problem with waiting for lock contention to go away before locking a page/table is that you may be gazumped by other locks while you are waiting and - in theory - never obtain the required lock. This is particularly so when an XLOCK is waiting for SLOCKs to be released or a transaction is trying to set a table lock. While the XLOCK is waiting there is a finite - albeit small - chance that other SLOCKs could be taken on the resource. Thus although the original locks are released, subsequent new locks prevent the waiting XLOCK from obtaining the page/table.

This is simply resolved by not allowing new SLOCKs on a resource which has a waiting XLOCK: quite simply determined in Sybase by the presence of a ULOCK.

Because of the limited lifespan of the SLOCK this will not occur often, but unfortunately it will tend to occur with the most used records and so it has to be catered for and the XLOCK given preferential treatment over SLOCKs once the ULOCK request has been registered. In practice Sybase allows up to 3 SLOCK requests before the XLOCK gets its turn. This is practical only because the Sybase SLOCKs are very short lived locks.

This is called **demand locking** and effectively puts a bar on SLOCKs once an XLOCK is requested on a resource.

Prior to v4.8 if there are several XLOCKs waiting for a resource to become free, there is no guarantee which task will get the free resource. When there is lock contention the task which is requesting the locked resource is put to sleep until the resource is available. Any further requests are queued for the resource. When the resource becomes free all tasks are woken and they contend for the resource. Therefore there is no guarantee that the first queued task will obtain the free resource and there is the obvious overhead of sleeping all the unsuccessful tasks again. From v4.8 the queue of waiting tasks is on a first in first out basis with only the longest waiting being woken to get the available resource.

6.3   **Client/server considerations**

The client/server environment that Sybase works in is one where the actions at the client and the server are independent of each other between message pairs. So a request for data by a client is responded to by the server by sending the data and then the server has no knowledge of what the client has or what the client is doing, until another request - possibly to update the data - is received and responded to.

The traditional sequence of display some data and update some or all of the data is two separate, independent transactions to the server. The most important aspect of the independence is that there are no locks held on the records between the select and the update, even if they are in the same transaction block. Sybase does not retain the SLOCK after the page has been read and therefore all records selected and displayed at the client are not locked by the server.

There is one exception to this: when the client leaves results pending at the server. Records read at the server are put into a server buffer. If more records are read than the buffer can hold, a buffer full condition is sent to the client to initiate transfer of the buffer records. Unfortunately the page that was read when the buffer full condition occurred remains in a "read state" and therefore the SLOCK remains on the page until the client has processed the records in the buffer and requested the next record from the database. When the records in the buffer are the result of a multi-table join, this can be a serious condition as many pages may be left with SLOCKs on. Try never to leave results pending from a Sybase client.

Therefore when a record is returned to the server from a client for update, there is no guarantee that the record has not been updated by another transaction between the select and the update. We now have the original lost update possibility of corrupt data. Figure 6.6 illustrates the problem.

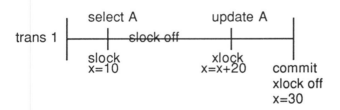

figure 6.6:   client/server lost update

Simply because transaction 2 retained the record at the client long enough, all lock conflictions of transaction 1 are released and the update of transaction 2 corrupts that of transaction 1.

This is not a new problem but it is exacerbated by the client/server environment where the client may be a workstation with processing power, storage capacity and a multi-tasking capability. In the dumb terminal environment you need to finish what you are doing before you can start another task. This minimises the time between events at the server and fixes the sequence of them. However in a multi-tasking, workstation environment you simply move the cursor to another window and carry out the new task...then answer the mail message...then send your own message...then update your diary...then remember what you were doing in the first place. All of this time the records have been sitting in your window minding their own business, happy for the rest, but potentially having the database version updated by another client. So when you finally decide to return the update, your version no longer reflects the current state of the database version.

Update in the Sybase client/server environment requires some type of version control to check to see if the version of the record being returned for update is the same as the version of the database record. Sybase implements this by a timestamping field on the record which is checked by including a special clause in the update command and updated by each insert/update command. This is shown simplified in figure 6.7.

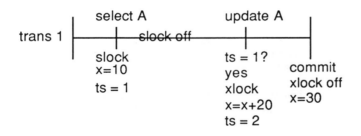

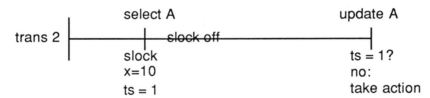

figure 6.7:   timestamp checking

The action that you take is application dependent, such as rollback or reread, but at least you do not corrupt the data.

There are some conditions that need to be met to allow this type of timestamp checking to be made in Sybase.

- the table must have a unique primary key

- the select must be issued with the FOR BROWSE clause

- the table must have a 'timestamp' field defined

- the update must include a dbqual clause for db_library or a tsqual clause for TSQL

- the select and update must be made on separate connections from db_library

These are not trivial, but not impossible or even out of the ordinary, and are essential to ensure data integrity in Sybase. You can, of course, set up your own field and processing to achieve this version control but Sybase's solution is quite adequate - the only real imposition being the requirement for FOR BROWSE in the SELECT.

For those of you who are used to the other Unix databases and consider this a weird situation, consider your alternative. Sybase requires this timestamp check on update to cater for not locking records between the select and the update or between the client and the server. For those who are used to the SLOCK being retained between the SLOCK and the XLOCK or a select for update and then display at the terminal, I hope that you are prepared for the contention of the client/server environment when the *locked* records - say 100 of them - are being browsed in a window by the user, the mail interrupt flashes, the user leaves the update window, reads the mail etc etc etc. You have records locked while this is happening.

Sybase is taking the more optimistic view of the locking situation. It may not be perfect but it is - in my opinion - preferable to the high contention that the ANSI standard SLOCK retention will cause. Most client/server applications will require an optimistic approach to locking - say read nolock, display, select for update to check locks and update - which you will need to design yourself with your own softlock field. Sybase gives you this automatically with timestamping.

6.4   **Administration considerations**

Contention in any database system is always one of the biggest problems and Sybase is no exception. If you suspect that there is a contention problem then the system procedure sp_lock will show the current locks and assist you to unravel the problem.

```
sp_lock

            sp_lock
```

Consider the transaction:

```
begin tran
      insert tab_1 values (1,2,'aaaaa')
      select * from tab_1 holdlock where fkey_col = 2
      select sum(balance) from tab_1 holdlock
      update tab_1 set name = 'bbbb'
                where fkey_col = 2
```

(where tab_1 has a clustered index on fkey_col)

An sp_lock at this stage will show the locks:

spid	locktype	table_id	page	dbname
1	ex_intent	122004611	0	fred
1	ex_page	122004611	509	fred
1	ex_page	122004611	1419	fred
1	ex_page	122004611	1420	fred
1	ex_page	122004611	1440	fred
1	sh_page	122004611	1440	fred
1	sh_table	122004611	0	fred
1	update_page	122004607	1440	fred
5	sh_intent	26004256	0	master
6	ex_intent	0	1128	tempdb

The insert is the heavy transaction here as it has locked an extent and 4 pages - 509, 1419, 1420, 1440. It is impossible to tell from this which each of these is, but we know that 1440 is the data page because it is locked by the 'select *' and the update. The other pages are probably the insert pages which are locked by the insert. The tempdb page lock is required by the sum(balance) which uses tempdb for the aggregate value.

The number of locks available to the server is configurable and set by the system procedure sp_configure.

sp_configure

```
sp_configure 'locks', 8000
```


This is the total available locks including all SLOCKs/XLOCKs at page and table level. If it is exceeded, the offending transaction is rolled back with an appropriate system error. Do not panic when this happens until you know why. Exceeding the maximum number of locks will happen but often it is because of an unusual configuration of events which may not happen again or happens so infrequently that it does not justify increasing the maximum.

Make sure that you know why it occurred so that you are forewarned and can prevent it happening again. If it occurs regularly or is caused by normal activity then you need to consider increasing the number of locks using sp_configure. And remember that the new value does not take effect until you have restarted the server.

A rule of thumb from Sybase - and I've no better - is to allow for 20 locks per connection. A Sybase user may have several connections - one to select and one to update - and the server views each connection as an independent transaction. So a 100 user system should be assumed to be 200 - 300 connections - let's overestimate and assume 300 - and will require a maximum lock setting of 6000. You will know your own system better than this average and will be able to judge the number of connections per user with more accuracy but, at initial system configuration, this is as good as it gets. Note that as the server views each connection as a separate transaction, you can lock yourself out of a resource!

Above all, do not panic when the maximum is exceeded. Reassure the user, watch them resubmit the command, take the applause when it works, find out what was happening when the maximum was exceeded and work at preventing it happening again or minimising it. If the resubmission of the command is also rolled back, mumble something intelligent and have an immediate look at what is happening with sp_lock. Usually it is one transaction retaining a large number of locks or one transaction locking the others out of a common resource.

What can you do about it? Nothing. All you can try is to minimise the effects of the Sybase locking strategy and get the number of locks as accurate as possible. Each lock requires 40 bytes of memory which is 40 K per 1000 locks so, although not a drastic problem, do not increase this without some thought.

6.5   Design considerations

6.5.1   Minimum records per page

Because Sybase locks at the page level a single lock will lock all the records in the page. The fewer records per page, the fewer unnecessary records are locked. At the extreme a highly active table with a high degree of concurrent usage will benefit by having one record per page to simulate record locking. This is only really possible by artificially padding the record with large char fields to make it greater than half a page. If all you do is update then a low fillfactor on a clustered index can achieve the same result but the large record is favourite.

Parameter style records, ie a small table with several very small records which are frequently updated, are the type of record to consider for this.

Having one parameter record with a large number of updatable parameter values in it is simply creating a contention bottleneck because almost every transaction in the system will be trying to lock and update this record. Splitting this single record into several with one parameter value per record will still leave all the records in one page which Sybase locks for each single record update. The small records must be padded to one record per page to simulate record locking in Sybase.

General usage may benefit from a lower fillfactor than normal on a clustered index to reduce the number of records per page. A large insert rate will negate much of the savings but if concurrent access is a problem this is worth trying.

6.5.2 Short transactions

Reduce the length of time that a page is locked by keeping the transactions short. As Sybase does not retain the SLOCK this effectively means to keep the time between the insert/update/delete and the end of the transaction as short as possible. Delay the XLOCK commands to as close as possible to the commit/rollback. And remember that XLOCK commands lock the page even if the command produces an error. If a delete is issued and the record does not exist, the page is still locked and remains locked until the end of the transaction.

Be very careful in this situation with a nested transaction as Sybase does not commit until the outer commit transaction.

```
begin tran
    . . . .
    . . . .
    begin tran
        . . .
        . . .
        update ctrl_tab set ctrl = ctrl + 1
        select @var_1 = ctrl from ctrl_tab
        . . .
        . . .
    commit tran
    . . .
    . . .
commit tran
```

The problem with this in Sybase is that the nested transaction is not committed until the outer transaction commit. Nested begin/commit do no more than keep track of the nesting level. The outer transaction controls the commit of the complete transaction.

Note that this means that any rollback is to the start of the nested transaction. This is particularly relevant in triggers and procedures which contain rollback commands.

Consider the sequence:

```
begin tran
...
...
exec jk_proc--------jk_proc
                        ...
                        ...
                        if...rollback tran
                        else commit tran
...
...
if...rollback tran
else commit tran
```

Both rollback tran commands will rollback to the beginning of the outer transaction: the second rollback reversing the effect of the procedure as well as any statements in the outer transaction.

To create transactions in triggers or procedures so that they may be rolled back without affecting other statements you need to use SAVE TRAN.

```
create proc jk_proc as
begin
      begin tran
      save tran jk_tran
      ...
      ...
      if .....
            begin
            rollback tran jk_tran
            commit tran
            end
      else
            commit tran
end
return
```

Note the commit tran after the procedure rollback: this is necessary as the rollback to a savepoint does not cancel a transaction and execution continues at the statement after the rollback.

Rollback tran in a trigger is all powerful and aborts the batch with no possibility of executing subsequent statements in the batch.

Commands executed via remote procedure calls are not rolled back from a rollback tran in an outer transaction. Remote procedure execution is independent of the calling transaction and therefore does not depend on either the commit or rollback of the outer transaction.

Commands which take or escalate to table locks will always cause contention, so avoid them as much as possible. Although indexes can be built while the system is operational, the create index takes table locks: SLOCK for non-clustered and XLOCK for clustered. Avoid doing this at the peak activity time of the day. Or at least take your phone off the hook.

6.5.3 Table access sequence

Although Sybase resolves deadlock it has to rollback one of the transactions to do so. The more traffic on the system the more this is likely to be of concern and you may wish to minimise it during the design of your update transactions.

Always do the selects before the updates (I include insert/update/delete when I say update) as this means that there cannot be any deadlock caused by SLOCKs. In other words, read every record you need data from before you update anything. With the SLOCK always being requested first, the requesting transaction has no other locks set and so deadlock is not possible. The SLOCK request may have to wait for the page but it cannot deadlock as the transaction has no other resource locked. This alters if you use holdlock because the SLOCKs will be retained and deadlock is now a finite possibility. **Try never to use holdlock**.

And watch the next sequential key processing:

```
BEGIN TRAN
    . . . .
    . . . .
    . . . .
    SELECT next_key FROM ctrl_tab HOLDLOCK
    UPDATE ctrl_tab SET next_key = next_key + 1
    . . . .
    . . . .
    . . . .
COMMIT TRAN
```

is a terrible sequence.

There is every possibility of deadlock here as we have a select with holdlock. All it needs is two transactions to select with holdlock and neither will be able to update. Simply do it as:

```
BEGIN TRAN
      . . . .

      . . . .
      UPDATE ctrl_tab SET next_key = next_key + 1
      SELECT next_key FROM ctrl_tab

      . . . .

      . . . .
COMMIT TRAN
```

You have the record XLOCKed until the commit so no-one else can change or access the value. You will have considerable contention for this type of control record so do not keep it XLOCKed for too long.

At a higher level you can minimise deadlock by updating the tables in the same sequence as often as possible. Most databases exhibit a hierarchical structure as shown in figure 6.8.

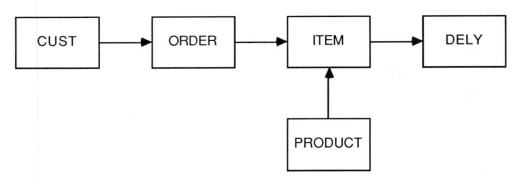

figure 6.8:   table hierarchy

By always updating these tables from the top of the hierarchy to the bottom ie CUST to ORDER to ITEM to DELY or PRODUCT to ITEM to DELY we eliminate inter-table deadlock. As most deadlock is caused between tables this is a significant gain. Intra-table deadlock will still occur between records in the same table and unless you can limit the transactions to one update, you will never avoid this in Sybase.

Of course there will still be some transactions which you cannot write from top to bottom, but at least you know which ones and could introduce a programming softlock to prevent potential deadlock transactions getting into the application at the same time.

6.6   **Memory allocation**

The other significant aspect of multi-user processing is the amount of memory that is needed to support the configuration. You cannot increase the number of concurrent users without a consideration of how much memory is needed to support them. The available memory is being contended for by programs, data and other system components, so it is not a simple equation.

The general comment is to throw as much memory as you can at a relational database but, although cheap, memory still costs money so it is worth calculating how much, if only to justify what your boss will view as outrageous.

All of the following will require memory allocation:

> operating system and network software
> Sybase server kernel
> connections
> open objects
> procedures
> data

6.6.1   **Operating system and network software**

Ask the vendors how much real memory should be allocated for the operating system and the network. Not disk or swap space but real memory. In general you will get away with 2-3 M bytes for most Unix systems and about the same for the network.

6.6.2   **Sybase server**

Sybase normally quote 4 M bytes for the server kernel. This may increase a little with new releases packed with long awaited new features...sorry, I cannot resist a little dig now and then...but 4 M bytes is reasonable. You can still run a few users in a 4 M byte Sybase allocation as the kernel is not quite that big, but do not expect to get that much in the way of response time as it is very tight and the operating system will be swapping for a high percentage of the time. So 4 M bytes for the Sybase kernel.

The default memory size is 2400 pages ie 4.69 M bytes of which the system component is:

executable code	1.2 - 2.0 M bytes
static server overhead	0.5 - 1.0 M bytes

which leaves about 2 - 3 M bytes for user conections, procedure and data cache.

6.6.3 Connections

Each connection to the server requires 34 K bytes of real memory for the standard server and 64 K bytes for the open server. (The v4.8 documentation quotes 40 K per user connection.) This is connections and not concurrent users. In general I estimate 3 connections per user. For standard front-ends isql takes 1 connection and dwb takes 2 connections. The more overlaid screens you use in dwb the more connections you use up to a maximum of 4. Program interfaces like apt and 3GL programs obviously depend on how you write the programs but a simple update will usually require 2 connections to enforce browse mode and timestamping.

The simple rule in your own front-end programs is that you need to generate your own cursor driven environment which requires one connection per emulated cursor. Db-library/apt return data in series into the buffer area. The two commands:

```
select a, b from tab_1
select a, b from tab_2
```

in the one connection will return all tab_1 records followed by all tab_2 records. If you require to compare record 1 from tab_1 with record 1 from tab_2 it is not impossible to do with program arrays but much simpler to open a second connection for the second command in which case the results will be in parallel in separate buffers to make record by record comparison easier.

Connections are not just required for users but also for each device defined in the disk allocation and for any "waitfor" commands. However I normally find that the 3 connections per user is a slight overestimate sufficient to ignore the devices and waitfor requirements. However if you have a large number of disks or devices it can amount to close to 1-2 M bytes which is not to be ignored. (The v4.8 documentation quotes 44 K per device.)

So 34/64 K per connection, estimated at 3 connections per user.

6.6.4 Objects

Each open object in Sybase requires 40 bytes of memory. (The v4.8 documentation quotes 72 bytes.) I always ignore this. The level of inaccuracy and overestimate in the procedure and data calculations makes this figure not worth calculating. However if you are calculating exactly or if memory is tight, you need to remember that every lock is an open object. If you have allowed for 8000 locks this will require 32 K of memory.

It is unlikely that you will need to consider more than 50 K for objects.

6.6.5 **Procedures**

Sybase reserves an amount of memory for the compiled procedures. This defaults to 20% of available memory and may be altered using the system procedure sp_configure

```
sp_configure "procedure cache", 10
```

This setting is very much an estimate and will depend on how much you use procedures and how big they are.

Let me recommend that you always use stored procedures except for ad-hoc SQL: by being pre-compiled they significantly reduce the load on the CPU and relational database software is surprisingly heavy on CPU. I know that there are potential optimisation problems with stored procedures - which I deal with in section 7.16 - but the decrease in CPU load gives an overall increase in throughput which far outweighs the small disadvantage of an occasional wrong execution plan.

Size is up to you but try to keep them on the small side. I normally aim for 12 K per procedure on average. The number of procedures also depends on how you have written them but I normally estimate 3 per connection. Of course if you have the luxury of knowing how many concurrent procedures you have with their sizes, then use these figures but usually you will need to guess prior to the procedures being written.

My 12 K size is twice the recommended estimate from Sybase. I feel that users are using procedures more and more with a subsequent increase in average size. Also any rule or trigger called by a command in a procedure is compiled into the size of the procedure. I think that 12 K is more practical.

So 12 K per procedure with 3 procedures per connection.

Once the system is operational you can do a rough calculation of procedure size:

procedure size (K) = number of records in sysprocedures * 256

6.6.6 **Data**

How large should data cache be? How long is a piece of string? (We have done that one.)

I like to have 20% of the data as data cache and never like to go below 5% of the data. I make no allowances for indexes when I quote these figures so they may be higher than you are used to. Do not neglect the size of the indexes but I like an easy life as an SA and if I can persuade the boss to 20% of the data I do not calculate index sizes, but if 5% is all that I can manage then I calculate index sizes to help my case for more data cache.

The more data cache the better, but do not waste it. I base my figures on the 80:20 rule of thumb that 80% of the processing takes place on 20% of the data. If I have this 20% cached then the system performs better. If I allocate more than 20% the extra is being used for low activity data. As it is low activity it will not be requested often, so it will be the first to be swapped out when cache is required. Therefore it will seldom be there when you need it again which means that you are wasting cache and money.

If you know that memory is going to be tight then you need to be a little pragmatic and have a careful look at the use of cache by the indexes. At the least we want the principal index levels to be cache resident ie all levels except the leaf levels of the non-clustered indexes. Remember that the index page gets no priority over the data page in cache, it simply resides longer because it is used more often. In v4.8 indexes are aged slower than data pages and so they get some priority in cache.

With enough cache for these index pages we then need some space for the data. How much depends on your knowledge of the activity but strive to get as close as you can to the 5% figure.

6.6.7 Memory size example

How much memory do we need for a 100 user system with 2 G bytes of data?

system overheads (OS, network, Sybase)	10 M
user connections	10 M
procedure cache	10 M
data cache	400 M
	-------
	430 M
	-------

where

user connections

      100 users: 300 connections @ 34 K: 10 M

procedure cache

    300 connections: 900 procedures @ 12 K: 10 M

data cache

    2 G bytes @ 20%:   400 M
    2 G bytes @ 5 %:   100 M

If you consider this large, let's look at it in more detail.

This is a reasonably large database and is probably made up of about 100 tables. Of these 20 or so will be quite small taking up about 100 M bytes. The other 80 will take up the rest of the space giving an average of 24 M bytes. If we assume that each table has one clustered index with an average size of 1 % of the data this adds 20 M bytes to the data size.

If we assume that each table has one non-clustered index with an average size of 15% of the data this adds 300 M bytes to the data size. The majority of this is leaf level pages and a more realistic caching figure is probably 8% ie 160 M bytes.

I'm sure that most designers would like to get most of the indexes (320 M) plus 5% of the data (100 M) into cache. So I normally use the rough guide of 20% of the data (400 M) as a first pass as it caters for all of the non-clustered index pages. And I know it is large but relational database software loves memory.

Note that the lowest limit of 5% of data - 100 M - does not even get our estimated index sizes - 180 M - into cache. Our minimum cache is about 180 + 100 to accommodate the indexes and about 5% of the data ie about 10% of the database.

Be very careful here with the latest releases of Sybase which use shared memory (4.8 upwards). They often have a limit on the number of pages per server and it can be quite low. Pyramid has a shared memory limit per server of 96 K pages ie 192 M bytes of shared memory. This severely limits the amount of cache which you can allocate to procedures and data. (I know of no others, but when one exists, it pays to check.)

6.7 **Summary**

Sybase uses an optimistic locking strategy of not retaining the SLOCK any longer than is necessary to read the data page and providing version control on the records being updated.

The version control on update is not mandatory but is provided by defining a timestamp field on the record which is checked and maintained by use of the Sybase dbqual and tsqual clauses in the update command. Use of this timestamp version control ensures 100% integrity of data.

Sybase has the page as the lowest level of locking granularity and therefore high performance systems need to consider this in their designs to minimise the amount of secondary record locking and update contention.

Memory allocation for a Sybase system is quite standard with consideration being required for system software, user connections, procedure and data. The only special from Sybase is that a single user transaction may have several connections to the server. Sybase does not use the common method of cursors for retaining context during a SELECT but requires a separate connection to simulate this.

Version 4.8 default values and bytes required are:

	default	bytes required
user connections	25	40960
open databases	10	644
locks	5000	32
open objects	500	72
devices	10	45056
memory	2400	2048

And finally....

The founders of Ashton-Tate launched their product with one of the micro-computer industry's most famous ads.

It showed the picture of a bilge pump with the headline, "This bilge pump sucks and so does most micro software."

It then went on to extol the merits of dBase II.

This caused a furore and even the manufacturer of the bilge pump complained that his product was used in a derogatory fashion. However he soon withdrew his complaint when Ashton-Tate promptly offered to print a retraction that his pump did not suck!

Chapter 7

Optimiser
and
index selection

This chapter investigates how the optimiser determines the execution strategy of the SQL. Throughout the chapter examples are given of the optimum index selection for SQL commands, using the information that we have on how the optimiser works.

The chapter borrows extensively from my previous book on database design.

O'Reilly's Seventh Law

That's not a bug, that's a feature.

Commands covered in this chapter:

> **set showplan on**
> **set noexec on**
> **update statistics**

System procedures covered in this chapter:

> **sp_recompile**

7.1   **Introduction**

We ask the database questions like:

```
SELECT NAME, LIMIT FROM CUSTOMER
      WHERE NAME LIKE 'K%'
          AND LIMIT > 50
```

and the optimiser decides how to access the CUSTOMER table to retrieve the records which satisfy the selection criteria. If indexes on NAME and/or LIMIT exist then the optimiser takes the decision on whether or not to use them. Such a decision is based primarily on the amount of disk accessing associated with each option.

There are three types of optimiser:

positional   where the position of the selection criteria is used to choose the optimum execution plan.
The assumption here is that the writer of the command will put the most selective criteria first in the command. Usually true but open to error.

syntactical   where the optimiser uses the syntax of the selection criteria to choose the optimum execution plan.
Each operator (=, >, between etc) is given a fixed percentage of records that will be retrieved with equality being the most selective, a closed limit next, less than / greater than next and so on. Not an unreasonable assumption but still liable to give a poor execution plan.

statistical   where the optimiser uses the statistics of the record distribution for the index to choose the optimum execution plan.
The best option as it uses actual record distribution but still incomplete in its implementation as the statistics are not dynamically updated and on occasion the statistical optimiser will revert to its roots of syntactical or positional.

Sybase operates a statistical optimiser except for the one case of 5 or more table joins when it groups the tables based on their position in the FROM clause.

Let's look at the various decisions that the optimiser will take in deciding on an execution plan.

7.2 Table scan

If we do not have any selection criteria ie no WHERE clause:

```
SELECT NAME, ADDRESS FROM CUSTOMER
```

then the optimiser will do a **table scan**. It will start at the first data page of the table and read to the last page using the internal page pointers which link the pages together. In general we must specify some selection criteria before the optimiser will consider using any index.

The basic, worst case plan of the optimiser is this table scan ie reading all of the data pages of the table. Therefore we need to be able to estimate what this will be to determine if our response times are acceptable or not.

This is quite simply done as:

no of pages = table size / page size

I/O time = no of pages / average I/O per second

So a 20 M byte table with a 2 K page size and a disk retrieval speed of 50 pages per second gives:

no of pages = 20,000,000 / 2,000 = 10,000

I/O time = 10,000 / 50 = 200 seconds

7.3 Viewing the execution plan

To see the plan that the optimiser has chosen - I shall call this the execution plan - you set the showplan environment variable.

```
set showplan on
go
```

If testing against the operational database you will usually not want to wait for the command to execute so you will also set the no execute environment variable.

```
set noexec on
go
```

Make sure that you do this in the above sequence, as the only command which executes under noexec is "set noexec off". You can stare at a non-responsive screen for a very long time before you realise what you have done.

The basic execution plan is the table scan:

```
select * from tab_1
```

STEP 1
The type of query is SELECT
FROM TABLE
tab_1
Nested iteration
Table scan

This is not too bad a display of the execution plan. It is quite readable but unfortunately does not include the expected number of reads for each index. The optimiser knows this and it would be extremely helpful if it would display this figure.

Notice also that Sybase use the term "nested iteration" throughout the showplan output. This is best treated as noise in the output as it contributes nothing to the meaning of the plan. The only time that it means anything useful is for the indexed join strategy which is called a nested iteration.

This now allows us to ask two questions of each SQL command: is it what we expected and is it acceptable. If the answer to either is no, we need to take corrective action.

7.4   Enquiry response time examples

Consider the above 20 M byte, 50,000 record table CUSTOMER with a composite, non-clustered index on (name, area_code).

7.4.1 enquiry 1:

```
SELECT NAME, ADDRESS, AREA_CODE FROM CUSTOMER
    WHERE NAME = 'KIRKWOOD' AND AREA_CODE = '05'
```

One record is returned with a response time of less than 1 second.

Is it what we expected?

Yes of course it is. We have an index on (name, area_code) which the optimiser has been able to use for fast retrieval.

Is it acceptable?

Yes.

7.4.2 enquiry 2

```
SELECT NAME, ADDRESS, AREA_CODE FROM CUSTOMER
    WHERE AREA_CODE = '05'
```

10 records are returned with a response time of 300 seconds.

Is it what we expected?

Yes. A table scan has been done (200 seconds access time for 20 M bytes). The composite index (name, area_code) is useless for an enquiry on area_code. For any index to be useful we must enquire on the most significant part of the index. Unless we give the optimiser a start point within the index it will have to search the complete index which is not as good a plan as a table scan.

Why is the table scan better than searching the complete non-clustered index? Because we have a non-clustered index which means that every data record has an index entry and to retrieve all of the records via the index requires one logical access per record (50,000 accesses). To retrieve all of the records via a table scan requires only one logical read per data page (10,000 accesses). This is a specific of a more general point which we shall discuss shortly.

Is it acceptable?

Depends on the user's requirements, but if not we need to see if an index on area_code will make it go faster. Well, will it? Yes. The enquiry returns 10 records only which will be retrieved faster by an index making 10 accesses than a table scan making 10,000 accesses.

If enquiries 1 and 2 are all we have to deal with the index combination:

> name, area_code
> area_code

is not optimum as both enquiries can be satisfied with the one index:

> area_code, name

7.4.3 enquiry 3

```
SELECT NAME, ADDRESS, AREA_CODE FROM CUSTOMER
    WHERE NAME LIKE 'KIRK%'
```

150 records are returned with a response time of 5 seconds.

Is it what we expected?

Yes. The index on (name, area_code) is useful as the most significant field (name) has been specified, so 150 index accesses are done. We need to be able to calculate if 5 seconds is reasonable for 150 index accesses. The (name, area_code) index entry will be of the order of 40 characters ie 50 per page so level 0: 1000 nodes; level 1: 20 nodes; root level: 1 node giving an average index I/O of 1 access. So each data record may be retrieved in 2 accesses - one to the leaf and one to the data - ie 300 accesses maximum or 6 seconds I/O time. So 5 seconds is not too unexpected.

This assumes that the 21 pages of root and intermediate levels will be predominantly cache resident during the enquiry. The first time the enquiry is executed this may not be reasonable but in general usage it is quite acceptable.

Is it acceptable?

Depends on the performance requirement but I would suggest that 8 screens of data in 5 seconds is not too bad.

7.4.4 enquiry 4

```
SELECT NAME, ADDRESS, AREA_CODE FROM CUSTOMER
    WHERE NAME LIKE 'S%'
```

12,000 records are returned with a response time of 250 seconds.

Is it what we expected?

Yes. It is the worst case of a table scan similar to enquiry 2. Remember that the table scan does 10,000 accesses. To read 12,000 records requires a minimum of 12,000 accesses which is greater than a table scan. This is a general optimiser result: if the number of records retrieved via a non-clustered index is greater than the number of pages in the table, then a table scan will be done.

Is it acceptable?

Possibly the wrong question here, as you have little choice. The combination of number of records and non-clustered index means that the table scan is the best result. A case where the index is useless. If you have the option, a clustered index will improve matters (to read 12,000 records takes about 2,500 page accesses, which is better than a table scan). If a clustered index is not available and it is imperative that this enquiry goes faster then a covered index of (name, address, area_code) is the only answer. This is an index entry of about 160 characters which gives 12 index entries per page ie about 1000 accesses.

Index covering is an important indexing technique which places all of the required data in the index. The Sybase optimiser recognises this and scans the leaf level pages instead of reading the data pages. This results in a saving in the ratio of the number of index pages to the number of data pages: in other words in the ratio of index entry size to data record size.

7.5   Search arguments

If we do not have an index on the selection field then the optimiser will do a table scan. So the first thing we are looking for is a WHERE clause with a search condition - called a search argument - which uses an index. The definition of a search argument is very specific.

search argument

> **column   operator   expression**

eg
VALUE	=	1500
LIMIT	>	1200
SALARY	>	1000 * 12

This is the only format which the optimiser will recognise as a search argument and therefore attempt to look at an index. The valid operators are:

=	equals
>	greater than
<	less than
>=	greater than or equal to
<=	less than or equal to
	like
	between

Note that != (not equal) is not considered a search argument operator and will always cause a table scan. In general any use of a not operator causes a table scan as the optimiser assumes a non-selective match with the data ie a lot of records returned.

If a search argument is not found in the selection clause then the optimiser will not use the index.

So:

```
SALARY * 12 > 12000
```

will not use an index on SALARY because SALARY * 12 is an expression, not a column.

```
SUBSTRING(NAME, 1, 4) = 'KIRK'
```

will not use an index on NAME because SUBSTRING(NAME, 1, 4) is an expression, not a column.

Having decided that it has a search argument, the optimiser then looks at the statistics of the index to determine if it is I/O efficient to use the index. If the optimiser finds that more records in a non-clustered index will be read than there are pages in the table then it abandons the index and does a table scan.

So:

```
SALARY > 12000
NAME LIKE 'S%'
```

may result in a table scan with a non-clustered index if more records in the table are accessed than there are pages in the table. A good rule of thumb is 20%: if a field normally returns more than 20% of the records for a specific value then there is little point indexing on it.

Why? Consider 50% of the table being accessed. The records are 1, 2, 3, 4 etc in a non-clustered index as in figure 7.1:

Ignoring the index, the number of data reads to retrieve 1, 3, 5, 7, 9 etc is approximately equal to the number of records ie 9. But there are only 5 pages in the table, so a table scan will be more efficient. I know that there will be a caching factor in the first case but even if it is 50% the table scan is still as efficient and we have not taken the index accesses into account in the first case. In a larger table the caching factor is less important and so the reasonable rule of thumb is that if more than 20% of the table is to be read to satisfy the command then the index is not efficient. Check this figure for each table as it is dependent on the number of records per page and I often find that as low as 5-10% will do a table scan. In general if I have a code field with up to 8 distinct values, I do not index it for retrieval purposes. In other words, I normally work at 12.5% as a cut-off point for non-clustered indexes.

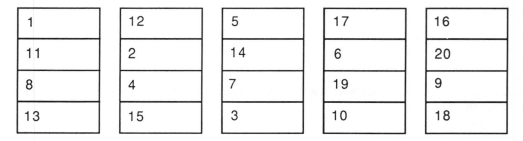

Figure 7.1 : Non-clustered index data storage

Note that this applies to a non-clustered index only. If the search argument is on a clustered index then the optimiser will always use the index. It comes to the same result to do a table scan as the data is in sequence except that the system knows which page to start or finish at. This makes any data scan no less efficient than the full table scan when the index is clustered ie the data is in index key sequence.

7.6   **Indexed execution plans**

```
SELECT NAME, ADDRESS, TEL_NO FROM CUSTOMER
      WHERE NAME = 'KIRKWOOD'
```

clustered index on name

STEP 1
The type of query is SELECT
FROM TABLE
CUSTOMER
Nested iteration
Using clustered index

```
SELECT NAME, ADDRESS, TEL_NO FROM CUSTOMER
      WHERE CUST_NO = '100'
```

non-clustered index on cust_no

STEP 1
The type of query is SELECT
FROM TABLE
CUSTOMER
Nested iteration
Index: cust_no

Note that the execution plan does not name the clustered index. This is extremely annoying as it is unlikely that you will remember what the name of the index is. I know that it is easy in the above example but a multi-table join with several where clauses could do with the clustered index being named.

7.7   **Index choice example**

Let's have a look at determining the optimum index configuration for a set of SQL enquiries on a table.

Consider a CUSTOMER table of 12,000 records, average record size of 300 bytes with a classification code grouping of:

class_code 1   6000 records

```
class_code 2    1500 records
class_code 3    1000 records
class_code 4    1000 records
class_code 5     500 records
```

The user requires three enquiries to run as fast as you can make them. The update overhead is minimal and the user is willing to accept slow updates to achieve fast enquiries.

(a)   SELECT * FROM CUSTOMER
            WHERE CLASS_CODE = 1

(b)   SELECT * FROM CUSTOMER
            WHERE NAME = 'KIRKWOOD' AND CLASS_CODE = 4

(c)   SELECT * FROM CUSTOMER
            WHERE NAME = 'KIRKWOOD' AND CUST_ID = 1234

The CUST_ID is unique and the name is evenly spread with a maximum of 600 records for a name.

The indexes available to us are clustered or non-clustered on:

(1)   name
(2)   class_code
(3)   cust_id
(4)   (name, class_code)
(5)   (class_code, cust_id)
(6)   (name, cust_id)
(7)   (class_code, name, cust_id)

(I have ignored for the moment, the opposite sequences of the composite indexes in 4-7 eg (class_code, name) for 4. If we determine that a composite index is going to be beneficial then we will consider the optimum sequence.)

I normally like to shorten the list by removing those that are obviously unsuitable. A table scan of this table will require a minimum of 2000 accesses (12,000 records at a maximum of 6 per page) so our non-clustered index on class_code will never satisfy enquiry (a) which retrieves 6000 records and the optimiser will always do a table scan. So scratch non-clustered index 2 on class_code. Also there is no SQL requirement for (class_code, cust_id) so scratch index 5. More importantly we have now fixed the clustered index of this table as class_code or at least beginning with class_code.

Our choice for enquiry (b)

(b)   SELECT * FROM CUSTOMER
              WHERE NAME = 'KIRKWOOD' AND CLASS_CODE = 4

is now non-clustered on:

(1)   name
(2)   (name, class_code)
(3)   (name, class_code, cust_id)

If we use name by itself then we need to read all the records for a name and test if the class_code equals 4. This will be a maximum of 600 accesses. If we index on (name, class_code) then we can immediately retrieve all of the class 4 records for the required name.

For example:

Name index			(Name, class_code) index	
Name	class_code		Name	class_code
KA	1		KA	1
KA	4		KA	4
KI	4		KI	1
KI	1		KI	1
KI	3		KI	1
KI	4		KI	1
KI	1		KI	3
KI	1		KI	3
KI	3		KI	4
KI	4		KI	4
KO	1		KO	1

With the name index we need to read 8 records whereas with the (name, class_code) index we need to read only 2 records. So the composite index is better. This is the general situation. Think composite index when the SQL statement has multiple selection clauses which generate search arguments and therefore may be indexed.

The (name, class_code, cust_id) index gives no advantage for this enquiry as cust_id is unique and supplies no further reduction to the number of records which will be accessed.

Our choice for enquiry (c):

(c)   SELECT * FROM CUSTOMER
            WHERE NAME = 'KIRKWOOD' AND CUST_ID = 1234

is non-clustered on:

    (1)   name
    (3)   cust_id
    (6)   (name, cust_id)
    (7)   (name, class_code, cust_id)

and by a similar logic to enquiry (b) the first choice would seem to be (name, cust_id). After all, the advice for this type of enquiry is to think composite index. But accept no general advice without thinking of the specific case. We have a different situation here. The cust_id is unique and therefore an index on cust_id will return one record only. So index (3) on cust_id is the fastest to satisfy enquiry (c).

The final result for the enquiries:

(a)   SELECT * FROM CUSTOMER
            WHERE CLASS_CODE = 1

(b)   SELECT * FROM CUSTOMER
            WHERE NAME = 'KIRKWOOD' AND CLASS_CODE = 4

(c)   SELECT * FROM CUSTOMER
            WHERE NAME = 'KIRKWOOD' AND CUST_ID = 1234

is three indexes - one for each enquiry:

        clustered (class_code) and
        non-clustered (name, class_code) and
        non-clustered cust_id

We are not finished of course, because the two indexes:

        clustered (class_code) and
        non-clustered (name, class_code)

may be replaced by the single index:

clustered (class_code, name).

The question is: which solution is more efficient for enquiries as the user is willing to accept overhead on updates.

Enquiry (a) will be satisfied equally by both solutions. There will be a difference in the size of the index entry and to the number of index levels, but not significantly so.

So the discussion is based on enquiry (b):

```
(b)     SELECT * FROM CUSTOMER
             WHERE NAME = 'KIRKWOOD' AND CLASS_CODE = 4
```

The maximum records retrieved for a name is 600. If these are all in class_code 4 we need 600 accesses for the non-clustered index and 100 for the clustered index. This logic applies to any distribution of name:class_code because we are asking for equality of both fields in the composite index.

So the optimum index configuration for the three enquiries is:

clustered on (class_code, name) and
non-clustered on (cust_id)

I've made the point of how useful composite indexes are. Let's have a closer look at when they are useful.

If a composite index exists on:

(A, B, C)

then it will be used only when the most significant field ie the leftmost is quoted in a search argument.

Therefore:

A, B, C
A, B

> A, C
> A

will all cause the optimiser to consider using the index.

However:

> B, C
> C
> B

will not be able to use the index as there is no start point to commence searching and therefore every record will need to be read and checked, which is more efficiently done by a table scan. The same logic applies to an index on name in that:

```
SELECT * FROM CUSTOMER
      WHERE NAME LIKE 'KIRK%'
```

will try to use the index as it can start at the first record starting with KIRK and read until it reaches KIRJ or greater.

But:

```
SELECT * FROM CUSTOMER
      WHERE NAME LIKE '%WOOD'
```

will not use the index as it is unable to locate the first record ending in WOOD as this could occur anywhere in the index. So a table scan must be done.

However even although the index:

> (A, B, C)

can support enquiries on:

> A, B, C
> A, B
> A,C
> A

the efficiency of each is different.

The most efficient is when all fields of the index are quoted as this clearly reads less records than any of the others. Quoting the fields in order of significance is next in efficiency. So it is better to request A, B than A, C. To satisfy the A, C enquiry all values of B must be read to check the C values.

So a composite index is more efficient the more fields that can be supplied and the more fields that can be supplied in order of significance.

Back to our enquiries:

(a)   SELECT * FROM CUSTOMER
            WHERE CLASS_CODE = 1

(b)   SELECT * FROM CUSTOMER
            WHERE NAME = 'KIRKWOOD' AND CLASS_CODE = 4

(c)   SELECT * FROM CUSTOMER
            WHERE NAME = 'KIRKWOOD' AND CUST_ID = 1234

which are brilliantly indexed as:

            clustered (class_code, name) and
            non-clustered (cust_id)

and the inevitable happens.

The user alters the requirement of enquiry (c) to:

        SELECT * FROM CUSTOMER
            WHERE NAME = 'KIRKWOOD' AND CUST_ID >= 1234

Now the non-clustered index on cust_id or any other non-clustered composite index starting with cust_id with no index on name will cause a table scan for enquiry (c). And we cannot have a clustered index on cust_id as we need this for class_code. So we need to rethink.

This is a very important point. Your index structure has been chosen based on the functionality. So when the functionality changes expect the indexes to change.

Going back to the first step (well almost) the possible indexes are:

(1)   clustered (class_code) satisfies (a)
(2)   clustered (class_code, name)   satisfies (a) & (b)
(3)   non-clustered (name, class_code)   satisfies (b)
(4)   clustered (cust_id, name)   satisfies (c)
(5)   non-clustered (name, cust_id)   satisfies (c)

Clearly we require index (2): clustered (class_code, name) to satisfy enquiries (a) and (b) and therefore any index to satisfy enquiry (c) must be non-clustered which eliminates index (4) and leaves us with index (5) for enquiry (c).

The final question is which way round is the (name, cust_id) index. We have looked at the (class_code, name) index and determined that it does not matter as the number of KIRKWOODs with class_code 4 is the same as the number of class_code 4s called KIRKWOOD. However the introduction of a range alters this argument.

Consider the values:

cust_id	name	name	cust_id
1232	JONES	JONES	1232
1232	KIRKWOOD	JONES	1234
1232	KIRKWOOD	KIRKWOOD	1232
1234	JONES	KIRKWOOD	1232
1234	KIRKWOOD	KIRKWOOD	1234
1234	KIRKWOOD	KIRKWOOD	1234
1234	SMITH	KIRKWOOD	1236
1236	KIRKWOOD	SMITH	1234
1236	SMITH	SMITH	1236
1236	THOMSON	THOMSON	1236
1236	WALTERS	WALTERS	1236

To satisfy enquiry (c):

```
NAME = 'KIRKWOOD'   AND   CUST_ID >= 1234
```

we need to read 7 records for (cust_id, name) but only 3 records for (name, cust_id). The equality on the first field in the index limits the search we have to make because we know that no further records can qualify once we go past the KIRKWOODs. However in (cust_id, name) we have to continue our search - in this case to the end of the index - because we may have other qualifying (cust_id, name) combinations later in the index sequence.

For composite keys, put the most selective field first in the index.

7.8   OR strategy

An OR is quite simply a union, or combination, of more than one query. The principal complication is that a record may qualify in more than one of the selection clauses but it must be shown only the once.

Therefore the OR strategy involves the creation of an internal work table of row ids which can be used to check for and eliminate duplicates. The simple internal approach to this is to create a work table of all row ids satisfying any of the selection criteria; sort the work table to eliminate duplicates and use the sorted work table to retrieve the row from the data table.

So if we have the query:

```
SELECT NAME, ADDRESS, SALARY FROM EMPLOYEE
     WHERE NAME LIKE 'KIRK%'
     OR SALARY > 1200
```

with indexes on NAME and SALARY, the OR clause will be evaluated as two separate queries and the results sort/merged to eliminate the duplicate rows. If the results of NAME LIKE 'KIRK%' are rows 1, 5, 7, 9, 10, 11 and of SALARY > 1200 are 2, 4, 5, 10, 12 we get a work table as shown in figure 7.2:

row	1		row	1
	5			2
	7			4
	9			5
	10	sort/merged as		7
	11			9
				10
row	2			11
	4			12
	5			
	10			
	12			

Figure 7.2 : OR strategy internal sort/merge

These row ids are then used to read the records directly from the data pages.

The execution plan is:

STEP 1
The type of query is SELECT
FROM TABLE
EMPLOYEE
Nested iteration
Using clustered index   (first pass through EMPLOYEE on name index)
FROM TABLE
EMPLOYEE
Nested iteration
Index: sal_ind   (second pass through EMPLOYEE on salary index)
FROM TABLE
EMPLOYEE
Nested iteration
Using Dynamic Index   (final pass through EMPLOYEE to retrieve records)

(The underlining and comments are mine: they do not appear on the showplan output.)

This plan is a little difficult to identify at first glance because it is not until you get to the end of the plan that you see the important words "dynamic index" which means that the two previous index accesses were to create the internal lists of row ids which are then merged into the dynamic index to read the qualifying employee records.

The simple rule of thumb is that if one of the selection criteria does not use an index and causes a table scan then the whole of the query will be solved by a table scan.


```
SELECT NAME, ADDRESS, SALARY FROM EMPLOYEE
        WHERE NAME LIKE 'KIRK%'
        OR TEL_NO LIKE '0734%'
```


STEP 1
The type of query is SELECT
FROM TABLE
EMPLOYEE
Nested iteration
Table scan

Because there is no index on TEL_NO the second where clause will need to do a table scan so the whole command does a table scan. Sybase is quite sophisticated in determining when to do a table scan and when to do a dynamic index strategy. Even when suitable indexes are available for each clause in the OR, Sybase will add up the expected number of records to read for each clause and if the total comes to more than the number of pages in the table, a table scan plan is chosen.

If there are indexes on CUSTID (unique), NAME and SALARY the dynamic index will be used for:

```
SELECT NAME FROM CUSTOMER
      WHERE NAME = 'KIRK%'
          OR SALARY > 12000

SELECT NAME, SALARY FROM CUSTOMER
      WHERE CUSTID IN (1234, 1235, 1236)
```

Where the IN is treated like an OR.

Note that in the last example it is intuitively obvious that, as the CUSTID is unique, it is sufficient to access by this index and not carry out the OR strategy which has the overhead of creating and sorting the dynamic index. Unfortunately Sybase does not recognise this and the OR strategy takes precedence.

The OR clause in an SQL statement gives considerable problems when trying to choose indexes. We no longer have the situation with the AND clause where one index may be used to select the records and then each of these tested for the other selection criteria.

```
SELECT * FROM CUSTOMER
      WHERE NAME = 'KIRKWOOD'
      AND COUNTY = 'BERKSHIRE'
```

This can be resolved with an index on NAME. Having selected all the records for KIRKWOOD we can simply test these records to see if they are in BERKSHIRE. Of course a composite index on (NAME, COUNTY) is better for retrieval.

However:

```
SELECT * FROM CUSTOMER
      WHERE NAME = 'KIRKWOOD'
      OR COUNTY = 'BERKSHIRE'
```

is not resolved by a single index either on NAME or composite on (NAME, COUNTY). What we want from this is all the KIRKWOODs plus all the people who live in BERKSHIRE. So an index is required for each clause in the OR statement. If any one of the OR clauses has no index or no useful index such that a table scan is required, the whole statement will be resolved by a table scan. In this case every record in the table is read once and the necessary tests made to see if the record qualifies.

7.9   Join clauses

A join clause involves two tables and takes the form:

table1.column = table2.column

eg   emp.empno = job.empno

Once it has been identified, the best index for the join clause is found as for the other clauses - search argument and OR clauses. Because of the non-procedural nature of SQL, the query can often be written as if there is no join clause. This is specifically found in nested statements:

```
SELECT TITLE FROM TITLES
      WHERE ISBN IN
            (SELECT ISBN FROM TITLE_AUTHOR
                WHERE AUTH_ID > 100)
```

This is the same as:

```
SELECT TITLE FROM TITLES, TITLE_AUTHOR
      WHERE TITLE.ISBN = TITLE_AUTHOR.ISBN
            AND AUTH_ID > 100
```

Be careful here as Sybase evaluates nested queries as join clauses when it is able to flatten the query. The results may surprise you. Consider two tables each with one column containing the values:

TAB_1: one column (A) with one record (a)

TAB_2: one column (B) with four records (a, a, b, c)

The expectation of the command:

```
SELECT A FROM TAB_1 WHERE A IN
      (SELECT B FROM TAB_2 WHERE B = 'a')
```

is one record from TAB_1 with value 'a'. However because the nested query is evaluated by the optimiser as:

```
SELECT A FROM TAB_1
      WHERE TAB_1.A = TAB_2.B
      AND TAB_2.B = 'a'
```

the join command returns two rows 'a' and 'a'. This type of flattening of nested clauses into joins is not unusual in optimisers but most will remove the duplicate outputs. (See 7.18 for a fuller discussion on nested query evaluation.)

If you wish to eliminate the extra rows in Sybase, always put a 'distinct' in the nested query:

```
SELECT A FROM TAB_1 WHERE A IN
      (SELECT DISTINCT B FROM TAB_2
            WHERE B = 'a')
```

But this is slower because of the internal sorted list required by the distinct and generates a different execution plan which we shall look at later.

7.10 Join strategy

So far we have worked with single tables in seeing how the optimiser processes the query once the various clauses and indexes are determined. With a join of two or more tables via join clauses, the optimiser has to determine another strategy to handle the join.

Sybase has two cases: nested iteration or reformatting, the former being used when indexes are available and the latter being used when table scans are required.

7.10.1 Nested iteration

When suitable indexes are available to action the join clause the optimiser will nest the tables and for each qualifying row in the outer table, it will perform a search of the inner table.

To satisfy the query (assuming suitable indexes):

```
SELECT EMP.NAME, EMP.DEPTNO, JOB.JOBNO, JOB.JOBDESC
    FROM EMP, JOB
    WHERE EMP.DEPTNO = 10
    AND EMP.JOBNO = JOB.JOBNO
```

the optimiser has two choices.

Nest EMP as outer and JOB as inner as in figure 7.3 which has to retrieve qualifying rows from EMP and for each of these to access JOB.

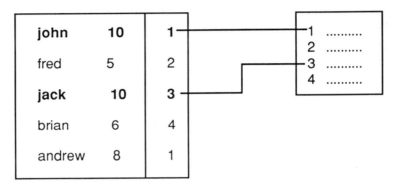

Figure 7.3 : nested iteration - most selective as outer

Nest JOB as outer and EMP as inner as in figure 7.4 which has to scan the JOB table and read each EMP record for the JOBNO to see if they qualify.

In this case the former requires two index accesses to EMP plus two index accesses to JOB; the latter requires a table scan of JOB and 5 index accesses to EMP.

Clearly the former is preferable - assuming reasonably similar table sizes - but the optimiser needs to determine how to make the choice.

There are two criteria used in nested iteration to decide on which table is the outer and which is the inner.

- how selective are the criteria on each table: most selective as outer

- is a table small enough to be cache resident: smallest as inner

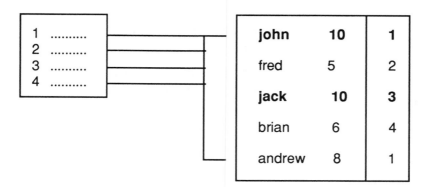

Figure 7.4 : nested iteration - least selective as outer

The optimiser then tries to make the smaller table the inner table and the more selective table the outer table. Thus the selection criteria which returns the smaller number of records will be made the outer table and the smaller table will be made the inner table. The nested iteration strategy is always a balance between these two decisions and it is in this area that the optimiser will sometimes get it wrong. Putting the most selective table as the outer table is given most weight and this will sometimes give an incorrect strategy.

In the above example the first approach of EMP as outer and JOB as inner is preferable (4 data record I/Os against table scan and 5 record I/Os) because the EMP selection criteria is more selective.

So the command:

```
SELECT EMP.NAME, EMP.DEPTNO, JOB.JOBNO, JOB.JOBDESC
    FROM EMP, JOB
    WHERE EMP.DEPTNO = 10
    AND EMP.JOBNO = JOB.JOBNO
```

gives the execution plan:

STEP 1
The type of query is SELECT
FROM TABLE
EMP
nested iteration
Using clustered index   (EMP as outer table, selection on DEPT NO)
FROM TABLE
JOB

Nested iteration
Using clustered index   (JOB as inner table, index access on JOB NO)

Notice how awkward the continued use of the term 'nested iteration' is as it is now meaningful: it is actually meaningful in all cases as a single table plan is simply a specific of the more general multi-table plan, but it would be much clearer if the output of the plan did not use the same term for a single table plan as it does for a multi-table plan.

Let's look at another two table join:

```
SELECT ORDER.CUSTNO, ITEM.QTY FROM ORDER, ITEM
     WHERE ORDER.ORDNO = ITEM.ORDNO
     AND ITEM.QTY > 10
```

this time with indexes on ORDNO and QTY.

First choice as in figure 7.5 with ORDER as outer.

ORDER

1
2
3
4

ITEM

ord prod	qty
1:1	5
1:2	10
2:8	20
2:10	4
3:1	80
3:8	16
4:5	4

Figure 7.5 : nested iteration - least selective as outer

Scan the order table and read corresponding records on the item table to see if the quantity qualifies. This requires a table scan of ORDER plus 7 record I/Os on ITEM.

Second choice as in figure 7.6 with ITEM as outer.

ITEM

ord	prod	qty
1:1		5
1:2		10
2:8		20
2:10		4
3:1		80
3:8		16
4:5		4

ORDER

1
2
3
4

Figure 7.6 : nested iteration - most selective as outer

Read the appropriate records for ITEM and retrieve the ORDER records. This requires 3 I/Os of ITEM and 3 I/Os of ORDER.

Again the more selective criteria as the outer table is the better strategy with the command:

```
SELECT ORDER.CUSTNO, ITEM.QTY FROM ORDER, ITEM
     WHERE ORDER.ORDNO = ITEM.ORDNO
     AND ITEM.QTY > 10
```

giving the execution plan:

STEP 1
The type of query is SELECT
FROM TABLE
ITEM
nested iteration
Index: qty idx   (ITEM as outer table, select on QTY index)
FROM TABLE
ORDER
Nested iteration
Using clustered index   (ORDER as inner table, index access on ORD NO)

Let's look at a three table join:

```
SELECT O.CUSTNO, P.PRODNO
      FROM ORDER O, ITEM I, PRODUCT P
      WHERE P.PRODNO = I.PRODNO
      AND I.ORDNO = O.ORDNO
      AND P.PRODDESC = 'RESISTOR'
```

Consider small tables of 4 orders, 7 items and 5 products with the only RESISTOR being product 2. If we search in the sequence of ORDER, ITEM, PRODUCT as in figure 7.7 we require to search the ORDER table and for each order search the ITEM table and for each item search the PRODUCT table.

ORDER

1
2
3
4

ITEM

ord prod	qty
1:1	5
1:2	10
2:8	20
2:10	4
3:1	80
3:8	16
4:5	4

PRODUCT

1
2
5
8
10

Figure 7.7 :   Three table join - least selective as outer

This means that we need 1 table scan of ORDER, 4 table scans of ITEM and 7 record accesses of PRODUCT.

The alternate nesting of PRODUCT then ITEM then ORDER is in figure 7.8.

Now we require 1 record access of PRODUCT which identifies 1 record - product 2 - and so we have only 1 access of ITEM which identifies 2 records and therefore we need to access ORDER only twice.

Again putting the most selective criteria as the outer table is the better strategy with the command:

```
SELECT O.CUSTNO, P.PRODNO
      FROM ORDER O, ITEM I, PRODUCT P
      WHERE P.PRODNO = I.PRODNO
      AND I.ORDNO = O.ORDNO
      AND P.PRODDESC = 'RESISTOR'
```

ITEM

PRODUCT

prod ord	qty
1:1	5
1:3	80
2:1	10
5:4	4
8:2	20
8:3	16
10:2	4

PRODUCT

1
2
5
8
1 0

ORDER

1
2
3
4

Figure 7.8 :   Three table join - most selective as outer

giving the execution plan:

STEP 1
The type of query is SELECT
FROM TABLE
PRODUCT
nested iteration
Index: desc idx   (PRODUCT as outer, selection on PRODDESC index)
FROM TABLE
ITEM
Nested iteration
Using clustered index   (ITEM next in nesting, selection on PRODNO index)
FROM TABLE
ORDER
Nested iteration
Index: ord idx   (ORDER as inner, selection on ORDNO index)

7.10.2 Reformatting

If there are no suitable indexes available, the optimiser will need to choose a table scan of the outer table and a table scan of the inner table for every qualifying row from the outer table. The number of logical I/Os for the nested iteration strategy is:

number of pages in outer table +

(number of qualifying rows in outer table *
number of pages in inner table)

This is going to be an expensive strategy when no indexes are available. Therefore when table scans are required in a join the optimiser will opt for the reformatting strategy which takes the inner table and sorts it into a clustered index to avoid a table scan for every qualifying row from the outer table. Even when indexes are available the above formula is checked against reformatting to choose the better strategy.

The sort on the inner table is done as a projected, restricted version of the table. Only those fields and those records which are necessary for the statement are put into the sort. This reduces the storage required and the sort effort. It also means that the normal reformatting tactic is to take the table which has a search criteria and make it the inner table. This is the opposite to the nested iteration which puts a table with a search criteria as the outer table.

If I have two equal tables TAB_1 and TAB_2 with no indexing:

```
SELECT TAB_1.A, TAB_2.B, TAB_2.C
    FROM TAB_1, TAB_2
    WHERE TAB_1.X = TAB_2.X
    AND TAB_2.B = 50
```

reformatting will create an internal work table of TAB_2.B, TAB_2.C for all records with TAB_2.B = 50 in the sequence of TAB_2.X. The reformatting strategy, having created a work table, looks like a nested iteration.

The execution plan is:

STEP 1
The type of query is SELECT
The update mode is direct
Worktable created for REFORMATTING
FROM TABLE
TAB_2
Nested iteration
Table scan   (TAB_2 chosen as inner table, no index)
TO TABLE
Worktable   (Worktable create from TAB_2)
STEP 2
The type of query is SELECT
FROM TABLE
TAB_1
Nested iteration
Table scan   (TAB_1 as outer table in nested iteration, no index)
FROM TABLE
Worktable

Nested iteration
Using clustered index   (clustered index access to worktable, index on X)

STEP 1 is the creation of the internal worktable and STEP 2 is then a nested iteration with TAB_1 as the outer table and the clustered index worktable as the inner table.

Altering the above to read:

```
SELECT TAB_1.A, TAB_2.B, TAB_2.C
    FROM TAB_1, TAB_2
    WHERE TAB_1.X = TAB_2.X
    AND TAB_1.B = 50
```

will create a work table of TAB_1.A for all records with TAB_1.B = 50 in the sequence of TAB_1.X.

The execution plan is:

STEP 1
The type of query is SELECT
The update mode is direct
Worktable created for REFORMATTING
FROM TABLE
TAB_1
Nested iteration
Table scan   (TAB_1 chosen as inner table, no index)
TO TABLE
Worktable   (worktable create from TAB_1)
STEP 2
The type of query is SELECT
FROM TABLE
TAB_2
Nested iteration
Table scan   (TAB_2 as outer table in nested iteration)
FROM TABLE
Worktable
Nested iteration
Using clustered index   (clustered index access to worktable on X)

If we take two tables: table 1 with 200 pages and 100 qualifying rows and table 2 with 100 pages, the maximum nested iteration cost of doing a table scan is:

$$200 + (100 * 100)$$

ie 10200 logical I/Os

The cost of reformatting is:

cost of a sort +

number of pages in outer table +

number of qualifying rows * 1 (access to clustered index)

where the cost of a sort is:

number of pages in the inner table +

number of pages in the inner table *
$\log_2$ (number of pages in the inner table)

For our example this evaluates to:

$$100 + 100 * \log(100) +$$

$$200 +$$

$$100 * 1$$

ie 1100 logical I/Os

In effect the sort is creating an internal clustered index of the inner table to minimise the number of accesses to retrieve the data. The formula assumes one access per qualifying row to the sorted table, which is reasonable. This is dependent on the size of cache and the sorted results but you have no choice if the practice is slower than the theory. The reformatting strategy will still produce better results over any other strategy when there are no useful indexes. If you have a serious performance problem with this strategy, try presorting the outer table before you present it to the join.

The Sybase optimiser has a finite - non-configurable - time limit before it produces an execution plan. When the statement has more than 4 tables in it Sybase may not have time to check all possible permutations of the tables and optimises the tables in groups of 4 from the left-hand side.

This is the only time Sybase exhibits any positional optimisation. At all other times the sequence of the tables or the where clauses has no effect on the execution plan.

Knowing this you can help the optimiser when you cannot avoid writing statements with many tables.

With indexes Sybase will try a nested iteration and so you can help it by following the nested iteration rules of placing the most selective tables on the left and the smallest tables on the right.

Without indexes Sybase will do a reformatting strategy and so you should build indexes, but if you cannot, put the most selective tables on the right to minimise the inner sort and loop.

7.11 Optimiser steps

The role of the optimiser is to analyse the query to identify the various clauses available to it:

> search argument clauses
> OR clauses
> join clauses

and then to choose the best index for each table. As each table is processed once only in the query - except for OR when it may be processed for each OR clause - the optimiser has to determine which index is best for each table to best execute the query.

```
SELECT NAME, SALARY FROM EMP, DEPT
    WHERE AGE > 30
    AND (DEPT.DEPTNO = 3  OR  DEPT.DEPTNO = 4)
    AND EMP.DEPTNO = DEPT.DEPTNO
    AND SALARY > 12000
```

emp table

search clause	age
	salary
OR clause	none
join clause	emp.deptno = dept.deptno

dept table

search clause	none
OR clause	dept.deptno = 3 OR dept.deptno = 4
join clause	emp.deptno = dept.deptno

The dept table presents little problem as deptno is the only field used in the clauses. So if indexed on deptno, the deptno index will be considered for use.

The emp table is more of a problem with 3 candidate indexes: age, salary, deptno. The optimiser has to determine the most selective of these to minimise the I/O cost.

To do this it needs to identify:

- is there an index for the clause or will a table scan be used

- number of rows to satisfy the clause

- number of pages to retrieve the rows

Assuming an index is available for the clause the optimiser has two basic tactics.

- if statistics are available the number of rows is calculated from the distribution steps

- if no statistics are available the optimiser reverts to syntactical optimisation

Note that when calculating from the distribution steps of the statistics, the data type in the clause must be the same as the index column. It might seem difficult to violate this rule in a simple select statement, but be wary of parameters in stored procedures or program calls especially as Sybase treats char and varchar as different data types and null and not null as different datatypes. The optimiser does no conversion of values when looking up the statistics and thus will simply not use them if the data types are different.

An unknown value will also cause the statistics to be ignored, which is why many SQL statements with expressions in them can give strange performance.

```
SELECT A FROM TAB1 WHERE COL1 > 2*1
```

is a bad idea as the expression 2*1 does not provide the optimiser with a known value. So although COL1 > 2*1 is evaluated as a search argument, the statistics are not used to determine if the index is useful. I know it's daft, but that's how it works.

Let's consider what the indexes might be on the emp table for the previous command.

```
SELECT NAME, SALARY FROM EMP, DEPT
     WHERE AGE > 30
     AND (DEPT.DEPTNO = 3  OR  DEPT.DEPTNO = 4)
     AND EMP.DEPTNO = DEPT.DEPTNO
     AND SALARY > 12000
```

The choices are:

(1)   age
(2)   salary
(3)   dept_no
(4)   (age, salary)
(5)   (age, dept_no)
(6)   (dept_no, salary)
(7)   (age, dept_no, salary)

Hopefully by this time you head first for the obvious choice of (age, dept_no, salary). But check it! Because all three fields are quoted, the three field composite index is more selective (ie returns less records) than any of the two field indexes. And, as none of the fields are unique, none of the single field indexes are any more useful. Note that, if one of these had been unique, the only index required would have been the index on the unique field.

So the (age, dept_no, salary) index is best for this enquiry. But in which sequence of fields? As before, the most selective should be the most significant and, in the absence of any other information, the equals operator should return less records than the greater than operator. There is no indication of selectivity between age and salary. So index the emp table on (dept_no, age, salary). And in the absence of any other information, use a clustered index.

7.12 **Statistics**

Sybase keeps the statistics in a single page (often called the distribution page) which means that there is 2 K available to retain the statistics figures. Each entry in the page is an index key value so the number of entries is:

number of distribution steps (n) = page size / key size

The value of the index key at each nth position is then recorded in the distribution page. The maximum number of rows per step is:

number of rows per step = (number of rows - 1) / number of steps

If we are indexing on an alphabetic field for a table of 20 rows and 5 distribution steps, we have:

index field	rec id	statistics page		step	key value
A	**1**			**step**	**key value**
A	10			0	A
A	40			1	C
B	12			2	F
C	**1 8**			3	N
D	7			4	S
E	6			5	W
E	35				
F	**2 1**				
G	23				
H	9				
M	8				
N	**6 4**				
S	68				
S	73				
S	75				
S	**108**				
S	100				
T	25				
W	**2 1**				

Since we know that there are 4 keys in each row we can now estimate that there are 2 steps less than F ie 8 records; 1 step between S and W ie 4 records and so on.

Notice the importance of the key size, which not only means a larger index but will give less accurate statistics. Because of this the statistics are held on the first field only of a composite index.

So if you have nothing in the statement to determine the field significance, put the one with the most values as the most significant. In the extreme if I wish to index on:

> marital_status
> name

the composite index (marital_status, name) will collect statistics against marital_status. As there are only a few values of marital_status, the statistics distribution will be useless and the index will look like an index on a field with few values. Such an index, when non-clustered, will normally do a table scan irrespective of the selectivity of the enquiry because of the expected number of records to be accessed.

However, the statistics on (name, marital_status) will be collected on name, giving a good, useful distribution.

The index key values distribution is created by the "create index" command and kept up-to-date using the command update statistics. Index statistics are not maintained dynamically as records are deleted and inserted: the only method is to execute update statistics.

update statistics

```
update statistics table_name [index_name]
```

Omission of the index name updates every index on the table.

This command should be run as often as you can on every index which has its distribution changed by deletion and/or insertion. This does not apply to every table: a table which is simply updated with little insert/delete activity does not need the statistics updated as the distribution of the key values does not change (as long as you are not updating the index key field).

The statistics are initialised when the index is created. This means that an index created on an empty table does not have any statistics as there is no data to build the statistics on. Therefore until you run update statistics the optimiser will be using syntactical optimisation on this index. Try to keep to the sequence of:

> create the table
> load the data
> create the indexes

7.12.1 **Density**

Information on the amount of replication of index key values is calculated when the statistics are collected. The density is the average percentage of duplicate keys for the index. The smaller this is the more unique the data and a density of 100% means that all keys have the same value. If we have a 1000 row table with 25% density then we expect to get back on average 250 rows per index value. The best density is 100/n% where n is the number of records in the table, which means that we expect 1 record per key value.

The density is used in the join strategy to estimate the number of records per join. The intuitive approach used if there are no statistics for the index is simply to divide the number of records in each table. So the average records per join between CUSTOMER and ORDER on cust_no is intuitively determined as:

number of records in ORDER / number of records in CUSTOMER

So for 1000 CUSTOMER records and 20000 ORDER records, the simple calculation is that every customer will have an average of 20 order records.

This obvious, but rather average, figure is replaced by the optimiser based on the index statistics using the density by multiplying the number of records in the table which contains the foreign key index by the density.

average records per join = records in table * index density

So in the above example, if the density of the cust_no index is 1%:

average order records per customer = 20000 * 1 / 100 = 200

7.13 **Optimiser assists**

Always try to write selection criteria to provide search arguments.

search argument	not search argument
NAME = 'KIRKWOOD'	SALARY < COMMISSION
SALARY > 12000	NAME != 'KIRKWOOD'
NAME LIKE 'K%'	NAME LIKE '%D'
	SUBSTRING(NAME,1,1) = 'K'
	SALARY * 12 > 14400

Note how the SUBSTRING is the same as the LIKE 'K%' but will not use a name index because it is not a search argument.

Do not create unnecessary joins but make the restrictions more explicit:

less efficient	more efficient
``` SELECT X FROM TAB1, TAB2 WHERE TAB1.A = TAB2.A AND TAB2.A = 100 ```	``` SELECT X FROM TAB1, TAB2 WHERE TAB1.A = 100 AND TAB2.A = 100 ```

Please beware of a cartesian product when adopting this technique. Only use it if there is a single value of the fields.

correct join	cartesian product
``` SELECT X FROM TAB1, TAB2 WHERE TAB1.A IN (1,2,3) AND TAB2.A IN (1,2,3) AND TAB1.A = TAB2.A ```	``` SELECT X FROM TAB1, TAB2 WHERE TAB1.A IN (1,2,3) AND TAB2.A IN (1,2,3) ```

The 'correct' join will display 3 output rows, the cartesian product will display 9 output rows.

Supply the optimiser with all possible join clauses as it will not try the implicit joins and these may be the best strategy.

```
SELECT TAB1.X FROM TAB1, TAB2, TAB3
     WHERE TAB1.A = TAB2.B
     AND TAB2.B = TAB3.C
```

The optimiser will not consider the join between TAB1 and TAB3 unless you give it a join clause.

```
SELECT TAB1.X FROM TAB1, TAB2, TAB3
     WHERE TAB1.A = TAB2.B
     AND TAB2.B = TAB3.C
     AND TAB1.A = TAB3.C
```

7.14 **Aggregates**

Aggregates in a select clause - count, avg, min, max, sum - use tempdb for working storage even if the result is one value. If CUSTOMER has a clustered index on NAME then:

```
SELECT COUNT(*) FROM CUSTOMER
     WHERE NAME LIKE 'K%'
```

gives an execution plan of:

STEP 1
The type of query is SELECT
Scalar aggregate
FROM TABLE
CUSTOMER
Nested iteration
Using clustered index   (index access to CUSTOMER on NAME)
STEP 2
The type of query is SELECT
Table scan   (table scan of aggregate worktable in tempdb)

The first step is the actual optimisation of the command - using the clustered index to create a temporary table in tempdb - and the second step is a table scan of the temporary table in tempdb to retrieve the results for display. Although this is a scalar aggregate with only one result value and will be a cache page read, the optimiser treats it as a table which has to be scanned.

If no where clause is specified the statement will table scan as always:

```
SELECT AVG(QTY) FROM ORDER_ITEM
```

STEP 1
The type of query is SELECT
Scalar aggregate
FROM TABLE
ORDER_ITEM
Nested iteration
Table scan
STEP 2
The type of query is SELECT

Table scan

There are two examples of this - **min** and **max** - where a table scan is not done. Because these need the information from one record only, the presence of an index on the field will cause the index to be used without a where clause being necessary.

```
SELECT MIN(QTY) FROM ORDER_ITEM
```

STEP 1
The type of query is SELECT
Scalar aggregate
FROM TABLE
ORDER_ITEM
Nested iteration
Index: qty_idx
STEP 2
The type of query is SELECT
Table scan

However Sybase does not do this if you combine the min and max in the one statement.

```
SELECT MIN(QTY), MAX(QTY) FROM ORDER_ITEM
```

STEP 1
The type of query is SELECT
Scalar aggregate
FROM TABLE
ORDER_ITEM
Nested iteration
Table scan
STEP 2
The type of query is SELECT
Table scan

This does a table scan so do not do it: execute two selects assigning the results to variables if need be. It is **much** faster.

Either a clustered or non-clustered index will be used for min and max. Note that the non-clustered index has the query covered, ie all the information is in the index, and therefore would appear to provide a faster solution. However the difference in levels between a non-clustered and a clustered index is normally one level and as only one record is being read, there is no difference between the covered non-clustered index and the clustered index as regards disk access. Remember that covering is effective when several records are being retrieved, it is no advantage over clustering for single record retrieval.

The aggregate may be qualified by GROUP BY and HAVING clauses. The optimisation effect of these is trivial as the tempdb table is not indexed and therefore is always table scanned. The use of GROUP BY does force the tempdb table to be held in sequence of the GROUP BY field(s), so clearly there is extra work involved: but it is not an optimisation overhead:

```
       SELECT PROD_NO, SUM(QTY) FROM ORDER_ITEM
            GROUP BY PROD_NO
```

STEP 1
The type of query is SELECT (into a worktable)
GROUP BY
Vector aggregate
FROM TABLE
ORDER_ITEM
Nested Iteration
Table Scan
TO TABLE
Worktable   (GROUP BY worktable created from table scan of ORDER_ITEM)
STEP 2
The type of query is SELECT
FROM TABLE
Worktable
Nested Iteration
Table Scan   (table scan of aggregate worktable in tempdb)

STEP 2 is identical but STEP 1 now states that a vector aggregate is being done for the GROUP BY. This simply means that each result stored in tempdb is made up of more than one value. In effect a temporary table of prod_no:sum(qty) is being created with one record per prod_no. Note that vector aggregate does not mean more than one aggregate record but more than one value per tempdb record.

```
       SELECT PROD_NO, SUM(QTY) FROM ORDER_ITEM
            WHERE PROD_NO LIKE 'ABC%'
            GROUP BY PROD_NO
            HAVING SUM(QTY) > 10
```

STEP 1
The type of query is SELECT (into a worktable)
GROUP BY

Vector aggregate
FROM TABLE
ORDER_ITEM
Nested Iteration
Index: prod_idx
TO TABLE
Worktable   (worktable created from index access of ORDER ITEM)
STEP 2
The type of query is SELECT
FROM TABLE
Worktable
Nested Iteration
Table Scan   (table scan of aggregate worktable in tempdb)

Identical format of execution plan with use of the prod_no index in STEP 1. Note that the existence of the HAVING makes no difference to the STEP 2 plan.

```
SELECT PROD_NO, SUM(QTY) FROM ORDER_ITEM
       GROUP BY PROD_NO
       HAVING PROD_NO LIKE 'ABC%'
```

STEP 1
The type of query is SELECT (into a worktable)
GROUP BY
Vector Aggregate
FROM TABLE
ORDER_ITEM
Nested Iteration
Table Scan
TO TABLE
Worktable
STEP 2
The type of query is SELECT
FROM TABLE
Worktable
Nested Iteration
Using Clustered index

Note the heavy overhead of putting the selection onto the worktable using the HAVING instead of onto the data table using a WHERE. Although the worktable is treated as a clustered index because it is in sequence of the selection field, the table is scanned instead of an index access when the WHERE is used. In this extreme example of equality the WHERE will do an index access onto ORDER_ITEM to extract a few records and then table scan the small worktable. However the HAVING will table scan ORDER_ITEM creating a large worktable which then has an indexed access.

This will always be a significant difference so restrict the records with WHERE and use HAVING only with aggregates.

Sybase does allow you to write:

```
SELECT PROD_NO, ORD_NO, PRICE FROM ORDER_ITEM
        HAVING PROD_NO LIKE 'ABC%'
```

and this gives the same execution as a WHERE:

STEP 1
The type of query is SELECT
FROM TABLE
ORDER_ITEM
Nested Iteration
Index: prod_idx

But when a GROUP BY is present, restrict the HAVING to aggregates and the WHERE to records.

7.15 Order by

The ORDER BY clause in a SELECT statement requests the output in sequence of the ORDER BY field(s). If any of these are requested in descending sequence there is little that we can do about it but if in ascending sequence the indexes may be used.

If there is a clustered index on the ORDER BY field(s) it will be used even without a WHERE clause being present.

```
SELECT NAME, TEL_NO FROM CUSTOMER
        ORDER BY NAME
```

STEP 1
The type of query is SELECT
FROM TABLE
CUSTOMER
Nested Iteration
Table Scan

I know that this says it is a table scan but remember that a scan of the data pages of the clustered index is the same as a table scan and as you can see from the next plan the clustered index is being used although the plan does not make this clear.

However even if there is a non-clustered index which covers the command by having all of the required data in the index, the optimiser will not take advantage of it unless you include a WHERE clause.

Non-clustered index on (ord_no, ord_date, name)

```
SELECT ORD_NO, ORD_DATE, NAME FROM ORDERS
        ORDER BY ORD_NO
```

STEP 1
The type of query is INSERT
The update mode is direct
Worktable created for ORDER BY
FROM TABLE
ORDERS
FROM TABLE
ORDERS
Nested Iteration
Table Scan
TO TABLE
Worktable   (creation of worktable from table scan of ORDERS)
STEP 2
The type of query is SELECT
This step involves sorting
FROM TABLE
Worktable
Using GETSORTED
Table Scan   (worktable sort)

This is the standard ORDER BY sort plan when no clustered index is available. The stutter FROM TABLE ORDERS is not mine but an actual example from version 4.2 of Sybase.

Notice the initial creation of a temporary table before the sort is done. This means that the ORDER BY does an initial projection (and restriction if there is a WHERE clause) to sort only the columns (and records) which are necessary - as explained in the reformatting join strategy. So try not to write 'select *' with ORDER BY.

If we have an index which covers the query then we can save a lot of time if we force it to use the index by including an appropriate WHERE clause.

```
SELECT ORD_NO, ORD_DATE, NAME FROM ORDERS
      WHERE ORD_NO > 0
      ORDER BY ORD_NO
```

STEP 1
The type of query is SELECT
FROM TABLE
ORDERS
Nested iteration
Index: ordno_idx

The WHERE clause allows the index to be evaluated and when it is found to cover the query an index scan is carried out. This can be a significant saving for ORDER BY statements and is always worth considering.

7.16 Nested selects with distinct

As stated earlier the Sybase optimiser will attempt to remove the nesting and flatten the command into a join. The advice is to prevent this where it will cause you problems with the extra records that the join can always produce by including a DISTINCT in the nested select. This not only removes any duplicates but causes it to produce a different execution plan.

```
SELECT DESC, PRICE FROM PRODUCT
      WHERE PROD_NO IN
      (SELECT DISTINCT PROD_NO FROM ORDER_ITEM)
```

STEP 1
The type of query is SELECT
FROM TABLE
ORDER_ITEM
Nested Iteration
Table Scan
TO TABLE
Worktable   (worktable create from table scan of ORDER_ITEM)
STEP 2
The type of table is SELECT
Scalar aggregate
Table Scan   (distinct aggregate processing on worktable)
STEP 3
The type of query is SELECT
FROM TABLE

Worktable
Nested Iteration
<u>Table Scan</u>   (worktable table as outer table, table scan)
FROM TABLE
PRODUCT
Nested Iteration
<u>Using Clustered Index</u>   (PRODUCT as inner, index access on PROD NO)

The inner select now has to create a tempdb table to store the product numbers from order_item to eliminate duplicates - in the same fashion as a group by.

STEP 1 and STEP 2 are the standard aggregate plan: a table scan of ORDER_ITEM because there is no WHERE clause and the table scan of the tempdb table of prod_nos to load the results to the outer query. STEP 3 is then a standard nested iteration join strategy between the temporary prod_no table as the outer and the indexed PRODUCT table as the inner table.

The same applies to other nestings where the optimiser cannot flatten the query. The general plan is to take the inner select and optimise it individually, merging the results with the outer select which is then optimised and so on. This is dealt with in more detail in section 7.18.

7.17 **Stored procedure optimisation**

SQL in stored procedures is optimised the same as SQL elsewhere: the difference is in the frequency and the timing. The stored procedure SQL is optimised when the stored procedure is loaded into procedure cache and while the procedure remains in cache it is not optimised again. With procedures which contain parameterised statements with range based retrievals, the first parameter values may generate an execution plan which is unsuitable for subsequent executions of the statement with different parameter values.

A WHERE clause such as:

> WHERE name LIKE @name + '%'

will probably use a non-clustered index if the parameter value is KIRKWOOD but may do a table scan if the parameter value is S.

Therefore stored procedures which have:

> parameterised statements

range based tests such as: like, between, >, <

a wide range of parameter values on different executions of the procedure

should be highlighted as potential performance problems.

The simplest answer is to recompile the procedure to force a new execution plan. This may be done in three ways:

create proc....with recompile

execute proc...with recompile

sp_recompile [table_name]

7.17.1 Create proc...with recompile

This causes a recompile of the procedure at every execution. This rather defeats the CPU savings which you are trying to gain with procedures, however all is not lost as it still reduces network traffic and modularises the programs at the server. However it is rather an extreme measure and not the usual one adopted.

7.17.2 Execute proc...with recompile

This recompiles the procedure for a specific execution. Figure 7.9 illustrates two clients executing the same procedure.

Before the second client uses the procedure, at the first execution by client_1 the procedure is not present in cache and must be loaded from the system tables on disk. At this point the procedure is optimised and compiled and all subsequent executions of the procedure by client_1 will be of this optimised version. If an atypical execution has been made on the first execution, executing the procedure with recompile forces a new execution plan. Once client_1 has executed with recompile the new execution plan remains with that cache version of the procedure. Of course procedure cache is a finite size and, especially if client_1 does not use the procedure for some time, there is a finite chance that the procedure will be swapped out of cache to make room for other client procedures. Having been swapped out, the next execution of the procedure by client_1 will find no cache version and have to read it afresh from disk which will cause it to be compiled and optimised.

When client_2 now wishes to use the procedure which is already being used by client_1, a copy of the cache version used by client_1 is made for client_2. Therefore no optimisation or compilation takes place for any user once the procedure has been loaded into cache. Client_2 may wish to execute with recompile to regenerate the execution plan but it is only the version being used by client_2 that is reoptimised and recompiled, the client_1 version remaining unchanged. Note that if client_1 is inactive for some time and the client_1 version is swapped out of cache, when client_1 requests use of the procedure again there is an existing cache version and client_1 will get a copy of the client_2 version. If this has been recompiled for new parameter values it may not suit client_1.

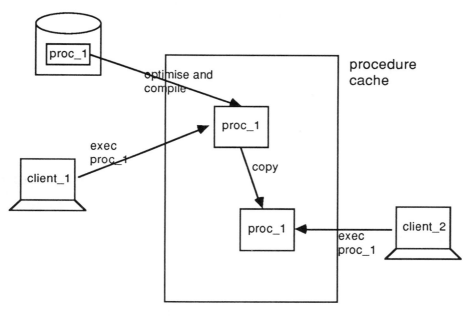

Figure 7.9:   Procedure optimisation

As complicated as this sounds it applies to only the heavily parameterised procedures which are executed with widely varying parameter values on non-clustered indexes. The incidences will be reasonably obvious and simple to correct with recompile. Do not panic: execute with recompile is usually sufficient to overcome this problem.

7.17.3 sp_recompile

Sybase uses procedure cache very efficiently and there is a reasonable chance that a frequently used procedure will remain in cache for long periods of time. So there is no guarantee that unused versions are no longer in cache and the performance problem may recur from an old version. Occasionally you will need to flush the procedure from cache to ensure that all cache versions have gone.

There is no command to flush a named procedure from cache. The common approach is to drop and recreate the procedure. This is not as daft as it sounds as most SAs will have scripts to do this and even have a routine in the operational system which automatically drops any procedure before loading it into the operational system. We are really discussing simple version control in the operational system here.

```
if exists (select * from sysobjects
              where type = 'P'
              and name = @name)
begin
      drop proc @name
end
go
create proc @name as
   .
   .
   .
etc
```

Sybase provide a system procedure sp_recompile which will recompile all procedures or all procedures for a named table.

sp_recompile

```
sp_recompile [table_name]
```

This does not recompile the procedures immediately but tags them in sysobjects and recompiles at the next execution.

This is a useful system routine available from version 4.2 but it adds about 6 K to each procedure recompiled so be careful of the size overhead.

7.17.4 Automatic recompilation

Sybase requires the table option on sp_recompile because it does not automatically recompile procedures for every change to a table.

If a procedure is in cache and does not need to be recompiled, Sybase simply checks that everything it needs is available. So it is only when an object is not available - dropping a table, index or column - that the procedure will initiate a recompile. When the recompilation happens, if the dropped object is essential to the execution of the procedure - a column or a table - then the compilation will fail. However if it is a non-essential object such as an index then a new execution plan is generated, the compilation is successful and the procedure executes.

Adding an index, rebuilding the index statistics or adding a new column does not force a recompile. If you have added an index or updated the index statistics to make the procedure go faster, you must recompile it to take advantage of the new situation.

It is important to realise that any new object will not cause an automatic recompilation of a procedure, so writing 'select *' in a procedure will not show all of the fields after you have changed the table without recompilation.

If you write:

```
create proc jk_proc as
begin
      select * from tab_1
end
return
```

and add a new field to tab_1, the procedure will not show the new field until you recompile it.

7.18 **Nested queries**

7.18.1 **Classification**

Sub-queries are classified by the type of WHERE test that is present.

expression

A simple nesting of a SELECT in a single equals test or an arithmetic expression. In other words anywhere in a predicate or an expression where a single value is expected.

```
WHERE  x = (SELECT a FROM tab_1
                  WHERE pkey = value)

SELECT @var_1 = isnull((SELECT sum(qty)
                              FROM ord_item),0)
```

existence

A nesting of a SELECT in a test where a value is checked as belonging to a set of values: most commonly identified with the IN, ANY or EXISTS operators.

```
WHERE x IN (SELECT a FROM tab_1)

WHERE EXISTS (SELECT * FROM tab_1
                       WHERE pkey = value)

WHERE x = ANY (SELECT a FROM tab_1)
```

non-existence   A nesting of a SELECT where a value is checked as not belonging to a set of values. Most commonly identified with the NOT operator but also with the ALL operator.

```
WHERE x NOT IN (SELECT a FROM tab_1)

WHERE NOT EXISTS (SELECT * FROM tab_1
                           WHERE pkey = value)

WHERE x > ALL (SELECT a FROM tab_1)
```

7.18.2 Nested query flattening to a join

Whenever possible the optimiser will flatten the sub-query into a join.

```
SELECT tab_1.a FROM tab_1
     WHERE tab_1.a IN (SELECT tab_2.a FROM tab_2)
```

is flattened to the join:

```
SELECT tab_1.a FROM tab_1, tab_2
     WHERE tab_1.a = tab_2.a
```

Prior to system 10 the join would display all matching occurrences of tab_1.a and tab_2.a. For example if tab_1 was a single row table with a=1 and tab_2 was a four row table with values of a = 1, 1, 2, 3 then the output of the above nested SELECT was 2 display rows of a = 1 and a = 1 ie the two records from the join between the tables.

In system 10 a special EXISTENCE JOIN is used that does not return duplicates. However this works only if the table in the sub-query is the inner table in the join execution plan. This is not always the case and a simple restriction on the nested table will tend to make it the outer table in a nested iteration plan.

```
SELECT tab_1.a FROM tab_1
     WHERE tab_1.a IN (SELECT tab_2.a FROM tab_2
                              WHERE tab_2.b = 10)
```

will be flattened to:

```
SELECT tab_1.a FROM tab_1, tab_2
     WHERE tab_1.a = tab_2.a
     AND   tab_2.b = 10
```

which will result in a nested iteration with tab_2 as the outer table as it is the most restrictive and will cause least passes through the inner table. Therefore the EXISTENCE JOIN will not be in effect and the output will display duplicates again.

A nice attempt by Sybase but I'm afraid that the old rule of thumb still applies: if the presence of duplicates in the output cannot be tolerated, then a DISTINCT must be included in the nested SELECT. This has two effects: it suppresses the duplicates and it prevents the flattening of the nesting by forcing a different execution plan (see section 7.16).

Nested queries cannot be flattened into joins if:

> the nested query contains a DISTINCT

> the nested query contains an aggregate or a GROUP BY

> the outer query contains an OR clause

The first two are reasonably obvious as it is impossible to construct a join when the nesting is of an aggregate:

```
SELECT tab_1.a FROM tab_1
     WHERE tab_1.a = (SELECT avg(tab_2.a) FROM tab_2)
```

Without too much thought it is easy to see that there is no join situation here between the two tables and the easiest way to execute the command is to evaluate the nested query first and pass the result to the outer query for evaluation.

However it is less clear why:

```
SELECT tab_1.a FROM tab_1
     WHERE tab_1.a IN (SELECT tab_2.a FROM tab_2)
     OR tab_1.b = 50
```

cannot be flattened into a join with an OR clause. The simple answer from Sybase is that the flattening does not work with empty tables. I really do not understand this one.

7.18.3 Non-join sub-queries

When the nested command cannot be flattened into a join, the command is evaluated from the inside out with the inner query being evaluated and the results joined with the outer query which is then evaluated and so on for each level of nesting.

This inner to outer evaluation requires the intermediate results to be presented to the outer query in as efficient a manner as possible. In doing this Sybase uses two internal aggregates - **any** and **once** - which operate as follows.

any   returns 1 if the WHERE clause is TRUE
                   returns 0 if the WHERE clause is FALSE

once   returns the single value that is supplied
                   returns NULL if no value supplied
                   returns error 512 if more than one value is returned

any

```
SELECT any(tab_1.a) FROM tab_1, tab_2
     WHERE tab_1.b = tab_2.b
```

Returns 1 if there is a match on tab_1.b and tab_2.b
Returns 0 if there is no match on tab_1.b and tab_2.b

once

```
SELECT once(tab_1.a) FROM tab_1
     WHERE tab_1.b = 5
```

Returns 5.

These are examples of how any and once work, they are not real executable SQL commands: any and once are not usable aggregates but are used internally in the evaluation of sub-queries. Similarly the explanations of the following nested evaluations do not show executable SQL but simply illustrate how the evaluation is done internally.

sub-queries returning a single aggregate value

This type of sub-query cannot be flattened into a join but it is really just a simple expression in the nested query which returns a value to the outer query. This is simply achieved by the use of a two step evaluation with a variable being used to hold the result of the inner query.

So:

```
SELECT tab_1.a FROM tab_1
WHERE tab_1.b IN (SELECT sum(tab_2.b) FROM tab_2)
```

is evaluated as:

```
DECLARE @sum int

SELECT @sum = sum(tab_2.b) FROM tab_2

SELECT tab_1.a FROM tab_1
     WHERE tab_1.b = @sum
```

outer query contains an OR clause

This nested query creates a work table containing the results of the inner query and then joins this with the outer query and the OR clause. The inner query evaluation uses the any aggregate.

```
SELECT tab_1.a FROM tab_1
     WHERE tab_1.b IN (SELECT tab_2.b FROM tab_2)
     OR tab_1.c = 5
```

The inner query is evaluated as:

```
SELECT b_res = tab_1.b, any_res = any(tab_1.b)
     INTO #work_tab
     FROM tab_1, tab_2
     WHERE  tab_1.b = tab_2.b
     GROUP BY ALL tab_1.b
```

If the tables are:

tab_1	a	b	c		tab_2	b
-------	---	---	---		-------	---
	1	1	1			1
	2	2	2			6
	3	3	5

then the work table will contain:

#work_tab	b_res	any_res
	1	1
	2	0
	3	0

The outer table tab_1 and the OR clause then join with the work table:

```
SELECT tab_1.a FROM tab_1, #work_tab
    WHERE (tab_1.b = #work_tab.b_res
                    AND #work_tab.any_res = 1)
    OR tab_1.c = 5
```

which returns the two values a = 1 and a = 3.

inner query contains a DISTINCT

```
SELECT tab_1.a FROM tab_1
    WHERE tab_1.b = (SELECT DISTINCT tab_2.b
                            FROM tab_2)
```

The inner query creates a work table of distinct tab_2.b values using the once aggregate.

```
DECLARE  @once   int
SELECT @once = once(DISTINCT tab_2.b) FROM tab_2
```

This is a single value which is merged with the outer query.

```
SELECT tab_1.a FROM tab_1 WHERE tab_1.b = @once
```

nested query contains a GROUP BY aggregate

This needs two work tables: one to evaluate the GROUP BY and one for the evaluation of the inner query using the any aggregate.

```
SELECT tab_1.a FROM tab_1
      WHERE tab_1.b IN (SELECT sum(tab_2.b) FROM tab_2
                                GROUP BY tab_2.c)
```

First of all the inner GROUP BY is evaluated using a work table.

```
SELECT c_res = tab_2.c, total_b = sum(tab_2.b)
      INTO #work1_tab
      FROM tab_2
      GROUP BY tab_2.c
```

If the original tables are:

tab_1	a	b		tab_2	b	c
	1	10			5	1
	2	20			5	1
	3	30			8	2
					10	2
					30	3

then we have:

#work1_tab	c_res	total_b
	1	10
	2	18
	3	30

The inner query is then evaluated into a second work table using the any aggregate.

```
SELECT b_res = tab_1.b, any_res = any(tab_1.b)
      INTO #work2_tab
      FROM tab_1, #work1_tab
```

```
WHERE (tab_1.b = #work1_tab.total_b)
GROUP BY ALL tab_1.b
```

This gives the result:

#work2_tab

b_res	any_res
10	1
18	0
30	1

which is joined with the outer table

```
SELECT tab_1.a FROM tab_1, #work2_tab
    WHERE tab_1.b = #work2_tab.b_res
    AND #work2_tab.any_res = 1
```

Non-existence checks

not in

```
SELECT tab_1.a FROM tab_1
    WHERE tab_1.b NOT IN (SELECT tab_2.b FROM tab_2)
```

As before the inner query is evaluated into a work table using the any aggregate and the result joined with the outer table.

```
SELECT b_res = tab_1.b, any_res = any(tab_1.b)
    INTO #work1_tab
    FROM tab_1, tab_2
    WHERE tab_1.b = tab_2.b
    GROUP BY ALL tab_1.b
```

If the original tables are:

tab_1	a	b		**tab_2**	b
	1	1			1
	2	2			4
	3	3			

This creates a work table of:

#work1_tab   b_res   any_res
                       1   1
                       2   0
                       3   0

which then joins with tab_1 as:

```
SELECT tab_1.a FROM tab_1, tab_2
    WHERE tab_1.b = #work1_tab.b_res
    AND #work1_tab.any_res = 0
```

not exists

```
SELECT tab_1.a FROM tab_1
    WHERE NOT EXISTS (SELECT * FROM tab_2
                            WHERE tab_2.a = tab_1.b)
```

Again we have a two stage process using the any aggregate:

```
SELECT b_res = tab_1.b, any_res = any(1)
    INTO #work1_tab
    FROM tab_1, tab_2
    WHERE tab_1.b = tab_2.a
    GROUP BY ALL tab_1.b
```

With original tables of:

tab_1   a   b   **tab_2**   b
                1   1   1
                2   2   4
                3   3

we have a work table of:

#work1_tab   b_res   any_res
                       1   1
                       2   0
                       3   0

which joins with the outer table as:

```
SELECT tab_1.a FROM tab_1, #work1_tab
    WHERE tab_1.b = #work1_tab.b_res
    AND #work1_tab.any_res = 0
```

7.18.4 Correlated sub-queries

Take time for a little thought when writing existence/non-existence sub-queries. I personally prefer to write in/not in sub-queries instead of exists/not exists. My preference is based on never writing correlated sub-queries where there is a join across the nesting. Use of in/not in involves no correlation but use of exists/not exists almost always requires some correlation.

For example the following are equivalent:

```
WHERE tab_1.b IN (SELECT tab_2.a FROM tab_2)

WHERE EXISTS (SELECT * FROM tab_2
                    WHERE tab_2.a = tab_1.a)
```

but the first is non-correlated as the nested query can be evaluated independently of the outer query, whereas the second is correlated as there is a join across the nesting.

Although Sybase creates the same execution plan for both of the above statements, I usually find that the non-correlated queries are easier to understand and often - even with Sybase - they execute faster than the equivalent correlated query.

However not all exists/not exists can be written as in/not in but I would recommend trying to do so as often as possible.

Of course not all correlated queries are exists/not exists statements.

```
SELECT tab_1.a FROM tab_1
    WHERE tab_1.b = (SELECT tab_2.c FROM tab_2
                            WHERE tab_2.c = tab_1.c)
    AND tab_1.d = 1
```

What Sybase does in this situation is to take any external search argument (tab_1.d = 1) into the nested query to find the best plan for the inner query.

So the above becomes:

```
SELECT c_res = tab_1.c, once_res = once(tab_2.c)
    INTO #work1_tab
    FROM tab_1, tab_2
    WHERE tab_1.c = tab_2.c
    AND tab_1.d = 1
    GROUP BY ALL tab_1.c

SELECT tab_1.a FROM tab_1, #work1_tab
    WHERE tab_1.d = 1
    AND tab_1.b = #work1_tab.c_res
    AND tab_1.b = #work1_tab.once_res
```

7.19 **Summary**

Sybase uses a statistical optimiser with very few surprises. Standard search argument definition of "column operator constant" is supported by an adherence to not doing more logical accesses than a table scan. Therefore a clustered index will always be used but use of a non-clustered index depends on the number of record accesses compared to the number of pages in the table.

OR statements are handled well by evaluating each clause separately and sort/merging the resulting row ids before retrieving the appropriate records.

Two join strategies are employed: nested iteration when useful indexes are available and a restricted/projected sort/merge, called reformatting, when no indexes are available.

One to watch for is the non-elimination of duplicate rows when a nested command is flattened to a join.

Optimisation of stored procedures can cause problems when they contain parameter statements with wide value ranges. Recompilation is the standard answer with three choices being available: at every execute, at specific executes or on request.

Two improvements to the optimiser output would be helpful: showing the number of disk accesses expected and naming the clustered index.

And finally....

Consultancy: the art of extracting money from another man's pocket without resorting to violence.

What's the difference between a dead consultant and a dead skunk in the middle of the road?

There are skid marks in front of the skunk!

What do you call four dead consultants at the bottom of a lake?

A good start!

What is the definition of waste?

A bus load of consultants going off the edge of a cliff with one seat empty!

Chapter 8

What If?

Problem
anticipation
and
solving
(hopefully)

This chapter is a collection of configuration, monitoring and problem solving techniques and tools.

O'Reilly's Eighth Law

If builders built buildings the way software vendors write programs, the first woodpecker to come along would destroy civilisation.

Commands covered in this chapter:

reconfigure
set statistics
dbcc

System procedures covered in this chapter:

sp_configure
sp_monitor

8.1   Server configuration

There is a set of parameters held in the master system table sysconfigures which defines the configuration of the server. These parameters are defined and displayed by the system procedure sp_configure. Only two of the configuration parameters - recovery interval, allow updates - are altered dynamically: all of the others require a restart of the server.

Sysconfigures contains the current setting of each variable but, as this may not yet be in effect, a temporary table - syscurconfigs - is created and displayed by sp_configure to display the current settings.

```
sp_configure
```

name	minimum	maximum	config_value	run_value
recovery interval	1	32767	0	5
allow updates	0	1	0	0
user connections	5	1024	0	25
memory	1000	2147483647	0	3200
open databases	5	2147483647	0	10
locks	5000	2147483647	0	5000
open objects	100	2147483647	0	500
procedure cache	1	99	0	20
fillfactor	0	100	0	0
time slice	50	1000	0	100
database size	2	10000	0	2
tape retention	0	365	0	0
recovery flags	0	1	0	0
serial number	1	999999	360156	360156
nested triggers	0	1	1	1
devices	4	256	15	15
remote access	0	1	0	0
remote logins	0	2147483647	0	0
remote sites	0	2147483647	0	0
remote connections	0	2147483647	0	0
pre-read packets	0	2147483647	0	0
upgrade version	0	2147483647	420	420
default sort order id	0	255	20	20
default language	0	2147483647	0	0
language in cache	3	100	3	3

The settings are changed by quoting the appropriate parameter and value.

sp_configure

```
sp_configure 'parameter', value
```

```
sp_configure 'recovery interval', 10
```

The two dynamic parameters - recovery interval and allow updates - are then reset immediately using reconfigure.

reconfigure

```
reconfigure [with override]
```

The with override option is used for the option 'allow updates'.

```
sp_configure 'recovery interval', 15
go
reconfigure
go

sp_configure 'allow updates', 1
go
reconfigure with override
go
```

8.2   Parameters

If you are in doubt about the units for each parameter have a look in the comments column of sysconfigures.

```
select comment from sysconfigures
```

Comment
Maximum recovery interval in minutes
Allow updates to system tables
Number of user connections allowed
Size of available memory in 2 K pages
Number of open databases allowed among all users
Number of locks for all users
Number of open database objects
Percentage of remaining memory used for procedure cache
Default fillfactor percentage
Average timeslice per process in milliseconds
Default database size in megabytes
Tape retention period in days

Recovery flags
Serial number
Allow triggers to be invoked within triggers
Number of devices
Allow remote access
Number of remote logins
Number of remote sites
Number of remote connections
Number of pre-read packets per remote connection
Upgrade version

recovery interval

```
sp_configure 'recovery interval', 10
go
reconfigure
go
```

The recovery interval is set in minutes with a default value of 5 which is as good as anything else.

The recovery interval determines the checkpoint frequency. The value is taken as the maximum amount of time that transaction recovery from a system failure should take. When the transaction management system determines that it has written enough images to the transaction log for recovery to take this long, it takes a checkpoint. So, although it determines when a checkpoint is taken, the figure is not the time between checkpoints but the maximum time it should take to recover from system failure. As mentioned in chapter 5, the time is the number of log records * 10 ms.

Note that the interval specified is not an upper bound for the recovery interval. If the server goes down during the execution of a long running transaction, the recovery interval may exceed this time by a considerable amount.

allow updates

```
sp_configure 'allow updates', 1
go
reconfigure with override
go
```

Allow updates is set as 1 (true) or 0 (false) with a default of 0.

Set this to 1 only under very special circumstances and have the database as 'dbo use only' to make sure that no-one else is allowed to use the database.

This setting allows updates to the system tables. This really is for emergency use only as users - including the SA - should not require update capability on the system tables. You need the system tables to operate the database so be careful. Speak to Sybase first about what you intend to do and, you may not get their approval, but at least they may indicate if you are about to cause a disaster.

If you create a procedure to do the changes to the system tables, this procedure will still be able to update the system tables after the 'allow updates' flag has been set to 0. So make sure that you revoke execute from public to prevent another user being able to execute the procedure.

user connections

```
sp_configure 'user connections', 30
```

This sets the total number of concurrent connections to the server.

The maximum is operating system dependent so check your specific system: Sun: 25-1024 depending on the system; Digital VMS: 500 depending on the Decnet limit; Ultrix 256-2000; Pyramid: 1024 and so on. Each connection requires 34 K (64 K for open server) of memory so, if you make a large increase to the number of connections, remember that you may need to increase the memory allocation.

The server requires 5 connections by default for master device, error log, console, network and mirror. Each device which you create requires one connection and each dbopen from an application requires a connection.

Sybase software requires:

isql	1 connection per user
dwb	1-4 depending on the level of screen nesting 2 when using the data dictionary
apt	It's up to you but 1 per channel (APT-Build uses at least 2)

memory

```
sp_configure 'memory', 8000
```

This sets the available memory for the server in units of 2 K pages. We have dealt with the size calculation in chapter 6 and the rules of thumb are:

system etc:	4 M
Sybase kernel:	4 M
connections:	3 per user @ 34/64 K each
procedure cache:	3 procedures per connection @ 12K per procedure
data cache:	5 - 20% of data

Set this for all that you need - all memory less the operating system if you have a dedicated server. At start-up the server will grab all that you have allocated and not release it when another process requests memory unless the server is quiescent. If this happens it will page fault to get back to full size again. This is not a good idea. Remember in Unix to allocate enough swap space to hold the server if it is swapped out. Even if not used, this swap space must be available. Try not to have the server paging in and out. Relational databases love memory so give it what it needs all of the time. Watch the use of shared memory in v4.8 as some vendors restrict it: Pyramid has an upper limit of 192 M bytes per server.

open databases

```
sp_configure 'open databases', 20
```

This sets the total number of concurrently open databases for the server. The default is 10. Every open database requires 40 bytes of memory as an object but this is negligible when compared with procedure and data requirements.

It is unlikely that you will need to set this very high but no point in setting it too low and having to restart the server. Depends quite simply on how many databases you expect to have on the server.

locks

```
sp_configure  'locks', 8000
```

This sets the total number of concurrent locks for the server. The default is 5000.

We dealt with this in chapter 6 and the rule of thumb is:

number of connections * 20.

open objects

```
sp_configure 'open objects', 2000
```

This sets the number of objects open at the same time on the server. The default is 500. On average each open object requires 40 - 50 bytes of memory.

You will need a lot of these - one for each entry in sysobjects for all databases. However the maximum is 10,000 which is only 0.5 M bytes, so even when memory is tight, don't worry about setting this high enough to have no problems.

procedure cache

```
sp_configure 'procedure cache', 10
```

This sets the percentage of 'leftover' memory which is allocated to hold the compiled procedures. Leftover memory is the memory available in that set by 'memory' after the server, connections and objects have had their share. In other words what is left for procedures and data. The default is 20%.

We have dealt with this in chapter 6 but be careful to alter the percentage when you increase memory to provide more data cache.

The error log after startserver shows the actual allocation of memory for data and procedures in 2 K pages.

number of buffers in buffer cache:	400	(data cache)
number of proc buffers allocated:	60	(procedure cache)
number of blocks left for proc headers:	70	

The first figure is the number of data cache pages: 400 * 2 K (0.8 M bytes).

The third figure is the number of procedure cache pages: 70 * 2 K (0.14 M bytes).

The second figure indicates how many compiled objects you can have in procedure cache at the one time. Note that triggers, views, rules, defaults used in a procedure are compiled into the procedure and qualify as separate compiled objects. A proc buffer is a structure used to manage a compiled object. A 2 K page can hold 21 proc buffers, so the above 60 proc buffers require 3 pages which increases the procedure cache to 73 pages.

fillfactor

```
sp_configure  'fillfactor', 75
```

This sets the percentage to which index and clustered data pages are filled during initial create. The default is 0, which means the clustered data pages are packed to 100% and the indexes to 75%.

When a new entry is added to a full index page it splits 50:50 into two. This is a very high overhead to the transaction and may be minimised by allocating an initial amount of free space in each index page via the fillfactor. The percentage used is application dependent but as full pages split 50:50 the index will navigate to 75% occupancy so - unless there is a good reason like a high insert rate - you might as well start at 75%.

The server wide fillfactor may be overridden in the individual index create.

timeslice

```
sp_configure  'timeslice', 100
```

This sets the time in milliseconds that the server allocates to each task in turn. The server has its own scheduler which allocates processing time to each task on a 'round robin' basis. Each process runs until it uses up its timeslice and then waits until it is its turn again. You should not need to adjust this but, if you feel that you must, please discuss it with Sybase.

database size

```
sp_configure  'database size', 10
```

This sets the default database size in M bytes. The default is 2 M bytes.

If no size is specified in the create database statement, the maximum of this value and the size of model is used. If other than 2 M bytes is required it is better to increase this value as increasing model takes up space on the master device. Use model as the template and this value as the default size.

tape retention

```
sp_configure 'tape retention', 5
```

This sets the number of days before a tape written by dump database should be reused.

A warning message is issued if you try to reuse a tape in dump database before its retention period.

recovery flags

```
sp_configure 'recovery flags', 0
```

If set to 1 (true) this displays all messages during recovery. The default is 0 (false).

Set to 1 is useful during testing to see what the recovery mechanism is doing. Once you have satisfied your curiosity - and it is useful to know what recovery does in case you have a problem - set if off. Do not set this on operational recovery as it will significantly slow down the recovery - which is slow enough.

serial number

No comment on this: it's set at installation and not something that you should alter.

allow nested triggers

```
sp_configure 'allow nested triggers', 1
```

This is set to 1 (true) to enable the firing of nested triggers so that a trigger may be invoked by action within a trigger. The default is 1. This is useful to allow the writing of modular triggers. If there is a hierarchy of tables as in figure 8.1 with deletion cascaded from the order table then with no nesting the order trigger must delete both items and deliveries. This requires duplication of the delete delivery code in the item trigger. With nesting the delete of item from order fires the item trigger which deletes the deliveries. So there is no duplication of code.

This option is provided for backwards compatibility only: it should be left at 1 unless you intend running very old applications - and consider recoding these to make use of nested triggers.

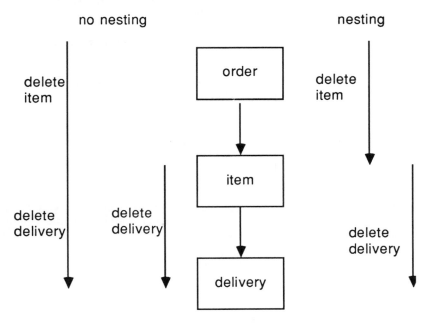

figure 8.1:   trigger nesting

max # of devices

```
sp_configure "max devices", 60
```

This sets the number of logical devices (vdevno in disk init) available to the server. The default is 10 configurable up to 256. Be careful: do not set this lower than the highest value currently in use or databases on these devices will not be recoverable.

allow remote access

```
sp_configure "remote access", 1
```

This is set to 1 (true) to allow other servers to function as remote servers for execution of stored procedure calls defined on other servers. Remote access must be configured to write Open Server programs. Configuring remote access allows the definition of four other parameters:

remote logins   The maximum number of users allowed to login

	remotely to another server from this server. Default is 1000.
remote sites	The maximum number of active remote sites. Default is 1000.
remote connects	The maximum number of user connections to remote sites. Default is 1000.
pre-read packets	The number of packets which are pre-read for a user over a connection. Default is 3.

Remember that all of these remote access features are system configuration options and so you need to restart the server before they take effect and before the remote servers/logins are known and you can execute remote procedure calls as discussed in chapter 4.

upgrade version

Simply the version you are running and not something you need to touch.

default sort order id

The default sort is binary sort order (ISO 8859-1): numbers followed by upper case alphabetic followed by lower case alphabetic, which is the only sort order supported in the current versions. This can be seen using sp_helpsort.

default language/language in cache

The default is US/English. This is used for the language of the system messages and the date internationalisation. New languages can be added using the system procedure sp_addlanguage and the current language may be altered using the "language" parameter of the "set" command.

Finally be careful when you alter configuration variables. They do not take effect until you restart the server - except for sp_reconfigure with "allow updates" and "recovery interval" - and so you can easily create a combination which the server is unable to accept and the startserver will fail. This is not checked as you change the variables, only when you start the server.

If you do get into this position you will have to rebuild the master device as described in chapter 5 using "buildmaster -r".

8.3   Monitoring system activity

Sybase does not provide much in the way of monitoring assists having really only 4 system procedures.

sp_spaceused	see chapter 3
sp_lock	see chapter 6
sp_who	see chapter 4
sp_monitor	

The activity system procedure sp_monitor shows CPU, I/O and network activity as a total and since the last sp_monitor.

sp_monitor

last_run	current_run	seconds
May 26 1992 18:55	May 26 1992 18:56	249851

cpu_busy	io_busy	idle
430(427)-0%	410(410) - 0%	0(0) - 0%

packets_received	packets_sent	packet_errors
4310(4124)	9901(9719)	5(5)

total_recd	total_work	total_errors	connections
28657(28556)	100890(100038)	0(0)	127(125)

The first set of figures is the cumulative values since the server was started. The second set is the values since the last issue of sp_monitor. Therefore this activity monitoring tool has a limited use and is really only effective at peak loading times to highlight any bottlenecks.

Individual SQL commands may be analysed by examining the execution plan as in chapter 7 and by examining the I/O using the "statistics" option of the "set" command. With the options on, an analysis of the I/O activity is output after the command has executed.

set statistics io on

Table: customer scan count 1, logical reads: 5, physical reads: 1
        Total writes for this command: 0

set statistics time on

Execution time 0
SQL Server cpu time: 0 ms   SQL server elapsed time: 5715784 ms

Execution time 1
SQL Server cpu time: 20 ms   SQL server elapsed time: 126 ms

8.4   Stored procedures

A general comment on Sybase is to use stored procedures for all of the frequently run SQL: in practice anything but ad-hoc SQL. This global statement is far too black and white of course, and not all SQL benefits greatly from being a stored procedure. However you will see little difference if you make all of the SQL stored procedures, but things will go rather slower if you do not use stored procedures at all. So follow the general rule but, as always, know why you are doing so. (This was dealt with in detail in chapter 7 but I have summarised it here for completeness.)

If the routine is large and run infrequently then there will be only a small saving in parse time. A procedure is parsed when it is created but then stored on the system catalog until executed. At the first execution it is read from disk, optimised, compiled and loaded into procedure cache. It will remain in procedure cache as long as it is used and/or there is room for it. Any other user who executes the procedure while it is in cache gets a copy of the optimised, compiled cache version.

So if you do not use the procedure often it will be one of the first targets to be swapped out when space is required in procedure cache. Once all versions have been swapped out the next execution reads the disk copy and optimises and compiles as before, negating the expected savings.

The timing of the procedure optimisation - when first loaded from disk - means that subsequent executions of the cache version will use this execution plan. If the procedure is parameterised then the first execution plan may not be suitable for subsequent executions.

```
create proc jk_proc
    (@low int, @high int)
as
begin
    select prod_no from ord_item
        where price between @low and @high
end
return
```

Depending on the values of the parameters, a non-clustered index on price could generate a table scan or an index search. The first value range will determine the execution plan for all executions and this may not be suitable causing a table scan when the index should have been used and vice versa.

When the user complains about an unusual response time on a procedure with parameter ranges as above, don't panic: recompile the procedure and try again. If it still runs slowly: then you start to worry.

This is not as serious a problem as it first seems, as it occurs only with ranges of parameter values such as:

```
where x between @var1 and @var2

where x like @var1+'%'
```

and non-clustered indexes. You can identify when these are liable to occur and keep them under control.

Control is based on recompilation to create an efficient execution plan.

```
execute jk_proc with recompile

create jk_proc ..... with recompile
```

The first recompiles the copy of the procedure in cache for that execution only and lasts until the cache copy is swapped out. The second recompiles the procedure at every execution.

The latter is a real sledgehammer to crack a nut and you should reconsider the use of such procedures: possibly rewriting them as isql scripts. It is not invalid to have such procedures as it still controls the code as small modules under the server dictionary control: but you have no performance savings (apart from a little parse time).

Execute with recompile is the normal solution but even this has its problems.

If user_1 and user_2 are executing proc_1 then user_2 has a copy of the optimised, compiled version of user_1. If user_2 executes with recompile only user_2's copy is recompiled and we have two different versions in cache. If user_2 stops using the procedure and this version is swapped out, the next execution by user_2 will be a copy of the original user_1 version which takes us back to the performance problem for user_2.

The reverse is also true if user_1's copy is swapped out as the next execution by user_1 will get a copy of user_2's version which may introduce performance problems for user_1.

Again this is not a serious problem - in fact a high incidence may indicate an underlying problem with the size of procedure cache - but be aware of it.

Also be careful when you adjust the indexing of a table to improve SQL performance: you need to recompile the procedures which are using that table. Any change which does not affect the optimisation plan or the compilation plan does not cause the procedure to be recompiled. The presence of a new index does not affect the execution of the compiled version as it does not know about the new index. You could wait until the next time the procedure is loaded from disk or execute with recompile, but the easiest way is to use the system procedure sp_recompile which will recompile all procedures or all procedures that access or modify a table.

sp_recompile

```
sp_recompile   [table_name]
```

This does not recompile the procedures immediately but sets a flag on sysobjects which the procedure checks before execution and recompiles if set. Use of sp_recompile adds a little (6 K) to the procedure so you might have problems with large procedures which are close to the maximum size of 64 K (192 K in the latest versions).

If this becomes a problem and you cannot use sp_recompile you will need to drop and recreate the procedure to ensure that all copies are flushed out of cache, or shutdown and restart the server to get them all.

8.5   DBCC

Sybase has a database consistency checker - largely undocumented, which is a great pity - which allows detailed investigation of the consistency of table and index information. This is a very powerful and dangerous piece of software with which you can easily corrupt your database and so I shall describe only the read features of dbcc: there are update facilities but I am not going to explain them and would strongly advise you not to touch them. If you have a problem which you believe involves the consistency of the data and requires you to use dbcc to find out what is causing the problem, and you decide that a piece of information needs altering, talk to Sybase - do not change it yourself using dbcc.

Having given this "government health warning" the read only investigative facilities of dbcc are extremely useful. Even if you are not having any problems with the tables and indexes, you can learn a lot about how Sybase structures its data layout by spending some time with dbcc.

During the examples of dbcc I shall use the table:

```
create table jk_tab (
     a      int,
     b      char(200),
     c      char(200),
     d      char(200),
     e      char(200),
     f      char(200),
     g      char(200))

create clustered index jk1_idx on jk_tab(a)

create nonclustered index jk2_idx on jk_tab(a)
```

with 5 records:

```
insert into jk_tab
     values(1,'1','2','3','4','5','6')
insert into jk_tab
     values(2,'1','2','3','4','5','6')
insert into jk_tab
     values(3,'1','2','3','4','5','6')
insert into jk_tab
     values(4,'1','2','3','4','5','6')
insert into jk_tab
     values(5,'1','2','3','4','5','6')
```

This gives a 5 page table with 2 indexes, each of which will require only the one index node.

8.5.1 **dbcc   checktable(table_name)**

This checks the consistency of the data and index pages of a table.

dbcc   checktable(jk_tab)

output
Checking jk_tab.

The total number of data pages in this table is 5.

Table has 5 data rows.

DBCC Execution completed. If DBCC printed error messages, see your System Administrator.

"dbcc checktable" carries out four main integrity checks:

- the page pointer chain is intact: each page points back to the page that pointed to it.

- the page offset table is consistent: each data row has an entry in the page matching its offset in the page offset table.

- index rows are located in the index pages in ascending key sequence.

- the nonclustered leaf index keys match the column(s) in the data row pointed to.

8.5.2 `dbcc    reindex(table_name)`

This is a fast dbcc checktable which looks at the indexes and rebuilds them if there is a problem. This command does not operate on the data of a table or on the system tables.

```
dbcc   reindex(jk_tab)
```

output
One or more indexes are corrupt. They will be rebuilt.

DBCC Execution completed. If DBCC printed error messages, see your System Administrator.

8.5.3 `dbcc    checkdb(database_name)`

This is a checktable on every table in the database. Note that if syslogs is on a separate device you get a report on used and free space during checkdb (or using checktable).

```
dbcc   checkdb(fred)
```

output
...
...

. . .
Checking syslogs

The total number of data pages in this table is 2.

> Space used in the log segment is 0.40 M bytes, 10%
> Space free in the log segment is 3.60 M bytes, 90%

DBCC Execution completed. If DBCC printed error messages, see your System Administrator.

8.5.4 **dbcc   checkcatalog(database_name)**

This checks for consistency of the system tables and reports on any defined segments.

dbcc   checkcatalog(fred)

output
Checking fred.

The following segments have been defined for database 20/ database name fred.

virtual start addr size	segments
4100	1536
	0
	1
	2

DBCC Execution completed. If DBCC printed error messages, see your System Administrator.

Some of the principal checks are:

- every type in syscolumns is in systypes

- every table and view in sysobjects has at least one column in syscolumns

- the last checkpoint in syslogs is valid.

8.5.5 dbcc   checkalloc(database_name)

This checks the consistency of the data and index pages with the corresponding extent structure.

dbcc   checkalloc(fred)

output
Checking fred.

Database "fred" is not in single user mode - may find spurious allocation problems due to transactions in progress.

```
****************************************************************
```

TABLE: jk1_tab   OBJID: 1500532379

INDID=0   FIRST=1048   ROOT=1072   SORT=1
          Data level: 1.   5 data pages in 2 extents.
          Indid: 1.   2 index pages in 2 extents.

INDID=2   FIRST=1088   ROOT=1088   SORT=0
          Indid: 2.   2 index pages in 2 extents.

TOTAL # of extents = 6

```
****************************************************************
```

TABLE: jk2_tab   OBJID: 1616008788

INDID=0   FIRST=817   ROOT=821   SORT=0
          Data level: 0.   5 data pages in 1 extents.

INDID=2   FIRST=1016   ROOT=1016   SORT=1
          Indid: 0.   2 index pages in 2 extents.

TOTAL # of extents = 3

```
****************************************************************
```

Processed 32 entries in the Sysindexes for dbid 20.

Alloc page 0   (# of extent= 32 used pages = 98 ref pages = 98)
Alloc page 256   (# of extent= 32 used pages = 119 ref pages = 111)
Alloc page 512   (# of extent= 32 used pages = 159 ref pages = 143)
Alloc page 768   (# of extent= 29 used pages = 206 ref pages = 86)
Alloc page 1024   (# of extent= 9   used pages = 17 ref pages = 17)
Alloc page 1280   (# of extent= 1   used pages = 1 ref pages = 1)

Total (# of extent = 135 used pages = 600 ref pages = 456) in this database.

DBCC Execution completed. If DBCC printed error messages, see your System Administrator.

The first display for jk1_tab is of the clustered index and the second of the non-clustered index.

The initial warning of "single user mode" is worth paying attention to as checkalloc can take some time and often page linkage errors are displayed which are caused by updates taking place while checkalloc is checking the page allocations. So run in "single user mode".

The output indicates that our database has 6 allocations with 600 used pages ie 600*2K: 1.2 M bytes and 135 extents ie 135*8*2K: 2.16 M bytes. This compares with a sp_spaceused:

sp_spaceused

database_name		database_size	
fred		3MB	

reserved	data	index_size	reserved
2118KB	658KB	384KB	1076KB

Close but not exact.

Checkalloc does the following consistency checks:

- checks the extent is for the correct table/index: object_id in the extent is the same as object_id in sysindexes.

- an extent occurs only once in the extent chain.

- checks the allocation bit map settings with the pages linked into the object page chain: pages marked as USED in the extent allocation bit map match those REFERENCED in the page chain.

8.5.6 `dbcc    traceon(setting)`

So much for the general consistency, let's look in more detail at dbcc options which allow us to investigate any problems highlighted by the previous options, especially checktable and checkalloc. I repeat for emphasis: if you need to fix a table or index do NOT do it yourself, talk to Sybase.

Most of the detailed dbcc output is directed to the console where the server was booted. To redirect it use the trace flag settings:

```
dbcc    traceon(3604)        to redirect to your terminal

dbcc    traceon(3605)        to redirect to the errorlog
```

These are turned off by:

```
dbcc traceoff(setting)
```

8.5.7 `dbcc    page(dbid,  page#,  printopt,`
`cache,  logical)`

Having run checktable we may have some problems with specific pages. We can look at the page and header contents using dbcc page:

```
dbcc    page(dbid,  page#,  printopt,
                    cache,  logical)
```

where
dbid	database id
page#	logical or virtual number
printopt	0: print page/buffer header only (default)
	1: print header information, data in row format and page offset table
	2: print header information, unformatted data and page offset table
cache	0: fetch disk version of page
	1: fetch cache version of page if possible (default)
logical	0: page# is virtual page number
	1: page # is logical page number (default)

dbcc page(20, 1049)

output
BUFFER
Buffer header for buffer 0x84ee41

page=0x8eb000	bdnew=0x7ebf9d	bdold=0x7ebf9d
bhash=0x0	bnew=0x7ec541 bold=0x7eb0c5	
bvirtpg=5149	bdbid=20 bkeep=0	bstd=0x1000
bwstat=0x0000	bpageno=1049	

PAGE HEADER
Page header for page 0x1345000

pageno=1049 nextpg=1050 prevpg=1048 objid=1500532379
timestamp=000100076a25
nextrno=1 level=0 indid=0 freeoff=1238 minlen=1206
page status bits=0x80,0x1

DBCC Execution completed. If DBCC printed error messages, see your System Administrator.

This does not tell the non-vendor SA much but, from checkalloc, we know that page 1049 is in jk_tab which this confirms. We can also see the previous and next page numbers and that the record is 1206 bytes long, free space is at 1238 (1026+32) and from our knowledge of the table we know that it is 1 fixed length record of 1204+2 bytes. Because the record is fixed length we do not have an offset table.

8.5.8 dbcc   prtipage(dbid, object_id, index_id, page#)

This prints the page number pointed to by each row in the specified index page.

dbcc   prtipage(dbid, object_id, index_id, page#)

where

dbid	database id
object_id	object_id of object that index is on
index_id	index_id to which page belongs
page#	logical page number

```
dbcc   prtipage(20,   1500532379,
                  2,   1088)
```

output
***INDEX LEVEL 0 - PAGE # 1088

Leaf row at offset 32 points to datapage 1048, row number 0
Leaf row at offset 43 points to datapage 1049, row number 0
Leaf row at offset 54 points to datapage 1050, row number 0
Leaf row at offset 65 points to datapage 1051, row number 0
Leaf row at offset 76 points to datapage 1052, row number 0

Page finished...

DBCC Execution completed. If DBCC printed error messages, see your System
Administrator.

From checkalloc we know that this is the nonclustered leaf index page which points to
the 5 data pages. The index entries are 11 bytes long which is consistent with a fixed
length field (a) index ie key (4 bytes) + record_id (6 bytes) + overhead (1 byte).

8.5.9 `dbcc   locateindexpgs(dbid,   object_id,`
`page#,   index_id,   level)`

This displays all references in an index to a specified page number.

```
dbcc   locateindexpgs(dbid,   object_id,   page#,
                               index_id,   level)
```

where
dbid	database id
object_id	object_id of object that index is on
page#	logical page number which we are looking for references to
index_id	index_id to search
level	level of index to search for references
	(0 for data page references)

```
dbcc   locateindexpgs(20,   1500532379,
                      1048,   2,   0)
```

output
INFO ON INDEX ROWS POINTING TO GIVEN PAGE

INDEX ROW ON:

Index page#:   1088
At offset: 32
Pointer to data row: 0

DBCC Execution completed. If DBCC printed error messages, see your System Administrator.

As we only have one index page and one data record per page, which is fixed length, this is not very informative.

8.5.10   **dbcc pglinkage(dbid, startpg#,**
                         #_of_pages, printopt,
                         targetpg#, ascending)

This traverses the page chain printing logical page numbers and checking the consistency of the page pointers.

```
dbcc pglinkage(dbid, startpg#,
                 #_of_pages, printopt,
                 targetpg#, ascending)
```

where
dbid	database id
startpg#	logical page number to start following the page chain
#_of_pages	number of pages to scan before stopping
printopt	0: print count of pages only
	1: print last 16 pages in scan
	2: print each page number in scan
targetpg#	logical page number at which to stop scan
ascending	0: descending
	1: ascending

```
dbcc pglinkage(20, 1048, 5, 0, 0, 1)
```

output
Object id for pages in this chain = 1500532379

End of chain reached.

5 pages scanned. Objectid=1500532379. Last page in scan=1052

DBCC Execution completed. If DBCC printed error messages, see your System Administrator.

This is fully consistent with our table jk1_tab which has 5 pages with logical page numbers 1048-1052.

```
dbcc pglinkage(20, 1048, 5, 2, 0, 1)
```

output
Object id for pages in this chain = 1500532379

Page: 1048
Page: 1049
Page: 1050
Page: 1051
Page: 1052

End of chain reached.

5 pages scanned. Objectid=1500532379. Last page in scan=1052

DBCC Execution completed. If DBCC printed error messages, see your System Administrator.

8.5.11   dbcc allocdump(dbid, page#)

This shows all of the extents on a given allocation page.

```
dbcc allocdump(dbid, page#)
```

where:
    dbid   database id
    page#   allocation page logical page number

```
dbcc allocdump(20, 1024)
```

output
*** DISPLAY ALL EXTENTS ON ALLOCATION PAGE

EXTID: 1024	objid: 5	indid: 0	alloc: ff	status: 2
EXTID: 1032	objid: 0	indid: 0	alloc: 0	status: 0
EXTID: 1040	objid: 1500532379	indid: 0	alloc: 1	status: 3
EXTID: 1048	objid: 1500532379	indid: 0	alloc: 1f	status: 3
EXTID: 1056	objid: 1500532379	indid: 1	alloc: 1	status: 3
EXTID: 1064	objid: 6	indid: 0	alloc: 1	status: 2
EXTID: 1072	objid: 1500532379	indid: 1	alloc: 3	status: 3
EXTID: 1080	objid: 1500532379	indid: 2	alloc: 1	status: 2
EXTID: 1088	objid: 1500532379	indid: 2	alloc: 3	status: 2

etc:

DBCC Execution completed. If DBCC printed error messages, see your System Administrator.

8.5.12   **dbcc   extentcheck(dbid,   object_id,**
index_id,   sortbit)

This displays the extents allocated to an object by scanning all allocation pages sequentially.

dbcc   extentcheck(dbid,   object_id,
index_id,   sortbit)

where

dbid	database id
object_id	object id to which extent belongs (else 0)
index_id	index id to which extent belongs (else 0)
sortbit	set to the same status as the sort bit in the status word of sysindexes

dbcc   extentcheck(20,   1500532379,
0,   1)

output
EXTID: 1040 objid: 1500532379 indid 0 alloc 1 status 3
EXTID: 1048 objid: 1500532379 indid 0 alloc 1f status 3

Total extents 2.

DBCC Execution completed. If DBCC printed error messages, see your System

Administrator.

Make sure that you get the sort bit correct otherwise you get no information on the object/index. Also the object_id:index_id columns function as a composite key to the extent entries.

$$\textbf{dbcc ~~ extentcheck(20, ~~ 1500532379,}$$
$$\textbf{1, ~~ 1)}$$

output
EXTID: 1056 objid: 1500532379 indid 1 alloc 1 status 3
EXTID: 1072 objid: 1500532379 indid 1 alloc 3 status 3

Total extents 2.

DBCC Execution completed. If DBCC printed error messages, see your System Administrator.

8.5.13   **dbcc extentdump(dbid, page#)**

This displays the extent information for a specific logical page number.

$$\textbf{dbcc ~~ extentdump(dbid, ~~ page#)}$$

where
dbid	database id
page#	logical page number

$$\textbf{dbcc ~~ extentdump(20, ~~ 1056)}$$

output
DISPLAY EXTENT FOR GIVEN PAGE REQUESTED

Logical page 1056:

> Extent ID 1056 on allocation page 1024
> Object ID is 1500532379
> Index ID is 1
> Allocation bit map: 0x1

Sort bit is on.
Reference bit is on.

DBCC Execution completed. If DBCC printed error messages, see your System Administrator.

8.5.14   **dbcc   findnotfullextents**
(dbid,
object_id,
index_id,
sortbit)

This displays all of the extents for the specified object which have free pages in them.

dbcc   findnotfullextents(dbid,   object_id,
index_id,   sortbit)

where
dbid   database id
object_id   object id to search
index_id   index id to search
sortbit   set to the same status as the sort bit in the status word of
                  sysindexes

dbcc   findnotfullextents(20,   1500532379,
0, 1)

output
** EXAMINE ALL NOT FULL EXTENTS ON ALLOC PAGES FOR SPECIFIED OBJECT

Id of extent not full: 1040
Id of extent not full: 1048

Total extents that are not full: 2

DBCC Execution completed. If DBCC printed error messages, see your System Administrator.

8.5.15   **dbcc   usedextents(dbid,   option,**
display)

This displays or counts the status of used/unused extents for specific databases and devices.

dbcc   usedextents(dbid,   option,   display)

where
dbid	database id
option	0: both data and log
	1: log only
	2: data only
display	0: display extents
	1: count extents

dbcc   usedextents(20,   0,   1)

output
Total used extents = 135

Total free extents = 57

DBCC Execution completed. If DBCC printed error messages, see your System Administrator.

8.5.16   **dbcc   memusage**

This displays the memory allocation and the current memory usage for the top 20 users of memory.

dbcc   memusage

output

	Meg	2K blks	bytes
configured memory	24.4141	12500	25600000
code size	0.1860	96	195052
kernel structures	4.9708	2546	5212273
server structures	5.2499	2688	5504964

page cache	10.9645	5614	11497136
proc buffers	0.0877	45	92004
proc headers	2.9550	1513	3098571

Buffer cache information (top 20):

Dbid	Object id	Index id	2K buffers
19	1042102753	0	682
19	274100017	0	566
etc			

Procedure cache information (top 20):

Type: stored procedure
Number of trees: 0
Size of trees: 0.000000 Mb, 0.000000 bytes, 0 pages
Number of plans: 1
Size of plans: 0.009693 Mb, 10164.000000 bytes, 5 pages
Database id: 1
Object id: 2144010669
Version: 1
Uid: 1
DBCC Execution completed. If DBCC printed error messages, see your System Administrator.

8.5.17   `dbinfo area`

This is an area in each database which contains information about the database. This is located in the syslogs entry in sysindexes, using the keys fields, as the log never has any indexes set on it. As the log row in sysindexes is always in the same location it gives a fixed reference to certain values. These values are of interest to some of the system routines but not a lot of use for general SA use.

If you do not believe me (and for completeness):

`dbcc  dbinfo(fred)`

output
DBINFO STRUCTURE:

dbi_lastrid:	page 136, rownum 0
dbi_dpbegxact:	page 1032, rownum 132
dbi_oldseqnum:	Jan 1 1900 12:00:00:00:000 AM

dbi_curseqnum:	Oct 29 1992 4:40:22:320 PM
dbi_nextseqnum:	Jan 1 1900 12:00:00:00:000 AM
dbi_deallocpgs:	0
dbi_drprowcnt:	0
dbi_pgcnt:	0
dbi_nextcheckpt:	page 0, rownum 0
dbi_dbid:	20
dbi_suid:	1
dbi_version:	2
dbi_status:	0x8
dbi_checkpt:	page 1032, rownum 1032
dbi_nextid:	1516532436
dbi_complete:	1207959552
dbi_crdate:	Sep 3 1992 10:30:13:340 AM
dbi_dbname:	fred
dbi_ldstate:	0
dbi_rambots:	0x0000 0x00000000
dbi_dmplastckpt:	page 0, rownum 0
dbi_dmplastrid:	page 0, rownum 0
dbi_pretruncpg:	0
dbi_posttruncpg:	0

DBCC Execution completed. If DBCC printed error messages, see your System Administrator.

There are many more uses for DBCC but these are the principal information displays. Please take care with DBCC. What I have shown you will help you determine what the problem is: **get Sybase to fix it.**

There are a few more display options to dbcc which you will not use very often - if at all - as they are not that helpful or the volume of output is prohibitive and the information is available elsewhere. The syntax for these is:

dbcc   allocmap(dbid)

> This shows the status of the allocation bit for all allocation units.

dbcc   ind(db_name,   table_name,   printopt)

> This shows all pages in use by indexes of the specified table.
> > printopt: 0 - all
> >
> > 1 - row
> >
> > 2 - header

dbcc   tab(db_name,   table_name,   printopt)
  This shows all data pages in use by the specified table.
    printopt: 0 - all
         1 - row
         2 - header

dbcc   showtext(db_name, logical_page_num)
  This shows the text or image data contained on the specified
  page.

dbcc   fixtext(table_name)
  This updates text values after a character set change.

8.6   **Summary**

Sybase is not the most helpful piece of software in assisting the SA to anticipate and solve problems. The system tables do contain a lot of necessary information but the system procedures are not extensive and a lot of home grown routines have to be created.

The monitoring tools do not supply much useful information: space and object placement is best retrieved yourself and activity monitoring is best done at the operating system level. System 10 is aiming to improve this with an activity monitoring server.

Nonetheless, you need to keep an eye on the system to ensure that it does not run out of resource at the wrong time. When you need to, sp_configure will allow you to make the necessary changes.

Regular monitoring of space with sp_spaceused and dbcc is essential and sp_lock and sp_monitor will be of occasional use to you.

And finally....

A computer salesman and his MD were making a trip to one of their major users in Scotland. Unfortunately there had been a mix up with the flights and they had to change airlines for a later flight.

They went to the ticket desk of the second airline to book two seats. Unseen by the MD the salesman handed his credit card to the reservations clerk for her to take his details. She keyed in the details and said to the salesman "Yes, that will be no problem, Mr Smith, your reservations are confirmed."

She then turned to the MD and asked
"And could I have your name please, sir?"

The MD, not having seen the credit card, was completely non-plussed by the fact that the girl knew the salesman's name and stood open mouthed, unable to answer the question.

The long silence was broken by the salesman who turned to the reservations clerk and said "It is Jones, B Jones" and then to his boss and said "Shall I get her to ask you an easier question?"

Appendix A

Sybase
System
Tables

This appendix gives the layout and indexes for the system tables in the system catalog. This is not intended to be a definitive description of the system tables but is included for completeness. The Sybase documentation gives a detailed description of these tables and is the real reference documentation for these tables as Sybase may change the structure of the system tables between versions.

sysalternates

One row for each user aliased to a user of the database.

column	datatype	description
suid	smallint	server user id of user being aliased
altsuid	smallint	server user id to whom user is aliased

indexes

clustered unique on (suid)

syscharsets

One row for each character set and sort order defined for use by SQL Server.

column	datatype	description
type	smallint	The type of entity represented by this entry. 1001: character set 2001: sort order
id	tinyint	The unique id for the character set or sort order. Sybase reserves 0-200.
csid	tinyint	For a sort order row, the id of the character set that the sort order refers to. Unused for a character set.
status	smallint	Internal system status information bits.
name	varchar(30)	Unique name for the character set or sort order.
description	varchar(255)	Optional description.
definition	image	Internal definition of the character set or sort order.

indexes

clustered unique on (id)
nonclustered unique on (name)

syscolumns

One row for each column in a table and view, and for each parameter in a procedure.

column	datatype	description
id	int	table or procedure id
number	smallint	sub-procedure number when procedure is grouped
colid	tinyint	column id
status	tinyint	indicates if NULL values are allowed or if unique position for bit columns
type	tinyint	physical storage type
length	tinyint	physical data length
offset	smallint	row offset where column starts; negative if variable length
usertype	smallint	user datatype id
cdefault	int	procedure id that generates column default value
domain	int	procedure id that generates column rule
name	sysname	column name
printfmt	varchar(255)	reserved

indexes

clustered unique on (id, number, colid)

syscomments

The SQL statements for views, rules, defaults, triggers and procedures. If the SQL is longer than 255 characters ie one row, it takes up multiple rows.

column	datatype	description
id	int	object id for text
number	smallint	sub-procedure number when the procedure is grouped
colid	tinyint	column id; 0 if not a column
texttype	smallint	0 for system supplied comments (views, rules, defaults, triggers and procedures) 1 for user supplied comments
language	smallint	reserved
text	varchar(255)	SQL text

indexes

clustered unique on (id, number, colid, texttype)

sysconfigures

One row for each user settable configuration value.

column	datatype	description
config	smallint	configuration variable number
value	int	configuration variable value
comment	varchar(255)	description of configuration variable
status	smallint	1: takes effect after reconfigure
		0: takes effect after server restart

Config values:

config	value	comment
101	0	maximum recovery interval in minutes
102	0	allow updates to system tables
103	0	number of user connections
104	0	size of physical memory in 2 K pages
105	0	number of open databases allowed
106	0	number of locks
107	0	number of open objects
108	0	procedure cache memory percentage
109	0	fillfactor percentage
110	0	average timeslice
111	0	default database size (megabytes)
112	0	tape retention period (days)
113	0	recovery flags
114	666666	serial number
115	0	allows nested triggers
116	50	number of devices
117	0	allows remote access
118	0	number of remote logins
119	0	number of remote sites
120	0	number of remote connections
121	0	number of pre-read packets per remote connection
122	400	upgrade version
123	50	default sort order id
124	0	default language
125	3	language in cache

indexes

clustered unique on (config)

syscurconfigs

Dynamic version of sysconfigures created when queried to contain an entry for each configuration variable with the current instead of the default values. Also contains four entries to describe the configuration structure.

Config values:

config	value	comment
1	1	major revision number of configuration data
2	0	minor revision number of configuration data
3	4	reconfigure revision number of configuration data
4	2	configuration boot source
101	5	maximum recovery interval in minutes
102	0	allow updates to system tables
103	25	number of user connections
104	2000	size of physical memory in 2 K pages
105	10	number of open databases allowed
106	5000	number of locks
107	500	number of open objects
108	20	procedure cache memory percentage
109	0	fillfactor percentage
110	100	average timeslice
111	2	default database size (megabytes)
112	0	tape retention period (days)
113	0	recovery flags
114	666666	serial number
115	0	allows nested triggers
116	50	number of devices
117	0	allows remote access
118	0	number of remote logins
119	0	number of remote sites
120	0	number of remote connections
121	0	number of pre-read packets per remote connection
122	400	upgrade version
123	50	default sort order id
124	0	default language
125	3	language in cache

sysdatabases

One row for each database in the server.

column	datatype	description
name	sysname	database name
dbid	smallint	database id
suid	smallint	server user id of database creator
mode	smallint	internal lock when database is being created
status	smallint	control bits, defined in chapter 3
		0x04 select into/bulkcopy
		0x08 trunc. log on chkpt
		0x10 no chkpt on recovery
		0x20 crashed while loading database
		0x100 database is suspect
		0x400 read only
		0x800 dbo use only
		0x1000 single user
		0x4000 dbname has changed
version	smallint	SQL server version when database was created
logptr	int	reserved
crdate	datetime	creation date
dumptrdate	datetime	date of last dump transaction

indexes

> clustered unique on (name)
> non-clustered unique on (dbid)

sysdepends

One row for each procedure, view or table which is referenced by a procedure, view or trigger.

column	datatype	description
id	int	object id
number	smallint	procedure number
depid	int	dependent object id
depnumber	smallint	dependent procedure number
status	smallint	internal status information
selall	bit	set if object is used in select * statement
resultobj	bit	set if object is being updated
readobj	bit	set if object is being read

indexes

clustered on (id, number, depid, depnumber, **dpedbid, depsiteid)**

The latter two are exactly as stated in the Sybase documentation but they are not in the table definition. A look at the table shows an index structure of:

clustered on (id, number, depid, depnumber)

sysdevices

One row for each device: database disk device, disk dump device and tape dump device.

column	datatype	description
low	int	first virtual page number for database devices
high	int	last virtual page number for database devices and dump devices
status	smallint	bit map indicating device type, default and mirror status

<table>
<tr><td></td><td></td><td>1</td><td>default disk</td></tr>
<tr><td></td><td></td><td>2</td><td>physical disk</td></tr>
<tr><td></td><td></td><td>4</td><td>logical disk</td></tr>
<tr><td></td><td></td><td>8</td><td>skip header</td></tr>
<tr><td></td><td></td><td>16</td><td>dump device</td></tr>
<tr><td></td><td></td><td>32</td><td>serial writes</td></tr>
<tr><td></td><td></td><td>64</td><td>device mirrored</td></tr>
<tr><td></td><td></td><td>128</td><td>reads mirrored</td></tr>
<tr><td></td><td></td><td>256</td><td>half-mirror only</td></tr>
<tr><td></td><td></td><td>512</td><td>mirror enabled</td></tr>
</table>

column	datatype	description
cntrltype	smallint	controller type

		0	database device
		2	disk dump device
		3-8	tape dump device

column	datatype	description
name	sysname	logical name
phyname	varchar(127)	physical operating system name
mirrorname	varchar(127)	physical name of mirror device

indexes

   clustered unique on (name)

sysengines

One row for each SQL Server engine.

column	datatype	description
engine	smallint	engine number
osprocid	int	operating system process id
osprocname	char	operating system process name
status	char	current status of engine online offline in create in destroy debug
affinitied	int	number of SQL Server process with affinity to this engine
cur_kpid	int	kernel process id of process currently running on this engine
last_kpid	int	kernel process id of process which last ran on this engine
idle 1	tinyint	reserved
idle 2	tinyint	reserved
idle 3	tinyint	reserved
idle 4	tinyint	reserved
starttime	datetime	date and time engine came online

indexes

sysindexes

One row for each clustered index; one row for each non-clustered index; one row for each table which has no clustered index and one row for each table that contains a text or image datatype.

column	datatype	description
name	sysname	index or table name
id	int	table id
indid	smallint	index id
		0 table
		1 clustered index
		2-254 non-clustered index
		255 text/image chain
dpages	int	number of data pages used (table or clustered index)
reserved	int	number of pages allocated (table or clustered index or text chain)
used	int	number of data and index pages (clustered index or text chain)
rows	int	number of rows (table or clustered index)
first	int	pointer to first data page of table or first leaf index page
root	int	pointer to last data page of table or root page of index
distribution	int	pointer to statistics distribution page
usagecnt	int	reserved
segment	smallint	segment number in which object resides
status	smallint	internal system status
		0x1 abort command if insert duplicate key
		0x2 unique index
		0x4 abort command if insert duplicate row
		0x10 clustered index
		0x40 index allows duplicate rows
rowpage	smallint	maximum number of rows per page
minlen	smallint	minimum size of row
maxlen	smallint	maximum size of row
maxirow	smallint	maximum size of a non-leaf index row
keycnt	smallint	number of keys
keys1	varbinary(255)	description of index key columns
keys2	varbinary(255)	description of index key columns
soid	tinyint	sort order id that the index was created with. 0 if no character data in the index
csid	tinyint	character set id that the index was created with. 0 if no character data in the index.

indexes

> clustered unique on (id, indid)

The above table layout is for versions up to 4.2. From v4.8 the layout of sysindexes has changed to:

column	datatype	description
name	sysname	index or table name
id	int	table id
indid	smallint	index id
		0 table
		1 clustered index
		2-254 non-clustered index
		255 text/image chain
doampg	int	a composite field for data pages
ioampg	int	a composite field for index pages
spare1	int	reserved field
spare2	int	reserved field
first	int	pointer to first data page of table or first leaf index page
root	int	pointer to last data page of table or root page of index
distribution	int	pointer to statistics distribution page
usagecnt	int	reserved
segment	smallint	segment number in which object resides
status	smallint	internal system status
		0x1 abort command if insert duplicate key
		0x2 unique index
		0x4 abort command if insert duplicate row
		0x10 clustered index
		0x40 index allows duplicate rows
rowpage	smallint	maximum number of rows per page
minlen	smallint	minimum size of row
maxlen	smallint	maximum size of row
maxirow	smallint	maximum size of a non-leaf index row
keycnt	smallint	number of keys
keys1	varbinary(255)	description of index key columns
keys2	varbinary(255)	description of index key columns
soid	tinyint	sort order id that the index was created with. 0 if no character data in the index
csid	tinyint	character set id that the index was created with. 0 if no character data in the index.

Page and row information is calculated using new functions:

data_pgs(id, doampg) for data
data_pgs(id, ioampg) for indexes

reserved_pgs(id, field_name)

rowcnt(doampg)

syskeys

One row for each primary or foreign key.

column	datatype	description
id	int	object id
type	smallint	record type
depid	int null	dependent object id
keycnt	int	number of non-null keys
size	int null	reserved
key1	int null	column id
key2	int null	column id
key3	int null	column id
key4	int null	column id
key5	int null	column id
key6	int null	column id
key7	int null	column id
key8	int null	column id
depkey1	int null	column id
depkey2	int null	column id
depkey3	int null	column id
depkey4	int null	column id
depkey5	int null	column id
depkey6	int null	column id
depkey7	int null	column id
depkey8	int null	column id

indexes

    clustered index on (id)

syslanguages

One row for each language known to SQL Server. The default us_english is not in this table but is always available.

column	datatype	description
langid	smallint	unique language id
name	sysname	language name eg french
alias	sysname	alternate language name eg francais
months	varchar(251)	list of full length month names
shortmonths	varchar(119)	list of short month names
days	varchar(216)	list of day names (Monday first)
dateformat	char(3)	date order eg dmy
datefirst	tinyint	first day of week: Monday=1
upgrade	int	SQL Server version of last upgrade for language

indexes

> clustered unique on (langid)
> nonclustered unique on (name)
> nonclustered unique on (alias)

syslocks

Information on active locks: built dynamically when queried.

column	datatype	description
id	int	table id
dbid	smallint	database id
page	int	page number
type	smallint	type of lock

1	exclusive table lock
2	shared table lock
3	exclusive intent lock
4	shared intent lock
5	exclusive page lock
6	shared page lock
7	update page lock
8	exclusive extent lock
9	shared extent lock
0x100	lock is blocking another process
0x200	demand lock

spid	int	id of process holding the lock

indexes

syslogins

One row for each server login.

column	datatype	description
suid	smallint	server user id
status	smallint	reserved
accdate	datetime	reserved
totcpu	int	reserved
totio	int	reserved
spacelimit	int	reserved
timelimit	int	reserved
resultlimit	int	reserved
dbname	sysname	default database name on connection
name	sysname	user login name
password	sysname null	password

indexes

clustered unique on (suid)
non-clustered unique on (name)

syslogs

The transaction log. Please do not even attempt to update syslogs as every change operation must be logged to syslogs which, because it is syslogs that is being updated, causes an infinite loop of log entries to syslogs which stops only when the log is full. As you have just filled the log you must dump with no_log and then dump the database as no_log does not create a recoverable transaction log. **Do not update syslogs.**

column	datatype	description
xactid	binary(6)	transaction id
op	tinyint	update operation number

indexes

sysmessages

One row for each system error or warning message.

column	datatype	description
error	int	unique error number
severity	smallint	severity level of error
dlevel	smallint	reserved for message descriptive level (terse, short, long)
description	varchar(255)	error description (includes parameter substitution)
langid	smallint	language

indexes

clustered unique on (error, dlevel)
nonclustered unique on (error, dlevel, langid)

One would question why there are two indexes on this table. A clustered index on (error, dlevel, langid) would seem sufficient, the only reason for the nonclustered index being the covering of an SQL command. Oh well, presumably this is the case and not just the introduction of a new index because a new field - langid - has been added to this table.

sysobjects

One row for each object: table, view, procedure, log, rule, default, trigger, temporary table. The temporary object entries are registered in tempdb only.

column	datatype	description
name	sysname	object name
id	int	object id
uid	smallint	user id of object owner
type	char(2)	object type
		S system table
		U user table
		V view
		L log
		P procedure
		R rule
		D default
		TR trigger
userstat	smallint	application dependent type information
sysstat	smallint	internal status information
indexdel	smallint	index delete count
		(incremented after an index is deleted)
schema	smallint	count of schema changes
		(incremented if a rule or default is added)
refdate	datetime	reserved
crdate	datetime	creation date
expdate	datetime	reserved
deltrig	int	id of delete trigger on table
instrig	int	id of insert trigger on table
updtrig	int	id of update trigger on table
seltrig	int	reserved
category	int	reserved
cache	smallint	reserved

indexes

> clustered unique on (id)
> non-clustered unique on (name, id)

sysprocedures

An entry for each view, default, rule, trigger and procedure. If the plan or sequence tree does not fit into one row it is spread across several rows.

column	datatype	description
type	smallint	object type
		0x1 entry describes a plan
		0x2 entry describes a sequence tree
id	int	object id
sequence	smallint	sequence number to link several rows for one object
status	smallint	internal system status
number	smallint	sub-procedure number when the procedure is grouped

indexes

clustered unique on (id, type, sequence, number)

sysprocesses

A dynamic table containing process information, built when queried by the user.

column	datatype	description
spid	smallint	process id
kpid	smallint	kernel process id
status	char(10)	process id status eg runnable, sleeping etc
suid	smallint	server user id of user who issued command
hostname	char(10)	name of host computer
program_name	char(16)	name of front-end module
hostprocess	char(8)	host process id number
cmd	char(16)	command currently being executed
cpu	int	cumulative cpu time for process
physical_io	int	number of disk reads and writes for current command
memusage	int	amount of memory allocated to process
blocked	smallint	process id of blocking process
dbid	smallint	database id
uid	smallint	user id who executed command
gid	smallint	group id of user who executed command

indexes

sysprotects

Permission information on objects.

column	datatype	description
id	int	object id to which permission applies
uid	smallint	user id or group id to which permission applies
action	tinyint	permission type

	193	select
	195	insert
	196	delete
	197	update
	198	create table
	203	create database
	207	create view
	222	create procedure
	224	execute
	228	dump database
	233	create default
	235	dump transaction
	236	create rule

column	datatype	description
protecttype	tinyint	permission

	205	grant
	206	revoke

column	datatype	description
columns	varbinary(32)	bit map of columns to which select or update permission applies. Bit 0 indicates all columns. Bit 1 indicates that column. Null indicates no information.

indexes

clustered on (id, uid, action)

sysremotelogins

One row for each remote user.

column	datatype	description
remoteserverid	smallint	remote server id
remoteusername	varchar(30)	user's login name on remote server
suid	smallint	local server user id
status	smallint	bitmap of options

indexes

clustered unique on (remoteserverid, remoteusername)

syssegments

One row for each segment.

column	datatype	description
segment	smallint	segment number
name	sysname	segment name
status	int null	indicates default segment

indexes

sysservers

One row for each remote server.

column	datatype	description
srvname	varchar(30)	server name
srvnetname	varchar(32)	interfaces file name
srvid	smallint	id number of the remote server
srvstatus	smallint	bitmap of options

indexes

clustered unique on (srvid)
non-clustered unique on (srvname)

systypes

One row for each system supplied and each user defined datatype.

column	datatype	description
uid	smallint	user id of creator
usertype	smallint	user type id
variable	bit	1 if datatype is variable length, else 0
allownulls	bit	1 if nulls are allowed, else 0
type	tinyint	physical storage datatype

34	image
35	text
37	timestamp
37	varbinary
38	intn
39	sysname
39	varchar
45	binary
47	char
48	tinyint
50	bit
52	smallint
56	int
60	money
61	datetime
62	float
109	floatn
110	moneyn
111	datetimn

(the duplicate 37 and 39 are not mistakes)

column	datatype	description
length	tinyint	physical length of datatype
tdefault	int	procedure id that generates default for datatype
domain	int	procedure id that contains integrity checks for datatype
name	sysname	datatype name
printfmt	varchar(255)	reserved

indexes

clustered unique on (name)
non-clustered unique on (usertype)

sysusages

One row for each contiguous allocation of disk space to the database.

column	datatype	description
dbid	smallint	database id
segmap	int	bit map of possible segment allocations
lstart	int	first logical page number
size	int	number of contiguous page numbers
vstart	int	starting virtual page number

indexes

clustered unique on (dbid, lstart)
non-clustered unique on (vstart)

sysusermessages

One row for each user message which may be used in procedures.

column	datatype	description
error	int	unique error number. Must be greater than 20000.
description	varchar(255)	user defined message
langid	smallint	language id for message
uid	smallint	id of message creator

indexes

clustered on (error)
non-clustered on (error, langid)   (I don't make these up. It comes directly from the manuals. I hope that there is a covered query to justify this index.)

sysusers

One row for each user and one row for each group.

column	datatype	description
suid	smallint	server user id
		1: dbo/sa
		-1: guest
		-2: public
uid	smallint	user id
		0: public
		1: dbo/sa
		2: guest
gid	smallint	group id
name	sysname	user or group name
environ	varchar(255)	reserved

indexes

> clustered unique on (suid)
> non-clustered unique on (name)
> non-clustered unique on (uid)

Appendix B

Command
and
System Procedure
Syntax

This appendix gives the syntax for the commands and system procedures. This is not intended to be a definitive description of the syntax but is included for completeness. The Sybase documentation gives a detailed description of these and should be used as the real reference documentation.

System commands

alter database

```
alter database db_name
[on device_name = size , device name = size]...]
[for load]


    alter database fred
    alter database fred on default = 20
    alter database fred on dev1 = 15, dev2 = 10
```

alter table

```
alter table table_name
    add   column_name datatype null
          [, column_name datatype null]...


    alter table jk_tab
        add   qty float null,
              price float null
```

begin

```
begin
```

begin transaction

```
begin transaction [tran_name]


    begin transaction
    begin tran tran_1
```

break

```
break
```

checkpoint

```
checkpoint
```

commit transaction

```
commit transaction [tran_name]


    commit tran
    commit transaction tran_1
```

continue

```
continue
```

create database

```
create database db_name
    [on device_name = size, device_name = size]...]
    [log on device_name = size
    , device_name = size]...]
    [for load]


    create database test_db
    create database systest_db on diska = 5,
            diskb = 4, diskc = 2
```

```
create database prod_db on diska = 20
            log on log_dev = 6
```

create default

```
create default default_name
            as constant_expression
```

```
create default date_def as getdate()
```

create index

```
create [unique]  [{clustered | nonclustered}]
    index index_name
    on table_name(column_name [, column_name]...)
    [with fillfactor= x,
    ignore_dup_key,
    sorted_data,
    [{ignore_dup_row | allow_dup_row}]]
    [on segment_name]
```

```
create index jk1_idx on jk_tab(a)
create unique clustered index jk2_idx
                    on jk_tab(a, b)
create nonclustered index jk3_idx
                    on jk_tab(a, c, b)
                    with fillfactor = 50
```

create procedure

```
create proc proc_name
    [(param_name datatype [=default] [output]
    [, param_name datatype [=default] [output]...])]
    [with recompile]
    as
    SQL statements
```

```
create proc jk_proc (@name varchar(3))
as
begin
select name, address from customer
      where name like @name + '%'
end
return
```

create rule

```
create rule rule_name as condition_expression
```

```
create rule date_rule as @fred <= getdate()
create rule qty_rule as @fred = 0
                or @fred > 100
```

create table

```
create table table_name
    (column_name datatype [{null | not null}]
    [, column_name datatype [{null | not null}]]...)
    [on segment_name]
```

```
create table jk_tab  (
      a   int,
      b float,
      c varchar(32) null)
```

create trigger

```
create trigger trigger_name on table_name
    for {insert, update, delete}
    as
    SQL statements
```

```
create trigger jk_trig on jk_tab
    for insert, delete
    as
    begin
        print 'update only'
        rollback tran
    end
    return
```

create view

```
create view view_name
    [(column_name [,column_name]...)]
    as
    SQL statements


    create view jk_view (description, average_price)
    as
    select description, avg(std_price)
        from product
        group by description
```

declare

```
declare   variable_name datatype
        [, variable_name datatype]...


    declare @var_1 int, @msg varchar(60)
```

delete

```
delete table_name
    [from table_name]  [, table_name]...
    [where search_conditions]
```

```
delete jk_tab where a > 10
delete ord_item
     from ord_item, orders
     where orders.cust_no = '12345'
     and orders.ord_no = ord_item.ord_no
```

disk init

```
disk init
     name  =  "logical_name",
     physname = "physical_name",
     vdevno = device_number,
     size = number_of_pages
     [, vstart = virtual_address]
     [, cntrltype = controller_number]
     [, contiguous]


     disk init
          name = 'test_dev',
          physname = '/usr/test.dir/test.dat',
          vdevno = 10, size = 1024
```

disk mirror

```
disk mirror
     name = "logical_name",
     mirror = "physical_name"
     [, writes = {serial | noserial}]
     [, reads = {mirrored | nomirrored}]
     [, contiguous]


     disk mirror
          name = "disk_mirr1",
          mirror = "/usr/u/mirr.dir/mirror.dat"
```

disk refit

```
disk refit
```

disk reinit

```
disk reinit
```

disk remirror

```
disk remirror
     name = "logical_name"


     disk remirror name = "disk1"
```

disk unmirror

```
disk unmirror
     name = "logical_name"
     [, side = {primary | secondary}]
     [, mode = {retain | remove}]


     disk unmirror
          name = "disk1", side = primary
```

drop

```
drop object  object_name  [, object_name]...


     drop database  fred_db
     drop default date_def
     drop index jk_tab.jk1_idx
     drop proc jk_proc
     drop rule date_rule
     drop table jk_tab
     drop trigger jk_trig
     drop view jk_view
```

dump database

```
dump database db_name to device_name


    dump database fred to dump_dev2
```

dump transaction

```
dump tran db_name to device_name
    [{with truncate_only |
     with no_log |
     with no_truncate}]


    dump tran fred to log_dev2
```

end

```
end
```

execute

```
exec [@stat=] proc_name
    [(param_name=value [, param_name = value]...)]
    [with recompile]


    exec jk_proc @name = 'KIR'
```

goto

```
goto label

label:
```

grant

```
grant command_list to name_list

grant permission_list on object_name to name_list


    grant create table to user_1
    grant execute on jk_proc to prog_group
```

if...else

```
if  boolean_expression
    statement_block
[else if boolean_expression]
    statement_block]


    if (select max(price)from ord_item) > 100
    begin
        print 'price too high'
    end
    else
    begin
        print 'price too low'
    end
```

insert

```
insert into table_name
    [(column_name [, column_name]...)]
    values
    (constant_expression [, constant_expression]...)

insert into table_name
    [(column_name [, column_name]...)]
    select_statement
```

```
insert into tab_1
    values (1, 2, 'dddd', 40, getdate())

insert into tab_1 (a, b, c)
select x, y, z*12 from tab_2
```

kill

```
kill spid
```

load database

```
load database db_name from device_name

    load fred from dump_dev2
```

load transaction

```
load transaction db_name from device_name

    load tran fred from log_dev2
```

prepare transaction

```
prepare tran
```

print

```
print  {"message_text" | character_variable}


      print  'hello'
      print  @msg
```

raiserror

```
raiserror  integer_expr
          {"message_text"  character_variable}


      raiserror 21000 @msg
```

readtext

```
readtext  table_name.column_name  text_ptr
          offset  size  [holdlock]
```

reconfigure

```
reconfigure  [with override]
```

return

```
return  [status_value]
```

revoke

```
revoke command_list from name_list

revoke permission_list on object_name from name_list

    revoke create table from user_1

    revoke execute on jk_proc from prog_group
```

rollback transaction

```
        rollback tran [tran_name]
```

save transaction

```
    save tran savepoint_name
```

select

```
select [distinct] select_list
    [into table_name]
    [from table_list]
    [where search_conditions]
    [group by column_list]
    [having search_conditions]
    [order by column_list]
    [compute aggregate_list [by column_list]]
    [for browse]

    select * from customer

    select name, address, ord_no
        from customer, orders o
        where customer.cust_no = o.cust_no
```

set

```
set option option_value
```

option	option_value
arithabort	on/off
arithignore	on/off
datefirst	number
dateformat	format
language	language
nocount	on/off
noexec	on/off
offsets	on/off
parseonly	on/off
procid	on/off
showplan	on/off
statistics	on/off
statistics io	on/off
statistics time	on/off
rowcount	number
textsize	number

setuser

```
setuser ['user_name']
```

```
setuser "dbo"
setuser "fred"
```

shutdown

```
shutdown [with nowait]
```

truncate

```
truncate table table_name
```

```
truncate table jk_tab
```

update

```
update table_name
    set column_name = expression
        [, column_name = expression]...
        [from table_list]
        [where search_conditions]


    update jk_tab
        set b = 10 where a = 40

    update ord_item
        set qty = 0
        from orders o, ord_item i
        where o.ord_no = i.ord_no
        and o.cust_no = '12345'
```

update statistics

```
update statistics table_name [index_name]


    update statistics jk_tab jk1_idx
```

use

```
use db_name
```

waitfor

```
waitfor    {delay "time" |
            time "time" |
            errorexit |
            processexit |
            mirrorexit}
```

while

```
while boolean_expression
    statement_block


    while (select max(price) from ord_item) > 50
    begin
        select price from ord_item
            where price = (select max(price)
                                    from ord_item)
    end
```

writetext

```
writetext  table_name.column_name  text_ptr
    [with log]
    data
```

System procedures

sp_addalias

```
sp_addalias login_name, alias_user_name

    sp_addalias student_1, dbo
```

sp_addgroup

```
sp_addgroup group_name

    sp_addgroup prog_grp
```

sp_addlanguage

```
sp_addlanguage language, alias, months, shortmons,
                days, datefmt, datefirst

    sp_addlanguage french,francais,
        "janvier, fevrier, mars, avril, mai, juin,
        juillet, aout, septembre, octobre,
        novembre, decembre",
        "jan, fev, nars, avr, mai, juin, jui,
        aout, sept, oct, nov, dec",
        "lundi, mardi, mercredi, jeudi, vendredi,
        samedi, dimanche",
        dmy, 1
```

sp_addlogin

```
sp_addlogin login_name
        [, password]
```

```
                    [, default_db]
                    [, def_language]


          sp_addlogin fred
```

sp_addmessage

```
          sp_addmessage    message_num,
                           message_text
                           [, language]


          sp_addmessage 30000, "cannot delete"
```

sp_addremotelogin

```
          sp_addremotelogin remote_server
                          [, local_name] [, remote_name]


          sp_addremotelogin test, john, rem_user
```

sp_addsegment

```
          sp_addsegment segment_name, device_name


          sp_addsegment seg_a, dev1
```

sp_addserver

```
          sp_addserver server_name [, local]


          sp_addserver production
```

sp_addtype

```
sp_addtype type_name, datatype [, {null | not null}]


    sp_addtype  date_type, datetime
```

sp_addumpdevice

```
sp_addumpdevice  "{tape | disk}",
                 device_name,
                 phys_name,
                 cntrltype
                 [, {skip | noskip}]
                 [, size]


    sp_addumpdevice  "tape",  tape_dump1,
                              "/dev/rmt8",
                              3, skip, 40
    sp_addumpdevice  "disk",  disk_dump2,
                              "/dev/rxy1d", 2
```

sp_adduser

```
sp_adduser login_name [, name_in_db [, grp_name]]


    sp_adduser john
    sp_adduser user_1, user_1, prog_grp
```

sp_bindefault

```
sp_bindefault def_name, obj_name [, futureonly]


    sp_bindefault date_def, "customer.create_date"
```

sp_bindrule

```
sp_bindrule rule_name, obj_name [, futureonly]

    sp_bindrule date_rule, date_type
```

sp_changedbowner

```
sp_changedbowner login_name [, true]

    sp_changedbowner prog_1
```

sp_changegroup

```
sp_changegroup grp_name, name_in_db

    sp_changegroup prog_grp, john
```

sp_checknames

```
sp_checknames
```

sp_clearstats   (VMS only)

```
sp_clearstats [user_name]
```

sp_commonkey

```
sp_commonkey tab1_name, tab2_name,
             col1_name, col2_name
             [, col1_name, col2_name]...


sp_commonkey orders, ord_delivery,
             ord_date, del_date
```

sp_configure

```
sp_configure [config_name [, config_value]]


sp_configure "recovery interval", 3
```

sp_dboption

```
sp_dboption [db_name, opt_name, {true | false}]


sp_dboption fred, "read only", true
```

sp_defaultdb

```
sp_defaultdb login_name, db_name


sp_defaultdb fred, prod_db
```

sp_defaultlanguage

```
sp_defaultlanguage login_name [, language]

    sp_defaultlanguage john, french
```

sp_depends

```
sp_depends obj_name

    sp_depends jk_tab
```

sp_diskdefault

```
sp_diskdefault logical_name, {defaulton | defaultoff}

    sp_diskdefault master, defaultoff
```

sp_dropalias

```
sp_addalias login_name
```

sp_dropdevice

```
sp_dropdevice device_name
```

sp_dropgroup

```
sp_dropgroup grp_name
```

sp_dropkey

```
sp_dropkey key_type, table_name [, dep_table_name]
```

```
sp_dropkey primary, jk_tab
sp_dropkey foreign, orders
sp_dropkey common, orders, ord_delivery
```

sp_droplanguage

```
sp_droplanguage language [, dropmessages]
```

```
sp_droplanguage french
```

sp_droplogin

```
sp_droplogin login_name
```

sp_dropmessage

```
sp_dropmessage message_num  [, language]
```

sp_dropremotelogin

```
sp_dropremotelogin remote_server
                [, login_name] [, remote_name]
```

```
    sp_dropremotelogin test, john, rem_prog
```

sp_dropsegment

```
sp_dropsegment segment_name [, device_name]
```

```
    sp_dropsegment "system", dev2
```

sp_dropserver

```
sp_dropserver server_name [, droplogins]
```

sp_droptype

```
sp_droptype type_name
```

sp_dropuser

```
sp_dropuser user_name
```

sp_extendsegment

```
sp_extendsegment seg_name, device_name
```

```
    sp_extendsegment seg_1, data_dev_1
```

sp_foreignkey

```
sp_foreignkey table_name, pkey_table_name,
              col_1 [, col_2]...

    sp_foreignkey orders, customer, cust_no
```

sp_getmessage

```
sp_getmessage   message_num,
                @msg_var output
                [, language]
```

sp_help

```
sp_help [obj_name]
```

sp_helpdb

```
sp_helpdb [db_name]
```

sp_helpdevice

```
sp_helpdevice [device_name]
```

sp_helpgroup

```
sp_helpgroup [grp_name]
```

sp_helpindex

```
sp_helpindex table_name
```

sp_helpjoins

```
sp_helpjoins table_1, table_2
```

sp_helpkey

```
sp_helpkey [obj_name]
```

sp_helplanguage

```
sp_helplanguage   [language]
```

sp_helplog

```
sp_helplog
```

sp_helpremotelogin

```
sp_helpremotelogin [remote_server [, remote_name]]

    sp_helpremotelogin glenlivet, rem_login
```

sp_helprotect

```
sp_helprotect name [,name_in_db]

    sp_helprotect jk_tab
```

sp_helpsegment

```
sp_helpsegment [seg_name]
```

sp_helpserver

```
sp_helpserver [server_name]
```

sp_helpsort

```
sp_helpsort
```

sp_helptext

```
sp_helptext obj_name
```

sp_helpuser

```
sp_helpuser [user_name]
```

sp_lock

```
sp_lock [spid_1 [, spid2]]
```

sp_logdevice

```
sp_logdevice db_name, device_name

    sp_logdevice fred, prod_dev1
```

sp_monitor

```
sp_monitor
```

sp_password

```
sp_password old_password, new_password [, login_name]

    sp_password null, jkjkjkjk
```

sp_placeobject

```
sp_placeobject seg_name, obj_name

    sp_placeobject seg_1, customer
    sp_placeobject index_seg1,
                    'customer.cust_idxnc1"
```

sp_primarykey

```
sp_primarykey table_name, col_1 [, col_2]...

    sp-primarykey ord_item, ord_no, prod_no
```

sp_recompile

```
sp_recompile [table_name]
```

sp_remoteoption

```
sp_remoteoption Xremote_server, login_name,
                remote_name,
                trusted, {true | false}]

    sp_remoteoption test, john, rem_prog,
                    trusted, true
```

sp_rename

```
sp_rename old_name, new_name

    sp_rename jk_tab1, jk_tab2
```

sp_renamedb

```
sp_renamedb old_dbname, new_dbname

    sp_renamedb fred, fred_test
```

sp_reportstats   (VMS only)

    sp_reportstats [user_name]

sp_serveroption

    sp_serveroption [server_name, option, {true | false}]

        sp_serveroption test, timeouts, true

sp_setlangalias

    sp_setlangalias language, alias

        sp_setlangalias french, francais

sp_spaceused

    sp_spaceused [obj_name]

sp_unbindefault

    sp_unbindefault obj_name [, futureonly]

        sp_unbindefault date_type
        sp_unbindefault "customer.cust_id"

sp_unbindrule

```
sp_unbindrule obj_name [, futureonly]


    sp_unbindrule date_rule, date_type
    sp_unbindrule id_rule, "customer.cust_id"
```

sp_who

```
sp_who [{log_name | "spid"}]


    sp_who john
```

Appendix C

Answers
to
Selected
Questions

Chapter 2

1   There are several steps which you can take to find out things about the installation. They are not sequential but I prefer to do them in this sequence.

    1.1   Use showserver to see what is running and make a note of the servers and device locations.

    1.2   Set DSQUERY and login as "sa" and change the password.

    1.3   Have a quick look at sysdatabases while you are in master.

    1.4   Back to the operating system and look at the interfaces file and each RUNSERVER file.

    1.5   Back into master and look at the databases, devices, segments, logins and any specially written system procedures.

    1.6   Into model and see what is set up in each database at create.

    1.7   You have found out about the overall set-up. Now you need to go into each database and look at the system tables to find out about: tables, types, rules, defaults, columns, procedures, triggers, users, groups, privileges and the configuration settings.

Chapter 3

1

1.1   disk init: 2 devices

1.2   sp_addsegment: 1 on each device

1.3   sp_dropsegment: default and system from second device

1.4   create database on device1 and device 2

1.5   create table on seg1

1.6   create index on seg2

2   System table information

2.1   Devices on the system.

An easy one to start with:

```
SELECT name, phyname, mirrorname
FROM sysdevices
ORDER BY name
```

Not really worth the bother, this one, as it is available from sp_helpdevice.

2.2   Size of each device

Again not very difficult:

```
SELECT name,
       size_in_db = (high-low+1)*2048/1048576
FROM sysdevices
WHERE cntrltype = 0
```

2.3   1: free space per database

```
set nocount on

DECLARE     @all int,
            @res int,
            @free int,
            @msg varchar(60)

SELECT @res = sum(reserved_pgs(id, doampg) +
            reserved_pgs(id, ioampg))*2048/1048576
FROM sysindexes

SELECT @all = sum(size) * 2048/1048576
FROM master.dbo.sysusages
WHERE dbid = db_id()

SELECT @msg = 'database name :    '+db_name()
PRINT @msg
SELECT @msg = 'allocated:   '
            +convert(varchar(12), @all)
PRINT @msg
SELECT @msg = 'reserved:    '
            +convert(varchar(12), @res)
PRINT @msg
SELECT @free = @all - @res
SELECT @msg = 'free:              '
            +convert(varchar(12), @free)
PRINT @msg
```

2: free space per device

```
CREATE TABLE #dev_free (
     dev_name              varchar(32),
     db_name               varchar(32),
     size_in_MB            int null,
     allocated_in_MB       int)
go

INSERT INTO #dev_free
     (dev_name, db_name, allocated_in_MB)
SELECT    d.name,
          db.name,
          allocated_in_MB =
                    sum(u.size)*2048/1048576
FROM sysdevices d,sysdatabases db,sysusages u
WHERE     d.name = 'input_value'
AND       db.dbid = u.dbid
```

```
AND          u.vstart BETWEEN d.low AND d.high
GROUP BY   d.name, db.name

UPDATE   #dev_free
SET   size_in_MB =
      (SELECT   (high-low+1)*2048/1048576
       FROM sysdevices
       WHERE   name = 'input_value')
WHERE   #dev_free.dev_name = 'input_value'
```

2.4   list of indexes with sizes

This is similar to 3.18.4: list of tables with sizes.

```
SELECT      name,
            indid,
            index_pgs = data_pgs(id, doampg),
            rows = rowcnt(doampg)
FROM   sysindexes
WHERE   indid BETWEEN 1 AND 254
```

Note that rows is valid only for the clustered index entry which is really the table entry.

2.5   list of columns for a table

```
SELECT c.name, c.colid, t.name, c.length
FROM syscolumns c, systypes t, sysobjects o
WHERE o.name  =   'input_value'
AND c.id = o.id
AND c.usertype = t.usertype
ORDER BY c.colid
```

2.6   list of indexes for a table

```
SELECT o.name, i.name, i.indid
FROM sysobjects o, sysindexes i
WHERE o.name = 'input_value'
AND o.id = i.id
AND i.indid  BETWEEN 0 AND 254
ORDER BY i.indid
```

Chapter 4

1

```
use master
go
sp_addlogin fred, NULL, test_db
go
sp_addlogin john, NULL, test_db
go

use test_db
go
sp_adduser fred
go
sp_adduser john
go

sp_dropuser john
go
sp_addalias john, fred
go

sp_addgroup progs
go
sp_changegroup progs, fred
go
```

2

```
use master
go
sp_addlogin jill, jill, test_db
go

use test_db
go
sp_adduser jill
go
```

login as jill

```
create table tab_1 (a int, b int)
go
```

login as sa

```
use master
go
sp_droplogin jill
go

use test_db
go
create proc read_tab_1  as
begin
select a, b from tab_1
end
return
go

grant execute on read_tab_1 to public
go
```

3   Remember that the login has to gain access to master to check syslogins. This is
done using "guest" in master. If this is missing then no-one will be able to
login except "sa" (and probe). If you deleted guest: be more careful. If you did
not delete guest: find out who did because either they know your sa password
or they have far too much privilege in master.

Bibliography

Bibliography

1 Sybase Inc.   System Administration Training Course
                        1989

2 Sybase Inc.   Performance and Tuning Training Course
                        1989

3 Sybase Inc.   Sybase System Administration Manual
                        1989/1992

4 Sybase Inc.   Sybase Commands Reference Guide
                        1989/1992

5 Sybase Inc.   Sybase Trouble-Shooting Guide
                        1992

6 Sybase Inc.   How Subqueries Work in the 5.0 SQL Server
                        1992

7 Al Huntley   The Unathorized Documentation of DBCC
                        Sybase International User Group
                        1991

8 R Frampton   IT's a funny thing
                        Digitus Ltd
                        1989

9 J Kirkwood   High Performance Relational Database Design
                        Ellis Horwood
                        1992

Index